RENEWALS 458-4574
DATE DUE

SEP 18			
JUN 2 4 2008			
JULY 8 2008			
GAYLORD			PRINTED IN U.S.A.

D1165877

WITHDRAWN
UTSA LIBRARIES

Strategic Sales Leadership

BREAKthrough Thinking for BREAKthrough Results

The Sales Educators

AMERICAN MARKETING ASSOCIATION

THOMSON ™

Australia · Brazil · Canada · Mexico · Singapore · Spain · United Kingdom · United States

Strategic Sales Leadership: BREAKthrough Thinking for BREAKthrough Results
The Sales Educators

COPYRIGHT © 2006 by Texere, an imprint of Thomson/South-Western, a part of The Thomson Corporation. Thomson and the Star logo are trademarks used herein under license.

Composed by: Interactive Composition Corporation

Printed in the United States of America by: RRD—Crawfordsville

1 2 3 4 5 08 07 06 05
This book is printed on acid-free paper.

ISBN 1-587-99203-5

This publication is designed to provide accurate and authoritative information in regard to the subject matter covered. It is sold with the understanding that the publisher is not engaged in rendering legal, accounting, or other professional services. If expert assistance is required, the services of a competent professional person should be sought.

ALL RIGHTS RESERVED. No part of this work covered by the copyright hereon may be reproduced or used in any form or by any means— graphic, electronic, or mechanical, including photocopying, recording, taping, web distribution, or information storage and retrieval systems, or in any other manner—without the written permission of the publisher.

The names of all companies or products mentioned herein are used for identification purposes only and may be trademarks or registered trademarks of their respective owners. Texere disclaims any affiliation, association, connection with, sponsorship, or endorsements by such owners.

For permission to use material from this text or product, submit a request online at http://www.thomsonrights.com

Library of Congress Cataloging in Publication Number is available. See page 273 for details.

For more information about our products, contact us at:

Thomson Learning
Academic Resource
Center 1-800-423-0563

Thomson Higher Education
5191 Natorp Boulevard
Mason, Ohio 45040
USA

Library
University of Texas
at San Antonio

CONTENTS

CHAPTER 1

REVOLUTION IN SALES MANAGEMENT

Introduction

This book is about the sales function, and the role it can and should play in 21st-century companies. As we shall see, this role is very different from the way sales has traditionally been approached. The majority of companies fail to realize the potential of their sales managers and salespeople. The tendency is to view sales as a somewhat mechanical set of activities, where salespeople are routinely hired and trained, territories are defined, quotas are set, incentives are offered, and performance is closely monitored and either rewarded or punished. All too often, salespeople are treated as replaceable objects where the trick is simply to put together the right combination of "carrots and sticks" to motivate employees to sell. Management is preoccupied with ensuring the salespeople are making the right number of calls, calling on the right accounts, pushing the right products, selling at the right price, and closing the right number of deals.

Today's competitive environment demands a radically different approach. Specifically, the ability of firms to exploit the true potential of the sales organization requires that company executives adopt a new mindset about the role of the selling function within the firm, how the sales force is managed, and what salespeople are expected to produce. The sales function must serve as a dynamic source of value creation and innovation within the firm. This new mindset is centered on a number of core principles, as follows.

- The sales function must become a source of competitive advantage in companies.
- Great sales organizations are run strategically and with strategic intent.
- Sales managers and salespeople must see themselves as entrepreneurs, and the sales department should be the most entrepreneurial area within companies.
- Sales must be an opportunity-driven, rather than a resource-constrained, activity.
- Innovation is a major responsibility of those in sales.

1

- The ability to create, develop, and manage relationships with customers is the single most important way salespeople create value in the marketplace.
- The sales function is not separate from the marketing function.
- Peak performance in sales is most likely when organizations have dynamic management systems to support the sales force.

These principles are the foundation on which this book is written, and represent themes that will guide the chapters to come. To appreciate the relevance of each principle, we have to first examine the fundamental changes taking place in the contemporary business environment. The changes are dramatic, and undermine many of the basic assumptions regarding what it takes to succeed in sales.

Evolution and Revolution in the Sales Environment[1]

A basic truism in organizations is that "external change forces internal change." In other words, what is happening outside the company has significant implications for how things are organized and managed inside the company. Unfortunately, as they grow and mature, companies tend to become more internally focused and insulated. Managers and employees become preoccupied with internal processes, procedures, budgets, bureaucracy, and politics. They lose sight of what is happening externally, and this is especially dangerous when the external environment is rapidly changing. The end result is that many large, established, and historically successful firms have become dinosaurs—they are out of touch with markets and technologies and competitive realities; they are slow to recognize and act on threats and opportunities; and they have lost the entrepreneurial edge.

The 21st century is a time of amazing change. The best word to describe the conditions in the external environments of most companies is "turbulence," and it applies to virtually every industry. Turbulence means three things: (a) external conditions are changing more rapidly, (b) they are becoming more hostile, and (c) they are becoming more complex. Experience tells us that highly turbulent environments force companies to change the way they do business. Firms have responded by downsizing, re-engineering, outsourcing, and making other fundamental changes in an attempt to become "lean and mean," more adaptable and flexible, and more aggressive.

---

[1] The discussion that follows builds on the work of Jones, E., S. P. Brown, A. Zoltners, and B. A. Weitz (2005). "The Changing Environment of Selling and Sales Management," *Journal of Personal Selling & Sales Management* (forthcoming).

Developments such as these create a major dilemma for those responsible for the sales function. Rackham and De Vincentis (1999, ix) explain:

> Sales forces are caught in the middle. On one side, their customers have changed dramatically in terms of how they purchase and what they expect. On the other side, their own corporations have shifted, going through downsizing, restructuring, and cost cutting. Traditional boundaries such as those between sales and marketing have crumbled. Salespeople have to cope with more products, introduced faster with shorter life cycles, and with less competitive differentiation."

While the external developments affecting the sales force are many, the major changes can be grouped into four categories: customers, competitors, technology, and the ethical and regulatory environment. These influences are depicted in Exhibit 1.1. Collectively, they challenge much of our existing knowledge and experience regarding what it takes to achieve excellence in sales. Let us consider each of these four areas.

Customers and Markets

Not too many years ago, those in sales and marketing commonly thought in terms of "mass markets" where large numbers of customers had similar needs and buying behaviors, and could be marketed to in the same way. Today, things could not be more different. Markets are highly fragmented and can only be expected to become more so. Terms like "relationship marketing" and "one-to-one marketing" have been introduced to describe an environment where the market is not only segmented into dozens and even hundreds of very narrowly defined segments (and narrow niches), but where individual customers must be approached as unique market segments.

Meanwhile, customer expectations of salespeople and the organizations they represent continue to ratchet upwards. Norms for achieving even minimally acceptable levels of customer satisfaction are a moving target. Evidence of this can be seen in declining customer satisfaction ratings of companies and their sales forces, even as these firms invest heavily in process improvements and customer relationship management (CRM) technology. In particular, customer expectations are rising in relation to (a) the salesperson's knowledge, (b) company response time, (c) amount and quality of communication, and (d) ability to customize information and product/service offerings. In fact, it is not unusual for customer expectations to change faster than organizations can effectively respond.

Exhibit 1.1   Environmental Conditions and the Sales Force

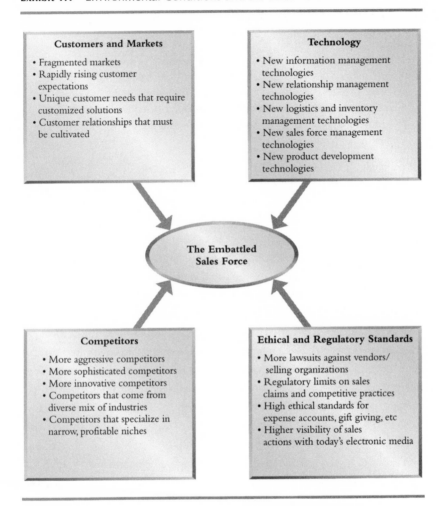

Customers and Markets

- Fragmented markets
- Rapidly rising customer expectations
- Unique customer needs that require customized solutions
- Customer relationships that must be cultivated

Technology

- New information management technologies
- New relationship management technologies
- New logistics and inventory management technologies
- New sales force management technologies
- New product development technologies

The Embattled Sales Force

Competitors

- More aggressive competitors
- More sophisticated competitors
- More innovative competitors
- Competitors that come from diverse mix of industries
- Competitors that specialize in narrow, profitable niches

Ethical and Regulatory Standards

- More lawsuits against vendors/ selling organizations
- Regulatory limits on sales claims and competitive practices
- High ethical standards for expense accounts, gift giving, etc
- Higher visibility of sales actions with today's electronic media

© Thomson

Salesperson Knowledge and the Availability of Information

In addition to the increasing burdens on salespeople in terms of their technological expertise and product knowledge, customers also expect the salespeople calling on them to know more about the selling organization's products and capabilities, and also about the buying organization's needs and operations. The customer may expect the salesperson to become familiar with information available in the public domain and over the Internet prior to making a sales call. One executive commented that the first call on an account used to serve the purpose of informing the salesperson about the firm, the set of people involved in the buying decision, the firm's buying procedures, and its buying requirements. In contrast, in today's environment, salespersons who attempt to use the first call to obtain background information—because they had not accessed available information prior to the call—would make a very poor first impression and likely fail to penetrate the account. Thus, pre-call preparation has taken on new meaning. New meaning is also attached to the sales organization's ability to collect and store the right kinds of customer data, analyze this data, and make specific recommendations that reflect the unique requirements of a given account.

The various dimensions of change in the selling environment discussed here also tend to create heavier cognitive demands on salespeople. The mental processes, thinking styles, and problem-solving approaches of those in sales are taxed mightily as they attempt to cope with increasing product complexity, customer demands, technological innovation, regulatory oversight, and competition. They must process, internalize, and manage increasing volumes of facts, figures, insights, and opinions, and yet are expected to respond to this information faster than ever. Not surprisingly, information overload is a common lament heard among salespeople.

The challenges of overwhelming amounts of information make it all the more critical that firms learn how to organize this information into actionable formats. These challenges influence how managers recruit and select salespeople, how they plan and implement sales force automation tools, and how they coordinate sales teams.

Speed of Response

Another characteristic of the 21st century is the movement toward "real-time marketing." In essence, the time between when a customer indicates that they want something (e.g., information, a product, a sales or service call) and the time they actually receive it is headed toward zero. Speed has become a key source of competitive advantage for companies, and those who cannot keep up with the pace quickly fall behind.

Buyers and sellers are increasingly online with one another 24/7. E-mail, the Internet, electronic blackboards, and other mechanisms have enabled salespeople to communicate more effectively with customers, as well as with their own firm. These advances have had the ancillary effect of increasing customer expectations regarding response time to their requests and inquiries. Given the capacity to communicate quickly and effectively, customers expect that salespeople will use it to serve their needs more quickly and completely. Collectively, customer demands for quick response can overwhelm salespeople who must simultaneously balance a multiplicity of other responsibilities. Thus, in addition to information overload, salespeople experience role overload (and burnout) as they struggle to fill all the different roles they are expected to play.

Breadth and Depth of Communication

To effectively serve customers' needs with increasingly sophisticated products, services, and applications, salespeople must become "leveragers" of organizational resources. That is, they must be adept at tapping into a variety of resources within their own firms on behalf of customers. They must be able to appeal to and coordinate the efforts of people in production, customer service, product development, credit and finance, senior management, and other areas within their companies—all in an attempt to serve the needs of a particular customer. As these needs continually change, so too does the need to elicit renewed support and leverage new resources from within the organization. So salespeople are not simply building relationships with customers, they are building them with key members of their own firm. The salesperson in effect becomes an orchestrator, mediator, and collaborator.

To establish and maintain strong customer relationships, salespeople must also deal with a greater number and variety of individuals within client organizations. Understanding influence dynamics and decision-making processes has become significantly more challenging as these processes center more around teams and networks (rather than around one or two individuals) embedded within the buying organization. The boundaries on both the selling and buying sides of the transaction are blurring. The growing reliance on strategic alliances between companies makes things even blurrier. Executives argue that such alliances better enable their companies to package "total solutions" for their customers. At the same time, depending on the circumstances, alliance partners are often competitors. Salespeople need to become, in a sense, social scientists capable of analyzing lines of power and influence across blurring boundaries in order to sell in today's business environment.

Customization . . . of Everything

Customers today are more empowered than ever. While there are certainly situations where demand is captive, the selling firm is a monopolist, and the product is a critical necessity for the buyer, these situations are the exception. Advancing technologies, the speed of information availability, and intense competition have created an environment where firms are forced to provide individualized solutions for each customer. Such solutions benefit both buyers and sellers, as both parties find themselves dissatisfied with commoditized "one-size-fits-all" products and services. For buyers, such products will generally require adaptation to provide a viable solution; for sellers, they represent low-margin, easily duplicated products with little differentiation from competitive offerings. Therefore, selling organizations generally seek ways to move these commodity products up the value chain with some form of differentiation (e.g., bundling services, adapting for specific types of applications, etc.). The need for customized solutions places additional burdens on salespeople in terms of information gathering and dissemination (e.g., to others in the organization assisting with sales and service, as well as to customers), and communication and coordination within both buyer and seller organizations.

Competitors and Competitive Strategies

Most markets today can be described as "hyper-competitive." It is not simply that there are more competitors, or that these competitors are more aggressive; it is that new forms of competition emerge and old ones fall away increasingly rapidly. Companies today find themselves competing with firms not just in their own industry. Competitors often come from completely unrelated industries, where a new capability or technology has led them to seek customers in new markets. These types of competitors are often the most threatening, as their underlying cost structures are often different from those of traditional competitors, as are their assumptions about how to compete. They often play by a different set of rules, and are not constrained by the traditional assumptions made by existing firms in the industry.

Competition is also changing the economics of selling. Performance expectations can be extreme, as salespeople find they are squeezed between tougher revenue and profit targets, higher costs of serving customers, and greater pressure to become more efficient. As product life cycles get shorter, competitors leapfrog one another with new products and features and new support services. Advantage seems anything but sustainable, forcing an ongoing quest for something new and better. For their part, salespeople struggle to manage their time, keep their market knowledge up-to-date, meet demanding performance metrics, maintain happy customers, and generate new business. All the while, the number of contingencies they must adapt to (e.g., different variations of competitive selling situations) continues to expand at a rapid rate.

Another implication of the changing competitive environment is that firms increasingly worry less about making a single sale to a given account, and more about customer lifetime value (CLV). That is, the real goal is to capture a certain percentage of what a customer will spend on a given product category over a number of years. In effect, companies are determining the actual worth of a customer by placing a dollar amount on what they can be reasonably expected to spend over time. The CLV concept has critical implications for how the sales organization allocates resources to market segments and individual accounts. Efficient and effective market strategies are those that differentiate customers based on their lifetime value. CLV is forcing the sales organization to approach client prospecting and account management in completely different ways.

New Technologies and Technological Developments

We live in an age of technology. Never in history has technology changed as fast as today. Every facet of business is affected by technological change, from product development and logistics management to customer service and human resource management. New technologies are changing how people work, when they perform different tasks, and their physical location when accomplishing a given task.

The sales function is no exception. Technologies enable salespeople to find and qualify prospects with much greater sophistication; interact with customers in unique ways at every stage of the selling process; know customers thoroughly; allocate their time much more efficiently; be instantaneously on top of changes in customer requirements; identify emerging patterns in the marketplace; and continuously assess the profitability of products, customers, territories, and distributors. Some of the major innovations in selling, such as customer relationship management (CRM) and sale force automation (SFA) systems, are predicated on continually changing technologies. In short, technology enables the sales force to customize, adds speed to the sales organization, and makes salespeople smarter and more efficient.

In reality, technology adoption by sales organizations is lagging, while managers continue to complain about the financial losses from huge technology investments and lackluster returns on investment. Moreover, technology is powerful and can be intimidating. It places heavy demands on salespeople. Unless it is carefully managed, technology adoption can lead to such unintended consequences as negative job attitudes and higher employee turnover.

Ethical Expectations and Regulatory Constraints

The legal and ethical environment plays a growing role in defining what is an acceptable, or unacceptable, sales activity. We live in a highly litigious age, and the sales efforts of companies are an increasingly popular target of lawyers and lawsuits. As a result, sales organizations are placing limitations on the claims that can be made to customers and establishing standards that must be upheld in sales transactions. Especially in highly competitive selling situations, salespeople are becoming more careful about the arguments used and inducements offered when attempting to win customers. Alternatively, long-term relationships with customers can encourage compromises of a different kind. Members of the buying and selling organization become so close that they engage in compromising behaviors in the name of the overall relationship. Moreover, as corporate scandals fill the pages of the business press and class-action lawsuits become commonplace, the public is demanding more transparency in corporate operations and better leadership. Sales managers are being held more accountable for ensuring that their salespeople are vigilant not only in following the law, but in behaving in a manner that reflects acceptable ethical standards.

For their part, salespeople have to be more judicious when managing expense accounts, giving gifts, addressing unethical demands from buyers, making promises about product performance and delivery, and selling products that can be perceived as "unnecessary." The challenges become all the more complex when operating internationally. Globalization has resulted in different interpretations of cultural expectations and has led to the need for more thoughtful consideration of cultural differences when selling globally. What's ethical in one country may be unethical in another.

The contemporary legal and ethical environment puts an additional burden on sales companies to select the "right" individuals. And with turnover costs continuing to skyrocket, sales companies can hardly afford to hire salespeople who make ethical and legal errors and then terminate them. Selecting and developing sales personnel has always been an important topic; today's environment raises the importance of doing this right.

An Alternative Concept of the Sales Force

The dramatic changes in the modern selling environment have led some to question whether the sales force as we know it is becoming obsolete (e.g., Jones, Chonko, and Roberts, 2004). Such obsolescence could occur for numerous reasons. In an age of relationships, a sales force that is highly skilled in generating new accounts may not be especially adept at building and managing relationships with existing accounts. In an age of speed, a sales force that is not empowered to make commitments to customers may find the decision-making processes in their own organizations are undermining sales. In an age of technology, buying and selling organizations are connected through electronic data interchange (EDI) systems, just in time (JIT) inventory management systems, materials requirement planning (MRP) systems, and other integrating mechanisms. The job of the salesperson comes into question when buying organizations are able to electronically purchase items, track deliveries, register problems, and ask questions.

In response to these environmental changes, some firms have attempted to eliminate, cut back, or outsource the selling function. Others have experimented with modifications to the structure, composition, objectives, and procedures of their sales forces. For example, key account and ad hoc selling teams are replacing "lone wolf" salespeople, and building and maintaining profitable long-term customer relationships is replacing short-term revenue goals. Firms are also beginning to recognize a need for changes in the sales culture and ingrained behaviors of salespeople, both of which can take considerable time.

We believe that the sales force can avoid obsolescence, and can actually become a significant source of sustainable competitive advantage in 21st-century companies. However, this cannot happen if companies move away from their commitment to the sales function, or simply make incremental modifications to sales operations. Instead, a new model of the sales force is needed. We believe that this new model should be built around six key elements which, when combined, produce what we call "the entrepreneurial sales organization" (see Exhibit 1.2). Each of these elements is discussed below.

Exhibit 1.2 A New Model of the Sales Force

© Thomson

The Creative Sales Force

Creativity must be the soul of the sales organization. It can be defined as the act of relating previously unrelated things. Creative thinking is vital in every facet of sales management and personal selling. To appreciate its role, let us consider creativity at the levels of the sales organization as well as the individual salesperson.

The Sales Organization and Creativity

Creativity in organizations is about destruction and construction. It requires the abandonment of certain assumptions, the rejection of accepted precepts, and the elimination of established methods. It also results in concepts or solutions that can disrupt the work lives of people in companies, making them break out of patterns and comfort zones. But creativity also brings with it a fresh start, a new way, a freedom from the constraints of what was and a path to what can be. It is a manifestation of the human spirit, such that the act of creativity is by itself a tremendous source of employee motivation and pride. To create is to matter, to count, to make a difference, to have an impact, and to be a source of value.

Organizations tend to be insensitive to the nuances and idiosyncrasies of the individual who is attempting to be creative. They typically are intolerant of failure, penalize rule bending or breaking, insist that people approach things from a logical point of view, discourage ambiguity, and assign people to jobs with very narrow job descriptions. While managers routinely encourage employees to "think outside the box," they in fact rigidly enforce the rules of the box, allocate resources only to things inside the box, and evaluate employees based on contributions to the box.

Although creativity will always be an art, organizations need not view it as unmanageable. On one level, creativity is messy, random, and unscientific. On another level, structure plays a role in creativity, and organizations that approach creativity from a more systematic perspective tend to come up with a lot more great ideas. Managers must emphasize practices that result in employees being challenged, provide them with freedom, and give them access to resources. Similarly, practices that result in well-designed, mutually supportive, and diverse work teams are likely to spur creativity. Also valuable are encouragement for creative outputs, and reinforcement of creativity in terms of the values, systems, and structures of the sales organization.

Fostering creative problem-solving also requires that managers figure out how to get different approaches and perspectives to grate against one another in a productive process that can be termed "creative abrasion." The point is not to create a scenario where colliding ideas or viewpoints or priorities simply battle each other, with one winning out or dominating and the other losing or being discarded. Nor is the objective to encourage compromise, alignment of positions, or watering down of one or both positions so as to achieve unity of direction. Creative abrasion serves to facilitate divergence, and it must be complemented by leadership styles and structures that ultimately produce convergence. Abrasion involves highlighting differences that are natural, and that increase the level of stimulation and variety in the organization. Examples of efforts to take advantage of abrasion could include hiring people who are not like current employees; putting together interfunctional teams (salespeople, design engineers, procurement managers, accounting personnel); giving a sales team two seemingly incompatible goals; introducing a perspective that threatens the positions and assumptions of those in the sales group; blurring responsibilities between departments or functions; and bringing in consultants, temporary staff, or speakers who hold very different points of view.

The Salesperson and Creativity

Employees are inherently creative. Some act on that creativity all the time, others stifle it, and most of us are somewhere in between. The reality is that employees often do not realize when or how they are being creative. Further, they fail to recognize the many opportunities for creativity that arise within their jobs on a daily basis.

The ability to be a continued source of creative contribution is tied to an understanding of (a) a salesperson's own immense creative potential; (b) a recognition of the many ways in which the individual is and can be creative; (c) an understanding of the nature of the creative process and some of the techniques for facilitating the mastery of that process time and time again; (d) an appreciation for one's own thinking or problem-solving style; and (e) a recognition of the different thinking styles of those with whom the salesperson works and to whom they report.

Creative thinking skills refer to the particular ways individuals approach problems and solutions, and the techniques they use for looking at a problem differently, seeking insights from other fields of endeavor, challenging assumptions, and so forth. Finding the appropriate path to a BREAKthrough solution is much easier if the employee approaches creativity as a process. Part of this process includes an ability to recognize and address creative blocks. Those in sales are more likely to come up with great ideas if they look for multiple solutions, are willing to think in impractical ways, are open to breaking existing rules, are playful and not worried about looking foolish, embrace ambiguity, and recognize that failure is a sign of progress. Salespeople also miss creative opportunities if they are too narrow and focused in their jobs. They may miss possibilities that do not fit their job description, or are outside of their educational, experiential, and professional backgrounds. Creative individuals are explorers, looking in other areas for ideas.

While there is latent creativity in every employee, people are not all creative in the same way. They have different thinking or cognitive styles. A popular way to label these styles involves distinguishing individuals based on whether they are more "left-brained" or "right-brained." The left-brained thinker arrives at solutions through a more analytical, logical, sequential approach, while the right-brained thinker relies more on an intuitive, values-based, nonlinear approach. Four distinct cognitive styles have been identified by researchers: (a) intuitive, rule-breaking, imaginative; (b) logical, fact-based, bottom-line oriented; (c) organized, planned, detailed; and (d) interpersonal, emotional, people-focused (Herrmann, 1995).

Over time, people develop a preference for a particular thinking mode. They develop skills for the types of tasks or methods associated with that thinking mode. The salesperson's style is reflected in work behaviors and decision-making activities, including a preference for working together versus alone, learning "about" something versus experiencing it, and making quick decisions versus generating lots of options no matter how urgent the matter at hand.

None of these four thinking styles is necessarily better than the others. Each is capable of producing significant creativity. As a result, thinking styles have important implications for creativity in work environments. People in companies have great ideas all the time. But they are often unheard, ignored, or discounted. The problem often lies not with the employee's idea or creative vision. Rather, it may be that his or her thinking or cognitive style differs from that of their boss or coworkers. People are judging both the methods someone uses to get to an idea and the idea itself from the unique perspective of their own thinking style. Similarly, when trying to sell an idea to someone within the organization, presenting it in a manner consistent with the thinking style of the recipient can be instrumental in obtaining their support.

The Expeditionary Sales Force

When applied within the sales organization, creativity can result in innovation. Sales innovations can take many forms, from novel methods for qualifying leads to unusual solutions that solve vexing customer problems. Innovation must become a core competency in sales. This competency consists of an ability to come up with meaningful innovations, and then champion them to the point that they are adopted by senior management, by other departments within the sales professional's own firm, and/or by customers.

Innovation is dynamic. It represents a moving target. New approaches have short lives, and are inevitably replaced by newer approaches. Accordingly, companies must create what we call an "expeditionary" sales force, meaning a sales organization that moves quickly in recognizing opportunity and acting on it. Moreover, an expeditionary sales force *leads* its customers, *leads* its competitors, and ultimately *leads* its own firm.

Let us begin with customers. A traditional perspective on innovation is that firms should ask customers what they want and then find a way to give it to them. In a sense, then, the sales organization is following the customer. A problem comes into play, though, when customers do not know exactly what they want, or are too busy and focused on their own problems to convey a clear sense of what sort of innovations might address their needs. The term "expeditionary" describes a sales force that leads customers instead of following them. Leading customers means taking them in new directions, and to modifications in how they buy. So again, the sales organization becomes a change agent.

The ability to lead customers implies that the sales professional knows the customer intimately. This awareness extends well beyond current and coming product needs. It includes an understanding of the core strategies being pursued by, the current and emerging capabilities and competencies of, and the competitive and other environmental challenges faced by the customer organization.

This leadership also applies to competitors. The expeditionary sales force does not mimic the moves of its adversaries. Rather, it learns from competitor successes (and failures), improves on them, and ultimately displaces them. Sales organizations have a tendency to believe that whatever the competition is doing must be right, and they tend to overreact to any new competitive action. While one cannot afford to ignore competing firms, their circumstances differ, including their resources, their capabilities and constraints, and the opportunities open to them. The expeditionary sales organization effectively competes with itself. Rather than play a game of "one-upmanship" with competitors, the expeditionary firm is continually trying to outdo its own achievements. A sense of "healthy dissatisfaction" pervades the organization, where managers are always seeking better ways to do everything.

Lastly, the expeditionary sales force leads its own company. With changes in the business environment occurring so rapidly, one of the most important and increasingly difficult tasks confronting the sales function involves monitoring the environment, deciphering patterns and trends, predicting how things might change, and developing strategies and plans that exploit and even modify environmental conditions. From its position on the front line of the organization, the sales force has the best perspective from which to observe and respond to market turbulence and to inform the organization about developments in the marketplace. The sales force becomes an instrumental source of guidance and direction in organizational efforts to adapt.

The ability to become expeditionary is tied to the ability to act strategically. Innovation does not happen by edict. Expectations and goals must be set for innovation. Resources must be allocated to support innovation. And company infrastructure must be developed to support innovation, including human resource management policies, management control systems, and the rules and processes that govern operations.

The Empowered Sales Force

Management control is vital in sales organizations. Without a variety of controls over budgets and sales personnel, it would be impossible to determine what is going on, distinguish high from low performers, satisfy customers on a consistent basis, or find ways to continually improve. And yet too much control limits the ability of salespeople to demonstrate imagination and creativity in their jobs. The challenge is to find a balance between the tightness and the looseness of control.

The approach in many sales organizations tends to be "top-down" as opposed to "bottom up." In top-down organizations, territories are defined, quotas are set, selling methods are prescribed, compensation approaches are put in place, and other operating decisions are made by senior management; and salespeople are then expected to implement the directives. With this approach, the salesperson has selling talent, and management's role is to ensure the holder of this talent is properly motivated, allocates his or her time in an optimal fashion, and sells enough of the right products to the right customers. The salesperson is simply a resource to be managed.

Sales managers and salespeople must be viewed as entrepreneurs. They should be opportunity identifiers, creative problem-solvers, and organizational value creators. The key to this alternative perspective is the empowerment of the sales force. Empowerment is an overused and frequently abused term in today's organizations. The popularity of this term suggests a general recognition that employees should be given more responsibility and authority in performing their jobs. However, in spite of this recognition, organizations fail to empower because (a) they do not really believe in it, (b) they do not understand the complexities and commitment involved in accomplishing it, or (c) their managers lack the requisite skills and are not especially good at it.

One approach to empowerment is simply to set high performance standards and let salespeople do whatever it takes to meet them. This approach is extremely shortsighted. It encourages expedient behavior, and can produce outcomes that are inconsistent with the core strategies of the firm. It also ignores the fact that sustainable innovation in companies requires discipline, team collaboration, and ongoing learning. Another faulty approach to empowerment is "tokenism," where managers allow employees the occasional freedom to make decisions for themselves but quickly withdraw that freedom when something goes wrong.

Empowerment involves risk and requires trust. It must be built into the design of sales jobs. Further, jobs themselves must be defined more broadly, with significant discretion to try new approaches and create novel solutions for customers. The salesperson in effect becomes responsible for tailoring elements of an entire marketing mix to serve an account, including the product configuration, pricing, customer communication, and logistics. He or she becomes accountable for value creation for customers and for innovating on behalf of the firm.

Empowerment does not mean that anything goes. A guiding principle of empowerment is "giving up control to gain control." By this we mean that the sales manager must be good at delegation, but it must be enlightened delegation. When a manager gives up control of some activity or area of responsibility (e.g., setting sales quotas, negotiating prices) and instead allows employees to handle it, control is being given up. And yet, if the empowered employee responds by being more conscientious, more creative, or harder working, then control is actually being gained. The control is not over the intermediate actions of the employee but over the employee's final output, as well as over the employee's sense of accomplishment and job satisfaction. Hence, giving the salesperson more discretion over some activity or decision variable must be coupled with a very clear sense of the larger objective.

The Strategic Sales Force

There is a tendency among sales organizations to focus almost exclusively on tactical maneuvers and operational considerations, while failing to think or act strategically. That is, they spend considerable time and effort hiring salespeople, designing sales incentives, developing sales appeals, and so forth, and they try to accomplish these day-to-day decisions are accomplished in a manner that ensures resources are being used efficiently. But efficiency does not imply effectiveness. Efficiency means that the activities that are being pursued are performed in the right way. Effectiveness means that the right opportunities are being exploited, the right activities are being pursued, and the right results are being achieved. Both efficiency and effectiveness are important for a sales force, and a strategic orientation helps to ensure that both are achieved.

There are two dimensions to a strategic orientation in selling. The first involves the connection between the company as a whole and the sales force. The second involves the connection between the overall role, direction, and priorities of the sales organization and the day-to-day operational decisions made by sales managers and salespeople. Let us consider each in turn.

The job of selling should not be managed in isolation. The strategic sales organization is one that is closely aligned with the strategic intent of the organization. Corporate strategy provides a clear sense of where the firm is going and the path for getting there. Overall strategy defines the firm's core value proposition; how the firm intends to position and differentiate itself; and the relative importance of existing versus new markets, existing versus new customers, and existing versus new products. The decisions in these areas should permeate every aspect of sales management and personal selling, from the types of objectives set for the sales force to the types of people hired for sales positions, and from the way the sales force is organized to the determination of sales force call patterns.

Linking the sales organization to the overall strategies of the firm is a two-way street. The sales organization should play a meaningful role in the formulation of a company's overall strategic direction. The goals of the sales organization must be central to the overall goals and strategies of the firm. Salespeople should drive company innovation efforts as much as these innovation efforts drive the way salespeople are approaching their jobs.

A related aspect of a company-level strategic orientation is the need to closely align the sales function with other areas of the firm. Sales must be integrated with production, marketing, logistics, and other core functions and units within a company. Customers will only invest in relationships when the selling firm is making meaningful investments and the investments are ongoing. The selling firm must be able to continually create new sources of value for the customer. A sales force cannot achieve this type of value creation in isolation. Salespeople must be able to speak the language, understand the resources and budgets, and appreciate the operational problems of other functions and departments in their own firms.

Previously we discussed how the sales organization must become an important source of innovation and value creation within companies. However, an important caveat is in order. As sales managers and salespeople discover and act on new opportunities, develop unique solutions for customers, or come up with whole new approaches to accomplishing sales tasks, they should not pursue new initiatives just because those initiatives are interesting, different, or expedient. Innovation that is random and unfocused can do more damage than good. It is vital that the creative efforts of those in sales be consistent with the strategic direction and core capabilities of the firm.

The second dimension of a strategic approach to sales concerns what happens within the sales organization itself, and the manner in which sales-related activities are accomplished. Sales management involves hundreds of decisions. Life inside a sales organization is filled with deadlines, daily pressures to perform, and periodic crises. These realities lead managers to make decisions in isolation, on the spur of the moment, and/or expediently. While some of this expediency cannot be avoided, in the strategic sales organization there is an attempt to "connect the dots" when making decisions. This means that the sales force itself has a clear sense of strategic direction. Decisions regarding who and what type of people to hire, how their jobs are defined, how their performance is assessed and they are compensated, and so forth are made in a manner that is consistent with the strategic direction of the overall sales organization.

Achieving a strategic orientation within the operations of the sales force requires that managers adhere to the discipline of what we call the "strategy cycle." The beginning point is the establishment of a set of measurable sales objectives. Next, based on these performance objectives, a sales strategy is designed. Then a range of sales tactics and action steps are formulated that are consistent with this strategy. Sales managers and salespeople then implement these tactics and action steps, with varying results. Finally, mechanisms are put in place to closely track or monitor performance outcomes to determine if sales objectives are being accomplished. Variances between sales objectives and performance outcomes lead to ongoing adjustments to the sales organization's goals, strategies, and tactics.

The Technological Sales Force

More than any other single factor, technology is transforming the capabilities of the company sales force. As a result, failure to embrace technology within sales undermines the firm's fundamental ability to compete. The integration of technology must happen both in sales management and in personal selling.

In sales management, new information technologies allow leading-edge companies to identify more and better candidates for sales positions, train salespeople continually and virtually, define sales territories in ways that optimize performance, and reward salespeople in novel ways and on a real-time basis. The sales manager is better able to estimate the lifetime value of a customer, and to group accounts based on their relative attractiveness. New systems for managing customer relationships find technology bringing sellers and buyers closer together. Other technologies also contribute to this closeness, such as electronic data interchange systems that place buyers and sellers online with one another, and just-in-time inventory systems that connect the operations of buying and selling organizations. Finally, the enlightened sales manager uses technology to better understand his or her sales force. Internal research is conducted regularly to identify patterns and relationships among a large number of sales force-related variables. Such research helps the manager anticipate salesperson failure before it happens, determine optimal call patterns, identify characteristics of top-performing salespeople, understand factors that drive the turnover of salespeople, and much more.

The impact is just as significant in personal selling. Technology is helping salespeople "sell smarter," while also greatly enhancing their efficiency. To a salesperson, the three most valuable resources are time, time, and time. Technology empowers the salesperson to do more with less, and to do things that heretofore she or he was unable to do. Specific tools exist for improving the salesperson's ability to generate, manage, and prioritize leads, conduct background research on customers and competitors, organize sales calls, design sales presentations, and rapidly respond to customer inquiries and requests. Just as important is the fact that customers are becoming more technologically sophisticated, and salespeople have no choice but to keep up.

There is also an important caveat here. Technology is dynamic. It will never stop improving. New and better software products become available to facilitate virtually every facet of sales operations on a weekly or monthly basis. These products leapfrog one another, often leaving the user confused regarding what to buy, when to upgrade, and when to move away from a given technology. Moreover, creating a "technologically enabled" sales force can become expensive, and the ability of any sales organization to calculate the return on investment for money spent on sales force-related technology is problematic. These realities reinforce the need for a technology strategy within the sales function, including a clear set of criteria for evaluating new technologies, and an ability to link the capabilities of a given technology to the practical needs of sales professionals.

The Collaborative Sales Force[2]

Collaboration is a prime requirement within the modern sales organization. It is vital for encouraging individuals to work together on inventive solutions, for enhancing the speed of the organization, and for supporting the growing emphasis on team selling. Internal collaboration also enhances the firm's ability to collaborate with and create value for customers. The implications of greater collaboration can be seen at the level of the senior manager, the field sales manager, and the individual salesperson.

At the senior leadership level, challenges come from both cultural and structural perspectives. Senior sales leaders must deal with the cultural issues of changing from an individualistic culture to one that is more collective, while refocusing the very nature of selling from "transactional" to "relational." Moving to a team culture impacts the criteria used in selection, rewards, and recognition. It also implies a clash of the old with the new in terms of strategy, systems, structure, and culture. Sales executives must understand that organizational change begins with value and belief change. Organizational and individual values must be aligned. The starting point is a transformation of senior managers and then field managers, followed by sales teams and salespeople.

A collaborative sales force results in a redefined role for the field sales manager. A blunt way of describing the change is the phrase "the boss is dead." Under the boss model, a person of authority emphasizes the maximization of self and the tendency to control. Authority, commands, and even fear are used to drive people in the organization with little concern for trust, empowerment, honesty, and the long-range impact of today's actions. In contrast, the collaborative sales environment emphasizes the need for coaching, plain talk, sharing authority and credit, inquiry instead of advocacy, and mutual respect of team members.

For the field sales leader, implementing changes in culture and cross-functional processes requires new skills. Change processes must be well communicated and led from the top. Salespeople and sales teams must be brought into a new world that values team-building dimensions such as cohesiveness, helping behavior, courtesy, peacekeeping, conflict management, and loyalty. The field sales manager plays a critical role in creating a preferred future for his or her organization. Relevant challenges center around an individual's ability to start a personal learning journey, adopt new mindsets, and behave in keeping with the desired cultural norms of the envisioned organization.

---

[2] For a more comprehensive discussion of collaboration in the sales force, see Ingram, T. N., R. W. LaForge, W. B. Locander, S. B. MacKenzie, and P. M. Podsakoff (2005). "New Directions for Sales Leadership Research," *Journal of Personal Selling & Sales Management* (forthcoming).

At the salesperson level, the challenge is multiplied. As sales organizations increasingly stress internal collaboration, those most important in accepting the changes are the most isolated from the senior and field leaders. Salespeople must learn to embrace their new roles and to trust the process of change. Putting team goals ahead of self-interests requires that trust in both the senior leaders and field sales managers be developed over time. Salespeople also must acquire and apply conflict resolution strategies and skills to work effectively within the organization.

For salespeople, the increasing importance of customer relationships is good news and bad. While frontline sales and service personnel have traditionally taken a customer advocate position, they generally have had to fight internally for the support necessary to implement a customer-focused strategy. As more importance is placed on relationships, the field sales force will come under increasing pressure to build strong linkages with a valued customer base. To accomplish this objective, salespeople will need greater expertise in problem solving and partnering skills, along with enhanced territory management skills. In addition, they may need better coping skills to deal with the likelihood of increased role conflict and role stress.

Getting There: The TSE BREAK Process

Creating the type of sales organization that we have been discussing requires change. Yet change of any kind is inherently resisted by both managers and employees. Change is threatening, brings significant uncertainty, requires considerable learning, and disrupts the patterns that enable people to be successful at their work. For this reason, no matter how promising a given change initiative appears to be, successful implementation of the initiative within the organization must begin with the recognition that there will be forces working against it. These forces will be built around both logical and illogical considerations.

Given the potency of the resistance that can be expected, it is important to approach change efforts from a perspective that is both systematic and enlightened. Stated differently, a perusal of the popular business press and available academic work suggests there is no shortage of new "high performance" concepts, "best or leading practices," and practices for becoming "great." However, there is a shortage of insights into how to successfully implement these new concepts and approaches. In brief, sales managers need a model or framework for making change happen.

This is where the BREAK process comes into play (see Exhibit 1.3). The Sales Educators (TSE) have developed BREAK as a logical and easy-to-use

Exhibit 1.3 The TSE BREAK Process

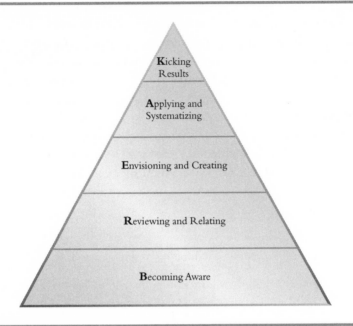

© Thomson

framework that can be applied to virtually any new sales initiative. Adopting this framework will significantly increase the likelihood that change efforts will be embraced by senior management and those within the sales organization. BREAK is central to the way we will approach each of the major topics discussed in the chapters to come.

There are five major steps or stages involved with the BREAK process:

1. **B**ecoming Aware
2. **R**eviewing and Relating
3. **E**nvisioning and Creating
4. **A**pplying and Systematizing
5. **K**icking Results to the Next Level

Let us consider each of these steps in greater detail.

Becoming Aware

As a foundation for BREAKthrough thinking, sales leaders must possess a high degree of self-awareness—about their own behaviors, the organizations they are leading, and the external environments in which they compete. Just as critically, they must be aware of the assumptions that guide their current way of doing things. Self-awareness requires more effort than simply looking in the mirror. A cursory glance in the mirror will reveal exactly what the person expects to see. More often than not, a critical evaluation does not take place. In fact, if the mirror gazers do not know what to look for while considering their reflection, personal insight about their true appearance may remain a mystery. However, if they had a list of questions to consider while reflecting in the mirror, they are much more likely to "see" themselves as they truly are.

Asking the right questions is an important part of "becoming aware," the critical first step in the BREAK process. As we address the major issues affecting today's sales organizations in the pages ahead, readers will be prompted to:

- look critically at their organizations and themselves,
- reflect on the questions posed at the opening of each chapter, and
- capture their preliminary thinking in response to the questions.

The reader will find the format of this book conducive to walking through the BREAK process in a very personal, hands-on way. Each chapter opens with a set of Becoming Aware questions that relate to the subject matter of that chapter. After each of these questions, space is provided to capture one's thinking. The Sales Educators encourage readers to use that space, and to take time to begin developing a keen awareness of the need for change and the types of change that are possible in their organizations.

Reviewing and Relating

Once the sales professional is aware (of shortcomings, opportunities, emerging challenges, new patterns, etc.), he or she must develop a richer understanding of these developments as they relate to the current mission, structure, capabilities, resources, and policies of his or her sales organization. This is the "reviewing and relating" stage of the process. The concern is with understanding how different facts and insights are connected to one another, why they matter, and the ways in which they might impact the performance of the sales force.

Again, this stage in the BREAK process is integral to the structure of this book. Each chapter contains a summary of current knowledge on a given topical area. As leading researchers in the sales and entrepreneurship area, The Sales Educators have collected and summarized the state-of-the-art thinking in the areas covered. *Strategic Sales Leadership* provides a review of current knowledge in an easy-to-read format. Academic formats of multiple citations and footnotes have purposefully been avoided to make the ideas easily accessible to all readers. The important part of the reader's job in the BREAK process is to review the knowledge contained in this text and to begin to relate such knowledge to the reader's organization. He or she must identify the practices that appear to be counter to the sales leader's current organizational practices (based on the Becoming Aware process). The reader is encouraged to carefully consider the leading edge practices described in the text, and relate those practices to the field sales organization's existing business practices and leadership behaviors.

Envisioning and Creating

The awareness and insights that result from the first two stages in the BREAK process provide the raw material with which the sales professional can innovate. Creative solutions to problems and innovative approaches to opportunities are the focus of the "envisioning and creating" stage. To build a high-performance sales organization, sales leaders have to develop new ways of thinking and new business practices, and these must be linked to the organization's existing ways of thinking and acting. Such leaders typically do not have the luxury of starting a field sales organization from scratch. The new must be connected to the old. The changed behaviors must clearly supplant old routines. Sales leaders have to envision what the new will look like. Like politicians stumping across the campaign trail, field sales leaders must first take their organizations through the change process *verbally*. They must describe for the organization where they have been and articulate the vision of where they are headed in each key area of change. Then they must co-create the steps for reaching the articulated vision for a particular area. Working in partnership with field sales representatives and others in the organization, readers of this text will create the steps necessary for adopting the "new."

Applying and Systematizing

New behaviors, business practices, and ways of thinking must be applied to the organization in a disciplined and systematic fashion. They must also be implemented in a manner that reflects the political realities that exist within any company. Otherwise, new behaviors are briefly (or never) adopted and then fade away. One of the biggest challenges for today's sales manager is to avoid becoming a "flavor of the month" leader. Qualitative research with sales professionals suggests that leaders both in the field and in the home office are notorious for identifying the latest "new thing" and pushing it out to the field. The new practice is introduced almost as a stand-alone phenomenon, with little regard for how it fits with other practices in the organization. For example, a new sales strategy leveraging the inside sales force to increase customer retention impacts multiple aspects of strategic sales leadership. The job description of the outside salesperson has just changed, suggesting a domino impact on his or her ideal candidate profile, supervisory system, compensation plan, etc. The goal of this book is to limit the reader's inclination toward a "flavor of the month" approach, encouraging the sales leader to consider how a change in practice impacts and can be integrated with other aspects of the sales management system.

As you work through the processes of Becoming Aware, Reviewing and Relating, and Envisioning and Creating, you will come out with a great set of ideas and notes for action. The Applying and Systematizing step is the *action step* in the BREAK process. In order to provide the maximum utility and value of this process to sales executives such as yourself, The Sales Educators invite you to join a community of sales professionals who use our Web site to apply and systematize what they have gleaned from this book. Using the Web site provides you maximum flexibility in developing your action steps, and also allows you to communicate directly with us about what your plans and strategies are. And, most importantly, our Web site allows us to keep the most current information possible at your fingertips so you can continually work toward Kicking Results to the Next Level!

Kicking Results to the Next Level

This is not a quick fix book offering a one-size-fits-all solution. The analogy to consider is learning to eat for health compared with going on a diet. The results from a diet typically are not sustainable. Learning to eat in a more healthy way really does provide a step-change in results.

Similarly, The Sales Educators are confident that readers, working openly and earnestly through the BREAK process, will actually experience a step-change increase in their sales organization's results. Sales professionals reading this text will think about their businesses differently. Becoming aware of one's practices, reviewing and relating best and next practices to one's organization, envisioning and creating the linkages between old and new practices, and creating and applying connections between the new practices and the sales management systems are key steps to effecting real change. They are steps toward a healthier, more prosperous, and more strategically relevant sales organization.

On The Sales Educators' Web site (www.TheSalesEducators.com) you will find continually updated ideas, exercises, and approaches for Kicking Results to the Next Level. We want this book, and the BREAK process you will learn herein, to become an ongoing, dynamic part of your organization and its leadership and management. In that spirit, beginning with Chapter 2 you will be invited at the end of each chapter to join us at our Web site for BREAK process worksheets and other resources. Also, we would like to hear from you about how the BREAK process is working for your sales organization! Through access and use of the materials on our Web site, you can ensure that you are always able to put best practices into play in your sales organization—facilitating Strategic Sales Leadership: BREAKthrough Thinking for BREAKthrough Results!

Where We Are Going: Overview of the Chapters Ahead

This opening chapter built the case that the company sales force, as we know it, is at risk. Salespeople and the infrastructure to support them are among the most expensive assets in a company. Fundamental questions are being raised about whether the benefits or returns on a sale force are worth the investment. Underlying such questions are concerns about the role and relevancy of a sales force given the nature of the competitors, customers, and technologies with which contemporary organizations are confronted.

Dramatic changes in the business environment are making traditional approaches to organizing and managing the sales force obsolete. These environmental changes have created a need for an entirely new concept of the sales function. By adopting this new vision, companies can get far more value out of the sales force—it becomes a major source of innovation and value creation, and ultimately a key competitive advantage for the firm. The chapter introduced the BREAK process, a step-by-step process for affecting meaningful change in a company's sales operations.

The purpose of this book is to encourage and empower sales leaders to:

- be reflective of their current business practices and leadership behaviors,
- identify best practices and next practices applicable to their leadership situation,
- transform their business processes and leadership behaviors, in order to
- become high-performance sales organizations.

It all starts with BREAKthrough thinking. The BREAK process, our foundational approach to BREAKthrough thinking, is a centerpiece of the coming chapters as we explore a wide range of issues that are central to the creation of a truly entrepreneurial sales force. While this opening chapter has introduced the BREAK process, subsequent chapters emphasize ways that sales managers can apply the BREAK process to particular areas within sales and to themselves. Although the specific chapters differ in format due to topic differences, each chapter prompts readers to assess their current situation, presents a synthesis of relevant sales research and best practices, and encourages the integration of new thinking for building improved results.

This opening chapter has described the dramatic changes in the environment sales organizations must operate in, outlined a significantly different view of the role and nature of the modern sales force, and presented a process for effecting innovation and change within the sales function. Following this introductory chapter, the book is divided into two parts. Strategic issues are discussed in Part One and leadership issues in Part Two. In Chapter 2, we delve much deeper into the concept of entrepreneurship and the nature of an entrepreneurial sales force. Entrepreneurship is approached as a logical process that can be applied to the day-to-day management of a sales force and to maximizing the potential of a sales territory.

Chapter 3 describes how to achieve peak sales organization performance. The chapter explores how sales managers must become aware of their critical roles, enhance their sales management skills, and improve their sales organization. New ways of thinking are encouraged and new business practices are introduced. The goal of the chapter is to help ensure that the methods learned will be adopted, maintained, and improved.

Chapters 4 and 5 examine new perspectives on customers and how they should be approached. Chapter 4 is concerned with customer relationship management. It explores what it means to be market driven, and how a market orientation should drive sales strategy and practice. Drawing on the notion that market-oriented firms develop competitive advantage by selecting their customers wisely and focusing their core competencies on serving these strategically relevant customers exceptionally well, the notions of customer relationship strategy and management are developed in sales force terms. The objective of Chapter 5 is to identify ways the sales organization can forge strategic, profitable relationships with key customers. An enterprise-level perspective is provided on strategic customer relationship choices and practices in achieving world-class sales performance.

Chapter 6 focuses on sales compensation systems. The challenge is to achieve a balance between the needs of the organization, customers, and salespeople in designing compensation programs. More than ever, it is crucial to tie sales compensation to strategic priorities, which can be largely achieved by carefully specifying salespeople's roles and rewarding strategically relevant sales activities. The chapter provides a process for designing and implementing effective sales compensation systems.

Chapter 7 provides readers a comprehensive system for defining the ideal sales candidate profile (CP) for the organization. The CP will then serve as the springboard for selecting a set of recruiting sources to facilitate a flow of appropriate candidates. Chapter 7 delineates how the CP guides the development of a strategic or goal-based selection system to ensure that appropriate candidates meeting are chosen. The recruiting and selection process is important not only for hiring new sales associates, but to facilitate the managers' goal of keeping top performers in the sales organization.

Teamwork is becoming increasingly important to most sales organizations. Chapter 8 discusses different types of teamwork and suggests several strategies for encouraging it. A process for integrating teamwork considerations into all sales management decisions and a method for building sales organization teamwork are also presented and discussed.

Finally, Chapter 9 provides some concluding ideas to the BREAK process, and especially encourages you to take the next critical steps of Applying and Systematizing what you have developed so far, vis-à-vis the templates and resources on our Web site.

References and Suggested Readings

Colletti, J. A. and L. B. Chonko (1997). "Change Management Initiatives: Moving Sales Organizations from Obsolescence to High Performance," *Journal of Personal Selling & Sales Management,* Spring, 1–30.

Dixon, A. L., J. B. Gassenheimer, and T. F. Barr (2003). "Identifying the Lone Wolf: A Team Perspective." *Journal of Personal Selling & Sales Management,* 23 (3), 205–219.

Herrmann, N. (1995). *The Creative Brain,* Lake Lure, NC: Ned Herrmann Group.

Ingram, T. N., R. W. LaForge, W. B. Locander, S. B. MacKenzie, and P. M. Podsakoff (2005). "New Directions for Sales Leadership Research," *Journal of Personal Selling & Sales Management* (forthcoming).

Jones, E., L. Chonko, and J. Roberts (2004). "Antecedents and C of Sales Force Obsolescence: Perceptions from Sales and Marketing Executives," *Industrial Marketing Management,* 33, 439–456.

Jones, E., S. Sundaram, and W. Chin (2002). "Factors Leading to Sales Force Automation Use: A Longitudinal Analysis," *Journal of Personal Selling & Sales Management,* 22(3), 145–156.

Parthasarathy, M. and R. S. Sohi (1997). "Sales Force Automation and the Adoption of Technological Innovations by Salespeople: Theory and Implications," *Journal of Business and Industrial Marketing,* 12(3/4): 196–208.

Rackham, N. and J. De Vincentis (1999). *Rethinking the Sales Force,* New York: McGraw-Hill.

Speier, C. and V. Venkatesh (2002). "The Hidden Minefields in the Adoption of Sales Force Automation Technologies," *Journal of Marketing,* 66(3), 98–111.

Szymanski, D. M. (1988). "Determinants of Selling Effectiveness: The Importance of Declarative Knowledge to the Personal Selling Concept," *Journal of Marketing,* 52(January), 65–77.

von Oech, R. (1998). *A Whack on the Side of the Head,* New York: Warner Books.

Widmier, S. M., D. W. Jackson Jr., and D. B. McCabe (2002). "Infusing Technology into Personal Selling," *Journal of Personal Selling & Sales Management,* 22(3), 189–198.

Zoltners, A. A., P. Sinha, and G. A. Zoltners (2001). *The Complete Guide to Accelerating Sales Force Performance.* Chicago: Amacom.

Chapter 2

Developing an Entrepreneurial Sales Organization

Introduction

Entrepreneurship is traditionally associated with innovative individuals who recognize opportunity and create growth-oriented ventures. However, this concept has important implications for the way companies of all sizes and types are managed. And, as we shall see, the sales organization is the natural home for entrepreneurship within a company.

Entrepreneurship represents a way of thinking and a way of acting. It requires a mindset that is opportunity driven, not resource constrained. It involves a manageable process that can be applied to the job of the sales manager and to the work of those in the sales force. The sales manager not only must be an entrepreneur, but must create work environments that encourage those within the sales force to act on their own entrepreneurial potential. This chapter will elaborate on each of these issues. A beginning point for those seeking to achieve higher levels of entrepreneurship in their organizations is the BREAKthrough Questions found in the Becoming Aware box on the next page.

Entrepreneurship as Competitive Advantage

Twenty-first-century companies find themselves operating in a new competitive landscape. Today's business environment can be characterized in terms of increased uncertainty, decreased ability to forecast, fluid firm and industry boundaries, and a reduced sense of control. Markets are more complex, competition is more predatory, and technologies continue to change every facet of how a company operates. As a result of these and other forces, the contemporary organization has never confronted so many threats, but also has never had such an abundance of opportunities available to its managers.

In response to a turbulent external environment, firms are learning new ways to compete. They are creating flatter organizational structures, broader spans of control, smaller staff functions, looser controls, customized rewards, formal goals for innovation, and greater individual autonomy. Processes are re-engineered, activities are outsourced, and new alliances are formed. Managers

---

BREAK BOX: Becoming Aware

1. How would you rate yourself in terms of the following characteristics?
   - desire for achievement
   - comfort with ambiguity
   - willingness to take calculated risks
   - internal locus of control (strong sense that you can effect meaningful change in your work environment or any other environment).
2. How many innovative concepts have you introduced into your sales organization over the past 24 months?
3. What is your attitude toward failure? How many failures have you experienced on the job in the past 24 months?
4. Which of the following better characterizes your leadership style: promoter (bold entrepreneurial leadership) or trustee (quality administrative leadership)?
5. How would you assess your skill set in the following four areas: coming up with innovative ideas, managing risks, leveraging resources (bootstrapping), and identifying guerrilla (unconventional) approaches to accomplishing tasks?
6. Does the work environment in your organization discourage or encourage your employees to engage in entrepreneurial behavior? What are the key constraints or facilitators?

---

at all levels are encouraged to tolerate failure, permit rule bending, support informal innovation projects, reward risk taking, and sponsor (or play the role of) champions. Established rules of thumb are abandoned as managers attempt to "unlearn" traditional principles and practices.

In short, turbulent change in the external environment is forcing internal transformation, as companies strive to achieve sustainable competitive advantage. And this brings us to the most fundamental aspect of the new competitive landscape: the source of sustainable competitive advantage. No longer are a better product offering, a lower price, or superior customer service sufficient. This is the battleground where all firms operate, and so the bar continues to rise in each of these areas. Stated differently, "one-upmanship" does not produce sustainable advantage.

Instead, companies are learning that advantage lies in creating a different kind of organization, one built around flexibility, adaptability, speed, aggressiveness, and innovation. Leading-edge firms are increasingly those that are more flexible in responding to diverse customer requirements, and more adaptable as conditions change and new opportunities appear. They move quickly in recognizing and exploiting opportunities. They bring an aggressive approach to developing their employees, satisfying their customers, outperforming their competitors, and growing their ventures. They create an ongoing sense of urgency within the organization, with innovation defined as a normal part of everyone's job.

In the new competitive landscape, the winners will be those companies better able to nurture the entrepreneurial spirit in every facet of company operations. Nowhere is this more critical than the sales function. Sales is arguably the single greatest source of ongoing interaction between a firm and its external environment. As such, it is in a unique position to recognize and exploit new opportunities, and to help the firm adapt to emerging customer and competitive circumstances.

Understanding Entrepreneurship in Established Companies

Entrepreneurship is a process by which individuals—either independently or inside organizations—create value by bringing together unique combinations of resources to exploit opportunities. Corporate entrepreneurship has been defined as a process of organizational renewal and new business creation. In a corporate context, entrepreneurial activities revolve around organizational constraints and resource commitments for the purpose of innovative results. These activities can take place on the corporate, division, functional, or project levels.

Approaching entrepreneurship as a process has important implications for the sales function. As a process, entrepreneurship can be broken down into steps or stages that can be managed. Further, the entrepreneurial process can be applied in a wide variety of sales contexts, ranging from new account selling or trade selling to customer relationship management. The process itself includes the set of activities necessary to identify an opportunity, define a novel concept or idea for exploiting the opportunity, assess the needed resources, acquire those resources, implement the concept, and manage and harvest the concept or approach.

Companies, and the sales organizations within them, can also be expected to vary in terms of how entrepreneurial they are. To fully appreciate this point, it is necessary to recognize that entrepreneurship has three underlying dimensions or components: innovativeness, risk taking, and proactiveness. *Innovativeness* refers to the seeking of creative, unusual, or novel solutions to problems and needs. It includes the development of new products and services, as well as new processes for performing organizational functions. In sales, such process innovation might include new approaches to territory design, goal- and quota-setting, prospecting, customer service, sales promotions, or sales administration, among many possibilities. *Risk taking* involves the willingness of managers to commit resources to opportunities having a reasonable chance of failure. The risks are not extreme and uncontrollable but instead are moderate, calculated, and manageable. *Proactiveness* is concerned with implementation and making events happen through whatever means necessary. It frequently entails breaking with established ways of accomplishing a task and requires a hands-on management style. It usually implies considerable perseverance, adaptability, and a willingness to assume some responsibility for failure.

Entrepreneurial activities within sales will reflect different degrees of innovativeness, riskiness, and proactiveness. Further, any number of entrepreneurial events can be produced by a sales organization in a given time period. Accordingly, all sales organizations demonstrate some level of entrepreneurship, but they differ in terms of degree (how much), and frequency (how often). The combination of degree and frequency can be referred to as *entrepreneurial intensity*. Exhibit 2.1 illustrates how sales organizations can be

Exhibit 2.1   How Does Your Sales Organization Rate?

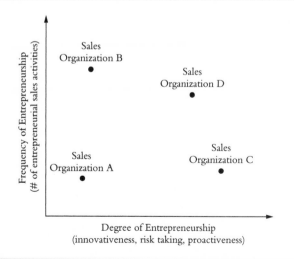

© Thomson

characterized in terms of their entrepreneurial intensity, and includes the following four sample profiles.

- *Sales Organization A:* Relatively low in both degree and frequency, this organization innovates very little, and the new approaches it does develop tend to be incremental changes from the status quo.
- *Sales Organization B:* This organization is continually experimenting with new approaches to a range of different sales activities, but the changes tend to be fairly incremental.
- *Sales Organization C:* This organization does not innovate very often in terms of sales management, but when it does, the new approaches represent fairly radical change.
- *Sales Organization D:* This dynamic organization is continually innovating, with a portfolio of new approaches at any given time, some of them major breakthroughs and others representing incremental changes.

The relevance of a given approach depends on the industry, markets, and competitive environment within which the firm operates. For instance, in situations where the product sells itself, or the firm is alone in the marketplace and has a product that the customer views as a necessity, there is less need for innovative, risk-taking, proactive behaviors. In such situations, Sales Organization A can be expected to perform reasonably well. Alternatively, when operating in a competitive market that is relatively saturated, where ongoing relationships with existing accounts constitute the core of a firm's business, the ongoing but incremental innovation of Sales Organization B might be more effective. If we assume that the market is quite volatile, with continual changes in technologies and product offerings, aggressive competitors, and ongoing changes in buyer organizations, then Sales Organization D is likely to be the winner.

Researchers have uncovered two key relationships when studying entrepreneurial intensity. First, companies that demonstrate stronger levels of entrepreneurial intensity also score higher in terms of how customer driven they are. The firm's entrepreneurial orientation may be the key to achieving a true customer orientation. The entrepreneurial firm is able to produce innovative solutions in response to customer needs, but is also capable of leading customers in new value-creating directions. Second, entrepreneurial intensity has a positive relationship with a number of measures of corporate financial performance (Morris and Kuratko, 2002). Quite simply, highly entrepreneurial companies tend to perform better. This second relationship appears to be most marked under conditions of environmental turbulence. When competitive conditions are especially challenging, the winners tend to be those best able to tap into the entrepreneurial spirit. These relationships reinforce the importance of entrepreneurship as a source of sustainable competitive advantage.

The Sales Function as Home for Entrepreneurship

No function, department, or area within a firm should be more entrepreneurial than sales. To appreciate why this is the case, let us first consider the elements that sales and entrepreneurship share in common, and then explore the nature of the entrepreneurial process.

Commonalities Between Entrepreneurship and Sales

Sales has much in common with entrepreneurship (see Exhibits 2.2 and 2.3). First, consider the nature of the work that must be done. The sales profession can be characterized as involving ample opportunities for personal initiative, moderate freedom of action, periods of high pressure and stress, a variety of challenging job-related tasks, a strong "results" orientation, significant potential for career development, and the possibility of large financial rewards. Each of these is also a core characteristic of the task facing entrepreneurs as they create and grow new ventures.

The similarities can also be seen if we look at the people involved in these two activities. When compared to their less successful counterparts, those

Exhibit 2.2   Similarities Between the Work of Entrepreneurs and Salespeople

- Deal with a variety of both routine and nonroutine tasks on a daily basis
- Work independently with a great degree of personal freedom
- Perform challenging work due to high level of business uncertainty
- Operate in ambiguous situations
- Develop creative solutions to business problems
- Driven by opportunities rather than resources
- Work under significant pressure and stress
- Receive fairly immediate feedback from job performance
- Define success largely in measurable, financial terms
- Income tied to job performance
- Organize own time and work schedule
- Directly responsible for performance

© Thomson

Exhibit 2.3   Common Characteristics of Entrepreneurs and Salespeople

- Achievement oriented
- Persistent
- Persuasive
- Assertive
- Take initiative
- Versatile
- Perceptive
- Energetic
- Self confident
- Internal locus of control
- Independent
- Calculated risk taker
- Creative
- Resourceful
- Opportunity seeker
- Comfortable with ambiguity
- Hard worker
- Well organized

© Thomson

who achieve success in sales tend to be more confident, independent, socially satisfied, adaptive, and aggressive. They also tend to be better educated, more adept at planning, to have stronger leadership qualities, and to demonstrate a stronger preference for commission-based compensation programs. These qualities also apply to the entrepreneur. For instance, the entrepreneurial personality has been described as independent, achievement motivated, tolerant of ambiguity, a calculated risk taker, having a strong internal locus of control, and being well organized. These traits mark sales as one of the more entrepreneurial of occupations.

Management of the sales function has the potential to be an entrepreneurial pursuit as well. In fact, there are reasons to believe sales management should represent one of the more entrepreneurial areas within firms. Most of the activities that comprise the sales manager's job (e.g., defining territories, recruitment and training of the sales force, design of compensation systems, motivating sales personnel, establishing quotas, determining overall sales strategies) demand a high degree of innovativeness, calculated risk taking, and proactiveness. Sales managers are in a position to give salespeople a sense of territorial proprietorship, granting authority and responsibility in a number of decision areas, encouraging experimentation while not punishing failure, and implementing creative methods for evaluating and rewarding individual performance. They can also influence the amount of paperwork and the number of bureaucratic obstacles facing a given salesperson, including the nature of the relationship between sales and other functional areas within the firm (e.g., production, R & D, order processing).

There is also evidence that sales managers embrace the importance of entrepreneurship in sales, and have clear ideas regarding how it applies. In a major national survey of sales managers, respondents were able to convey a clear concept of entrepreneurship, viewed it as a key source of strategic direction within sales, believed they could influence the level of entrepreneurial behavior demonstrated by their salespeople, and had clear priorities regarding the sales areas where entrepreneurship should play the biggest role. Exhibit 2.4 summarizes some of the key findings of the study.

Exploring the Entrepreneurial Process Within Sales

Central to understanding its role within sales is the recognition that entrepreneurship is a manageable process. This process can be applied in an unlimited number of ways at the level of both the sales manager and the salesperson. Whether the sales manager is dealing with the general challenge of motivating the sales force, or a particular sales rep is looking for better ways to generate referrals or close sales, the ability to produce innovative solutions is enhanced by approaching entrepreneurship as a logical process. Let us briefly consider each of the stages in the process.

1. *Opportunity Identification*   An opportunity is defined as a favorable set of circumstances creating a *need* or *opening* for a new business concept or approach. It is a situation where something can be improved at a profit. Some opportunities are perennial, meaning they are always there, such as the ability to do something cheaper, quicker, more reliably, in a higher-quality manner, or incrementally better. Other opportunities are occasional, such as the emergence of a new market segment, the development of a new capability, the withdrawal from the market of a key competitor, a temporary surge in demand, or a market hole. Opportunities are everywhere, and derive from a large number of sources. Some of the ways they can be identified include challenging assumptions, recognizing patterns or trends in internal or external data, researching markets, looking for new ways to apply existing capabilities, and exploiting underutilized resources. It is also important to note that

Exhibit 2.4   What Sales Managers Think About Entrepreneurship

In a large national survey of sales managers by one of the authors, strong evidence was found for the relevance of entrepreneurship within a sales context. Some key findings included:

- Sales managers believe that entrepreneurship is a term which applies within established companies, is driven by individuals within those firms, and is a major factor for continued company success;
- The entrepreneurial person is largely a product of his/her environment, and can be characterized in terms of drive, self-confidence, and action-orientation, persistence, and risk-taking skills;
- Attributes associated with entrepreneurship tend to also be those identified as most critical for success in sales;
- Entrepreneurship represents a source of strategic direction for firms. The entrepreneurial firm can be characterized as maintaining a sense of smallness, having a long-term focus, planning well, investing in new product and service development, being tolerant of failure, and being creative in problem solving.
- Organizations are capable of developing the entrepreneurial spirit in their employees;
- Sales managers identify the sales function as one of the most entrepreneurial areas in their firms. They see themselves at the leading edge of their companies, affecting meaningful change in spite of organizational obstacles;
- Strategy development appears to be the area within sales where entrepreneurial approaches are most important. Other priorities include salesforce recruiting, design of compensation programs, and finding ways to motivate the salesforce;
- Incentive-based compensation systems appear to be most consistent with entrepreneurial thinking;
- The leading obstacles to fostering entrepreneurship within sales include excessive control by top management, and the tendency for employees to be change resistant and risk aversive.

© Thomson

there is a "window of opportunity" that applies to any new idea. This is the optimal time period in which the sales manager must move on an innovative idea, with failure often occurring because he or she acted before the factors creating the opportunity had come together, or after the opportunity was well exploited and the window had begun to close.

2. *Concept Development*   While the opportunity centers on an untapped need, the concept is the *specific value-creating method* for capitalizing on this need. As noted above, the concept can be a new product, service, or process. While sales managers frequently come up with ideas for new products and services the organization can sell, the greatest number of innovative possibilities can be found in the processes or ways in which selling and sales management tasks are accomplished. Developing concepts involves putting resources together in new and different ways. For instance, if the opportunity was a move by customer organizations toward decentralized purchasing operations, the concept might be a new approach to organizing sales force call patterns. Importantly, entrepreneurial efforts frequently fail because of a lack of fit between the concept and the opportunity.

3. *Identification of Resource Needs*   The tendency is to assume that the key resource when pursuing an entrepreneurial opportunity is money. The evidence suggests a more complex picture. While new ideas fail because they do not attract enough financial support, the more typical problem is a shortage in other resource areas. All the money in the world will not ensure the success of a particular new idea if other key resources are not in place. For example, if the person behind the innovation has not put together the right skill set in terms of the sales team, obtained access to the right distribution channel, achieved buy-in from other key units or departments in the company, or gotten customers to modify some aspect of their operations, the idea may flounder.

4. *Acquisition of Resources*   When it comes to resources, the traditional mindset it that the manager must own or control all the needed resources, or an idea should not be pursued. Entrepreneurship is about pursuing opportunities that go well beyond one's current pool of resources. As a result, the sales manager must develop skills at leveraging the resources controlled by others, and bootstrapping new ideas until they show enough promise that the organization will formally allocate resources to support them. These skills are elaborated on in the next section.

5. *Concept Implementation*   Implementation involves moving beyond analysis and acting on an opportunity. It requires an action orientation. It also requires considerable tenacity, as anything new and different is going to be resisted. The sales manager must expect unplanned and sometimes arbitrary

obstacles, and his or her ability to persevere with a concept, while also making key adjustments to the concept and to the implementation approach as things unfold, becomes vital. Implementation requires rapid learning regarding what is working and what is not, and quick adaptation as circumstances change and new possibilities emerge. He or she must also have the insight to know when to bend or break a rule, and when to follow a rule. A willingness to "ask forgiveness instead of permission" is also important.

6. *Management and Harvesting of the Concept*   Innovations in the sales area have finite lives. Especially in the new competitive landscape, a new idea will become obsolete or ineffectual much more quickly than in times past. A novel approach to compensating the sales force may have a dramatic impact on sales force performance for 12 or 24 months, but ultimately the compensation system requires further innovation. As a result, it becomes important to consider the useful life of a new concept up front, and to think through how it will be implemented, how it will be expanded or grown, and what the exit strategy will be.

While presented as a logical set of steps, entrepreneurship is not a linear process. The stages can overlap, with activities often occurring in tandem. The manager frequently must go back and forth between stages, such as when problems with the concept force him or her to revisit the opportunity and redefine the need, or when resource issues require the manager to modify the concept or idea. It is also important to recognize that entrepreneurial thinking is necessary not only when coming up with innovative concepts and ideas (stage 2), but at every stage in the process.

Fostering Entrepreneurship in Sales: Changing the Mindset

Where does the sales manager begin when attempting to foster the entrepreneurial spirit within the company? Attention must be devoted to two major challenges: (a) creating the right mindset among all those involved in managing and implementing the firm's sales effort, and (b) creating the kind of work environment that encourages those within sales to recognize and act on their own innate entrepreneurial potential. In this section, we will explore the first challenge, focusing initially on sales leadership styles.

Styles of Leadership: Promoter Versus Trustee

Achieving higher levels of entrepreneurship begins with the leadership of the overall sales organization and of individual sales units. A useful distinction can be made between two general types of leadership styles: the "promoter" and the "trustee" (Stevenson, et al, 1999). The promoter is strongest on entrepreneurial competence, while the trustee is strongest in terms of administrative competence. These two styles can be distinguished along six major dimensions, as discussed below.

1. *Strategic Sales Orientation* When plotting strategic direction for the sales organization, the promoter is opportunity driven, while the trustee is resource constrained. The promoter views strategy as a disciplined approach to capitalizing on bold new opportunities, and is willing to pursue opportunities that are bigger than the resources currently at his or her disposal. If the opportunity is real, and is pursued with energy and insight, the promoter believes the resources can be found. The trustee is concerned with managing existing resources (e.g., budget, salespeople, distributors, market intelligence, logistics) as efficiently as possible, and will only pursue new directions that fit the resources he or she currently controls.

2. *Action Orientation* The promoter moves quickly to capitalize on opportunities, often without the complete commitment of those higher in the organization. Once a new direction is taken, he or she is also able to move away from an opportunity that proves to be less attractive just as quickly. The trustee moves slowly on new or emerging opportunities, attempting to virtually guarantee they will produce results before acting.

3. *Commitment Orientation* While quick to act, the promoter does not jump in with both feet. He or she invests in a new course of action in stages, experimenting with different approaches and investing incrementally more in the paths that appear to be producing results. The trustee more exhaustively analyzes the new course of action and, when finally ready to act, makes a complete resource commitment to a given plan or approach.

4. *Resource Control Orientation* The promoter will "beg, borrow, or steal" resources from wherever they can be found. He or she is adept at resource leveraging and bootstrapping, concepts discussed in more detail in later chapters. The promoter emphasizes flexibility when it comes to resources, meaning he or she attempts to avoid longer-term commitments to a given resource. The preference is to use resources only when they are needed, for as long as needed. Alternatively, the trustee is more conservative, and is uncomfortable with borrowing, sharing, or temporarily employing resources. The trustee seeks to control all the required resources, believing the sales organization must own the resources it uses, and must permanently commit to resources if they are to be employed. He or she often views resources as a reflection of status and influence.

5. *Structure and Control Orientation* The promoter prefers flatter structures, open channels of communication between and among sales employees at all levels, and decentralized decision making. The sales organization is designed and managed with a priority on flexibility and speed. The trustee is more

comfortable with a highly structured organization and a command-and-control style of management. He or she believes in hierarchy, the chain of command, and a top-down approach to managing the sales force.

6. *People and Task Orientation*   The promoter sees employees as the ultimate source of innovation and value creation in the company. He or she strives to help employees recognize and act on their innate entrepreneurial potential. The trustee views employees in terms of their competence at the specific sales tasks that must be performed (e.g., prospecting, closing, relationship management), and expects them to follow a fairly well-defined set of directives and procedures in accomplishing those tasks.

The effective sales manager must be capable of wearing the hats of both the promoter and the trustee. This implies that he or she is adept at recognizing and pursuing innovation opportunities, but also has strong administrative skills. The more a company finds itself in a turbulent and threatening competitive environment, the more the sales manager must wear the promoter hat. Stated differently, in the new competitive landscape, the promoter style becomes critical for company success. Yet organizations are political entities, and the people within them resist change. This forces the sales manager to occasionally wear the administrative hat, playing the role of competent trustee. Unfortunately, many managers are better at one of these approaches and not especially good at the other. Highly entrepreneurial managers will often fail because they lack the necessary administrative and political capabilities.

Innovating Intelligently: A Different View of Risks and Resources

Successful innovation requires that those who lead the sales effort view themselves as "risk managers." Any type of innovation in sales involves risk of failure and some probability of loss. Fear of failure and loss is a rampant problem in contemporary organizations. The challenge for the sales manager is to transform what others in the company may initially view as extreme or undue risk into a more calculated or manageable risk.

Entrepreneurial individuals do not like risk, and they do not blindly pursue new directions regardless of risk. Based on sound assessment of an opportunity, they are keenly aware of the key financial, market, technical, career-related, and other risks associated with an innovative course of action. However, they are not risk averse. Rather, they are very good at finding ways to mitigate risk and to share risk with others. They will act decisively while at the same time engaging in behaviors that lessen the amount of risk exposure. To the creative sales manager, there are many ways to manage risk. Four examples follow.

- Keep new initiatives "under the radar screen" as long a possible so that problems can be identified and worked out before attracting a lot of higher-level attention.
- Pursue innovative projects in stages, with clear benchmarks that determine an increasing level of resource commitment to a given initiative as it evolves from small pilot project to full-fledged implementation.
- When interacting with senior executives, manage their expectations regarding a new initiative by following the adage "promise less but deliver more."
- To the extent possible, pursue initiatives by using resources without locking them in or making long-term commitments to them.

This final example suggests that sales managers must also adopt a different view of resources. Resources always seem scarce, when in fact they are usually more abundant than meets the eye. It all depends on how the manager thinks about resources. The conventional view is that the primary resource is money and that other resources are purchased with the sales budget. However, buying a resource is a more permanent and less flexible approach. Entrepreneurial sales managers are not constrained by the resources they currently have at their disposal. They are able to leverage resources in a number of different ways, including:

- stretching resources much farther than others have done in the past;
- getting uses out of resources that others are unable to realize;
- using the resources of others to accomplish one's own purpose;
- complementing one resource with another to create higher combined value; and
- using certain resources to obtain other resources.

Sales managers need to develop a creative capacity for resource leveraging. Recognizing that a resource is not being used optimally, seeing how the resource could be used in a nonconventional way, and convincing those that control the resource to let the marketer use it require insight, experience, and skill. The same can be said for getting team members to work extra hours, convincing other departments in the company to perform activities they normally do not perform, or putting together unique sets of resources that, when blended, are synergistic.

Perhaps the most critical form of leveraging involves using other people's resources to accomplish the marketer's purpose. Examples of this include bartering, borrowing, renting, leasing, sharing, recycling, contracting, and outsourcing. These efforts can be directed at other departments and units within the firm or at suppliers, distributors, customers, and other external organizations. The efforts frequently entail both informal initiatives such as the exchange of favors and the use of networks, and formal initiatives, such as strategic alliances and joint ventures.

Making Things Happen: The Guerrilla Approach

At the heart of entrepreneurship is the ability of the sales manager to think and act as a guerrilla leader. In guerrilla warfare, the military takes unique advantage of natural surroundings, uses nonconventional tactics, and is highly creative in exploiting the weaknesses of an opponent. When applied in the sales arena, the guerrilla approach involves doing more with less; finding nonconventional ways to accomplish sales tasks; and the creative use of reciprocity, partnerships, and networks. Consistent with the leveraging principle, the sales manager takes advantage of other people's resources, and taps underutilized resources in the organization and in the marketplace.

There are unlimited innovation possibilities once one adopts the guerrilla mindset. Some represent major initiatives, such as the "sales force in reserve" program at PSS/World Medical, where 5 percent of the current sales force does other jobs in the company, waiting in reserve (and getting ongoing sales training). This allows the company to move amazingly fast when a given territory needs extra help, a new territory is opened, or a field rep leaves the company or is promoted. When they hit the field, they are better qualified, more confident, and more productive than would otherwise be the case (Kelly, 1998). Other guerrilla initiatives are simple tactical moves, such as the sales team at a major rental car company that delivered complimentary boxes of donuts early in the morning to car repair shops, significantly increasing client referrals. A large company with dozens of product divisions having distinct sales forces organized mini trade shows at customer sites to demonstrate a wide range of company capabilities. Or consider the sales organization with a clever program for getting referrals from prospects that decide not to buy from them. Another example is the sales rep who prepares and sends helpful report cards to his customers that remind them when they need maintenance or upgrades, shows them how to save money on supplies, and advises them when equipment should be replaced.

In general, guerrilla initiatives are low-cost, relatively simple, and slightly un-orthodox (but effective) ways to accomplish sales tasks. A good beginning point in identifying guerrilla opportunities is to ask the following three questions:

1. *"What resources do we have that we are not fully utilizing?"* Are we making full use of our Web site, salespeople, vehicles, computer resources, sales support materials, and any other assets or resources under the sales manager's control? Are there clever things we could be doing with any of these resources?

2. *"Are there ways we can leverage relationships with suppliers, distributors, producers of complementary products, or customers to generate sales?"* Can we do some joint selling programs with any of these partners? Are there opportunities to share sales-related resources with any of these members of our network? Are there ways we can use any of these relationships to facilitate our selling efforts?

3. *"Do untapped or underutilized resources exist in the marketplace?"* Examples could include external databases useful in prospecting or qualifying accounts, key gatekeepers inside of prospect firms, or events that members of the firm's target market might be expected to attend.

Fostering Entrepreneurship in Sales: Changing the Work Environment

The second challenge when attempting to foster entrepreneurial behavior in the sales organization concerns the work environment. While some companies attempt to designate people from whom they expect entrepreneurial behavior, the more productive approach is to create the right work environment that lets the entrepreneurs emerge from anywhere in the sales organization. To use a baseball metaphor, if the circumstances are properly designed, sales entrepreneurs will step up to the plate.

While many variables combine to create a given work environment, sales managers are encouraged to focus on four key variables: structure, controls, human resource policies, and culture.

Structuring the Sales Organization

Structures are created to bring order and logic to sales operations. The design of a sales organization includes a wide range of structural decisions, including the number of management levels that exist in the sales organization, the span of control or number of salespeople that report to a given sales manager, the degree of specialization of tasks or assignments built into the structure, the extent to which decision making is centralized or decentralized, and the formality of relationships and communications within the organizational hierarchy.

Unfortunately, as companies grow, structures become increasingly bureaucratic and entrepreneurship suffers. The challenge today is to design sales organizations that balance the need for coordination and consistency against the need to empower employees to develop innovative approaches to acquiring and keeping customers. Leading-edge companies have come to realize that structures must be subject to continuous change, as the appropriate structure for a company today may be dysfunctional two years from now.

Our experience suggests that entrepreneurship flourishes where management creates a sense of smallness within what is otherwise a large enterprise. Generally, there should be fewer layers or levels in the sales organization, while spans of control for managers should be broader. The overall goal should be for a flatter or more horizontal sales organization. Decentralized decision making and empowerment of salespeople and sales teams are coupled with clear vision and strategic direction from senior sales executives. Where sales teams are appropriate, they operate with significant autonomy. The dominant direction in terms of the flow of new ideas in the organization is bottom up, not top down. Vehicles are put in place to facilitate extensive and rapid communication among salespeople, between salespeople and sales management, and between those in sales and those in other key functional areas within the firm.

Designing the Control System

A control system comprises those formal and informal mechanisms that help individuals regulate what they do with themselves and other resources on the job. It is concerned with harnessing company resources in a manner consistent with the organization's purpose. Controls are intended to guard against the possibility that people will do something the organization does not want them to do, or will fail to do something they should do. Without controls, it would be impossible to determine what is going on in the organization, distinguish high from low performers, satisfy customers on a consistent basis, be cost competitive, and find ways to continually improve.

In sales, the control system has a large number of elements, and these are continually modified and expanded. Examples of control measures include sales goals and quotas; call frequency standards; sales budgets; sales activity reports; travel and expense reports; tests of salesperson knowledge; customer satisfaction surveys; and efficiency measures such as cost per sales call, repurchase rates, and new accounts as a percentage of total accounts. Each of these is intended as a way to accomplish a particular managerial purpose.

While controls prevent chaos and waste, they also tend to steadily evolve to the point where every penny is being counted and every job-related behavior is being monitored. The by-products are overwhelming paperwork, slow approval cycles, and significant bureaucracy, and it becomes almost impossible to implement anything new or different. Rather than serve as a means to accomplishing some managerial purpose, the control measures become the sole focus. They often have unintended consequences as the employee simply does what is necessary to look good in terms of the control measure. The concern with efficiency (doing things right) takes precedence over effectiveness (doing the right things).

The entrepreneurial sales manager believes in control systems that have simultaneous loose-tight properties, where trust and empowerment are coupled with a clear sense of direction and demanding goals. He or she believes in the concept of "giving up control to gain control," where employees are given discretion in how they use resources to accomplish the organization's goals, and management focuses more on what gets accomplished and less on how it gets accomplished. He or she also believes in the concept of "resource slack," where money and other resources are not allocated on a detailed, line-item basis. Rather, resources are put into larger "buckets" and can be used flexibly so long as overall goals are being achieved. In this manner, resources are freed up for generating and experimenting with new ideas. Early development and trial work can be done on new initiatives without having to first go through a long approval process and receive senior-level approval. Those that show clear promise can then be more easily sold to senior management.

Formulating Human Resource Management Policies

Human resource management (HRM) is a broad term that refers to the set of tasks associated with acquiring, training, developing, motivating, organizing, and maintaining the sales employees of a company. Much more than handling routine personnel matters such as benefits, HRM can serve as a major vehicle for achieving the company's strategic direction. Management faces a number of choices as it makes decisions regarding employee recruitment, selection, training, performance appraisal, and compensation, and how these choices are made can promote and reinforce particular employee characteristics and behaviors. Entrepreneurship is a case in point. For sales organizations seeking to attract entrepreneurial employees, or that wish to encourage existing employees to develop and act on their innate entrepreneurial potential, the appropriate mix of HRM policies can make a significant difference.

A starting point is the design of the sales job itself. A sales position must be fundamentally defined as an entrepreneurial pursuit. Entrepreneurial behavior is more likely where jobs are designed more broadly, with the salesperson responsible for creating total value solutions for customers by addressing a range of marketing tasks. The employee is given significant discretion in how the job is accomplished, with strong pressure for results. The job is less structured and less constrained by rigid organizational policies. Employees are also highly involved in designing their jobs. Turning to recruitment and selection processes, the entrepreneurial organization looks for employees who have demonstrated traits and characteristics associated with entrepreneurship, such as strong achievement motivation, comfort with ambiguity, an internal locus of control, calculated risk taking, and a results orientation. As a case in point, some companies (e.g., Nordstrom) hire salespeople based on their ability to run a business within a business. In addition, such companies devote significant effort to employee orientation and socialization, where the entrepreneurial values and behaviors are reinforced. Training and development programs, in addition to technical training related to selling skills, product knowledge, and an understanding of customers and markets, stress skills and methods related to opportunity identification, creativity, and innovation. Emphasis is also placed on political skills and techniques for gaining managerial support for new ideas and approaches.

The sales manager communicates performance expectations and reinforces desired employee behaviors through the performance appraisal and reward systems. Motivation to act in an entrepreneurial fashion requires that management make clear the types of behaviors expected, evaluate effort allocated to the behavior, assess results of the effort, and reward and reinforce the effort. Accordingly, appraisals of the sales force must go beyond standard performance measures such as exceeding quotas, generating new accounts, and building satisfactory relationships. Specific evaluative criteria must also assess the salesperson's innovative, risk-taking, and proactive behaviors in creating value for customers. In terms of rewards, the classic question in designing compensation programs for salespeople concerns the relative emphasis on incentive pay versus a fixed salary. Entrepreneurial behavior tends to be more associated with incentive compensation, and companies get quite creative in how they design the awards and rewards that support innovations by salespeople. They create point systems, bonus pools, stock options, on-the-spot cash awards, frequent-innovator clubs, and other novel programs. Entrepreneurial companies have cultures of celebration, where they regularly recognize employee innovativeness and award everything from plaques and pins to a desired parking spot, gift certificates, innovator jackets, vacation trips, and large-screen televisions. Some go so far as to create scholarships in a salesperson's name in their hometowns, or give to the salesperson's favorite charity.

Building the Culture

Culture captures the personality of a sales organization. It includes basic beliefs and assumptions regarding the company, how employees should behave, and how the company defines itself in relation to the competitive environment. The culture of an organization is a complex phenomenon, and much of it is unstated and not readily observable. It is reflected in the firm's values, rules of conduct, methods for getting things done, vocabulary, rituals, and myths or stories. Yet, in spite of its intangible nature, the culture touches and influences everything that employees do.

Entrepreneurship is not simply affected by the company's culture, it must be a core element of the culture. A culture that is very risk averse, or very process driven, is almost by definition discouraging employees from acting in an entrepreneurial manner. Alternatively, entrepreneurial cultures tend to emphasize the following elements:

- a focus on people and empowerment
- value creation through innovation and change
- attention to the basics
- calculated risk taking
- hands-on management
- doing the right thing
- freedom to grow and freedom to fail
- commitment and personal responsibility
- emphasis on the future and an ongoing sense of urgency

Another important element of the entrepreneurial culture can be termed "healthy discontent." Employees in entrepreneurial firms reject the notion of "if it ain't broke, don't fix it." Instead, they believe there is always a better way. They are always critiquing, raising positive criticisms, and challenging the way things are. They are never complacent, even after a major achievement. The desire is to continually take it to another level. Finally, role models play a big part in an entrepreneurial culture. Sales managers and reps who have overcome internal and external obstacles and successfully implemented innovations are regularly held up as examples for others.

The Sales Territory as an Entrepreneurial Venture

A core challenge for the sales manager involves getting the salesperson to view his or her territory as an entrepreneurial venture. In this sense, every salesperson is defined as an entrepreneur, and is expected to exploit the opportunity

Exhibit 2.5   Ten Characteristics of a Sales Territory That Are Similar to an Entrepreneurial Venture

1. The territory is a self-contained unit, and a value can be placed on it.
2. Salesperson negotiates and structures deals that determine the value of the territory.
3. Performance is measured in terms of sales and profits over time.
4. Success or failure is tied to the salesperson's performance.
5. The salesperson must out-compete others to sustain the territory.
6. The salesperson allocates resources to different activities in attempting to manage the territory.
7. The salesperson seeks investments (from the sales manager) into the territory.
8. To get things done, the salesperson leverages resources from other departments within his or her company and from the external environment.
9. Possibility exists for expansion of territory through innovation.
10. The salesperson works with customers to develop innovative solutions to their needs.

© Thomson

contained within a territory. A sales territory is very much like an entrepreneurial venture. Exhibit 2.5 delineates ten similiarities between territories and ventures. Chief among these is the notion that a territory represents an opportunity to be exploited, that it has a value, and that realizing this value depends on the salesperson's innovativeness, calculated risk taking, and proactiveness.

A salesperson managing his or her territory deals with a fair amount of ambiguity, much like the entrepreneur. Sales may or may not happen, while customer requirements and buying behaviors can be difficult to decipher and continually change. A potential deal may fall apart after months of effort and significant commitment, suggesting a degree of risk, whereas another deal may close with only a modicum of work. Many leads and sales approaches prove to be dead ends, while being well organized in terms of time management, account prioritization, call planning, and follow-up activity is a key to success. The salesperson is constantly jumping from activity to activity, such that a given day might include some prospecting, first-time calls, paperwork, a follow-up call on an unclosed account, a service call to a current customer, direct mail correspondence, complaint handling, and so forth.

Approaching a territory as a venture encourages a mentality of ownership on the part of the salesperson, while also getting him or her to think more strategically. The salesperson supports his or her venture by leveraging resources from the company, such as by collaborating with those in production, logistics, information technology, marketing, and customer service. The salesperson allocates resources (e.g., field sales calls, product samples, design of customized solutions, customer incentives) across accounts within the territory.

As the person responsible for an entrepreneurial venture, the salesperson should be evaluated based on how well he or she successfully grows the territory. The sales manager becomes somewhat like a venture capitalist with a portfolio of ventures in which he or she invests. The overall sales budget is approached as a type of venture capital fund, and money is invested in territories based on their potential and the ongoing efforts of the salesperson. The salesperson regularly comes up with innovative ideas and pitches these ideas to the manager. A periodic valuation of each territory is performed, with rewards tied to appreciation of the territory's value.

Case Examples of Entrepreneurship in Sales

Some notable companies have come to appreciate the importance of achieving high levels of entrepreneurship in their sales organizations. Consider three examples.

Cisco Systems prides itself on a highly empowered sales force, and on giving salespeople high status within the company (Marchetti, 2000). Compensation reflects this status, with pay plans that allow for some salespeople to earn over $1 million. Innovative approaches are central to the Cisco approach to selling. Salespeople are expected to work closely with customers to produce innovative solutions that enhance a customer's operations. A number of creative approaches are employed in managing the sales force. One example is their use of technology in sales. Customized web pages are created for each member of the sales team from which they can manage relationships with customers, conduct all their travel and 401(k) transactions, monitor their current performance levels, access sales training videos and texts, communicate with internal departments, and more. The company encourages internal competition between the sales force and other operating departments to find the best ways to leverage the Internet in the ways they do business.

IBM has found that sales force innovation comes from freeing up salespeople to spend more time with customers. By organizing the sales force into teams that serve focused clusters of customers, creating a universal reporting system that brings consistency to performance numbers, having every sales-person follow the same selling process, and mandating a dramatic reduction in internal sales meetings (to a single 30-minute meeting per week with one's direct manager), salespeople have more time on their hands, and they are expected to spend it inside customer organizations. The result is that they are much more on top of customer problems and opportunities as they emerge, and can develop innovative solutions in real time.

AT&T has developed entrepreneurial approaches to dealing with specific problems in sales force performance (Henderson and Crawford, 2002). A case in point is the negotiation skills of their salespeople, a major problem area within the company. In addition to introducing classroom and online training that emphasizes the fact that successful negotiation involves coun-terintuitive skills and approaches, the company launched an online planning and knowledge management tool called "Dealmaker." The salesperson inputs information regarding a customer and then receives support on how to approach the negotiation and finalize a deal. The assistance helps the sales-person creatively identify unmet customer needs and requirements; think of ways to respond to difficult issues raised by customers; formulate concession strategies; and, ultimately, put together a plan of attack for a negotiation. The salesperson can also access case studies on best practices in similar negotia-tions. Finally, salespeople are encouraged to document their own experi-ences so that others in the sales force can benefit.

Challenges Posed by Entrepreneurship in Sales

Sales managers typically find themselves in uncharted territory when it comes to entrepreneurship. While many of their salespeople demonstrate entrepreneurial traits, implementing a systematic approach that fosters higher levels of entrepreneurship in the organization is not easy. A number of forces work against the innovator.

At the most fundamental level, the sales manager must confront two key "people issues." It is important to remember that entrepreneurship is about creating change. It is disruptive. Those affected by the change will inherently resist any new initiative. Sales managers who are not prepared for such resis-tance, with a systematic plan for addressing it, are likely to be frustrated. Entrepreneurship also entails risk, meaning that innovative ideas have a down-side. This leads to a second problem: fear of failure. Even where there are no apparent negative sanctions, employees tend to demonstrate a strong aver-sion to being associated with failed initiatives. As a result, they become more concerned with minimizing the downside than with maximizing the upside.

The key is to recognize that failure is a positive indicator of an innovative environment. Failure is the number one way employees learn what works and what does not, enabling them to adapt and adjust their innovative ideas, and to recognize entirely new possibilities. The entrepreneurial sales manager believes that "those who are not failing are those who are not trying anything new."

A major concern in ongoing attempts to foster entrepreneurship is the lack of support from top management. Sales managers feel senior executives fail to lead by example, provide little strategic direction in terms of entrepreneurship, and are unwilling to delegate the authority or permit the autonomy needed to implement entrepreneurial programs. This problem reflects one of the great dilemmas in organizational entrepreneurship. Entrepreneurial ideas tend to come from the bottom up, but they tend to go nowhere if entrepreneurial vision and overall direction do not come from the top.

Earlier it was noted that sales managers should focus on structure, controls, human resource management policies, and culture when creating a work environment that supports entrepreneurship. However, these same elements can also serve as significant obstacles. Entrepreneurship in sales can be difficult when the larger corporate environment is extremely hierarchical, with significant bureaucracy and red tape; when the firm has an overly rigid and tight approach to management controls; reward and measurement systems focus solely on short-term performance indicators; and the culture is defined in terms of conformity, mediocrity, stability, and risk avoidance.

A common lament in many companies is that there simply is no time to innovate. The sheer demands of day-to-day operations and the need to attend to periodic crises and recurring deadlines can make it difficult to identify, refine, and implement new ideas. If anything, intensified competition and the information age have resulted in less free time on the job. It is rare that a company designates a specific proportion of an employee's time to be spent on inventing new ideas and better ways to do the job.

Finally, the ability to make innovation happen with the sales organization requires that the sales manager have certain skills. Organizations are inherently political. Individuals have interests, departments or units have interests, and the overall firm has interests. To implement entrepreneurial ideas and concepts, the sales manager must be able to influence key stakeholders and resource providers. He or she must be able to obtain sponsors and achieve legitimacy. Insight is also needed in terms of knowing when to break a rule, bend a rule, or follow a rule. New concepts often require financial support, and financing requires good justification in terms of the numbers. Skill at financial projections and the ability to demonstrate a meaningful return on investment become important. The projections often depend on figures that are not readily available through the firm's normal financial reporting system. Another shortcoming can be people development skills. The ability to give up some control and allow employees to try new things and fail depends first on the manager's skills at mentoring salespeople and assisting them in recognizing and developing their entrepreneurial potential. In addition, and as discussed earlier, skills in leveraging resources, managing risks, and acting as a guerrilla are vital, and only come with practice.

Conclusions and BREAKthrough Directions

This chapter has introduced entrepreneurship as a central theme of the BREAKthrough process. Entrepreneurship in sales is not about chaos, or out-of-control innovation. It involves positive collisions between disciplined management and BREAKthrough concepts that fit the strategic direction of the firm. It involves a logical process that can be applied to the job of the sales manager and the sales rep. This process is opportunity driven, and requires certain skills and abilities, including the ability to think and act as a guerrilla.

Sales managers should be held accountable for creating work environments that encourage innovativeness, calculated risk taking, and proactiveness. This challenge can be met by developing goal structures, territory designs, evaluation mechanisms, administrative procedures, and the methods of resource allocation that allow for a level of autonomy, encourage experimentation, and reinforce healthy discontent.

Success requires that the sales manager develop a personal approach to the identification and pursuit of entrepreneurial opportunity. The approach should reflect skills in obtaining sponsors, building a flexible team structure, insulating projects, building project momentum, obtaining resources that have not been formally assigned to a project, developing internal support networks, and managing expectations. In effect, the manager is challenged to redefine the rules of the competitive game in terms of how sales resources are acquired and used.

Another focal point concerns the basic attitudes and perceptions of employees within the sales organization. Salespeople must see themselves as entrepreneurs, and their territories as entrepreneurial ventures. Training programs, resource pools, compensation systems, and symbolic recognition all represent vehicles for redefining the sales job, and for honoring attempts at innovation. Complacency, not failure, should be penalized. Tolerance for rule bending and skepticism toward established rules of thumb should guide the manager's behavior. The goal should be to get all the members of the sales force thinking innovation on a daily basis so that business as usual is subject to experimentation.

BREAK BOX: Reviewing and Relating

1. Consider the sample profiles of Sales Organizations A, B, C, and D discussed early in the chapter. What is an appropriate concept of entrepreneurship for your sales organization?

2. Consider the major responsibilities (e.g., recruiting, training, mentoring, evaluating, rewarding, etc.) in your position as a sales manager. Where do you see the greatest need for entrepreneurial behavior?

3. Consider your boss, yourself, and a salesperson who reports to you. Which of these three individuals is the most entrepreneurial? Which one should be the more entrepreneurial? What might be an example of entrepreneurial behavior at each level?

4. Review the discussion of the promoter and the trustee. Now rate your own skill set as an entrepreneurial manager. What are your major strengths and your major weaknesses in terms of making innovation happen in your sales organization?

5. To what extent are your sales territories run as if they were entrepreneurial ventures? What are the key factors that keep your salespeople from being more entrepreneurial in the way they do their jobs?

BREAK BOX: Envisioning and Creating

Identify a key priority for action in each of the following areas:

1. Enhancing my skill set as an entrepreneurial manager.

2. Setting goals for entrepreneurial behavior within my sales organization.

3. Creating a work environment that encourages employees to step to the plate by coming up with innovative ideas and acting on them.

4. Changing the attitudes and perceptions of employees so they recognize their own entrepreneurial potential and run their territories as ventures.

The BREAKthrough process introduced in Chapter 1 represents a useful framework for moving forward. Early in the current chapter, the reader was challenged to *become aware* of some of the basic issues in entrepreneurship by considering the BREAKthrough questions in the Becoming Aware box. The next step is to *review and relate* the core concepts introduced in this chapter to the reader's sales organization. The Reviewing and Relating box provides a set of five initial BREAKthrough questions to guide this effort. Based on your written answers to these questions, begin to chart a course of action for *envisioning and creating* a sales organization that truly reflects the entrepreneurial spirit (see the Envisioning and Creating box). How would this organization differ from the existing one? While a large number of potential issues may require attention, the reader is encouraged to set some initial priorities in four areas: personal skill development, goal setting, modifications to the work environment, and changes in employee attitudes and perceptions. These priorities for action should set the tone for capitalizing on the sales organization's innate entrepreneurial potential.

> Visit The Sales Educators Web site for further BREAK process materials on this chapter's topics. www.TheSalesEducators.com

References and Suggested Readings

Godin, S. (2002). *Purple Cow,* New York: Portfolio Books.

Henderson, J. and G. Crawford (2002). "Ten Ways to Wire Sales Training," *T+D,* 56(4), 48–57.

Jones, E., J. A. Roberts, and L. B. Chonko (2000). "Motivating Sales Entrepreneurs to Change: A Conceptual Framework of Factors Leading to Successful Change Management Initiatives in Sales Organizations," *Journal of Marketing Theory and Practice,* 8(2), 37–49.

Kelly, P. (1998). "Fast Track," *Inc. Magazine,* 20(10), 33–36.

Levinson, J. C. (1992). *Guerrilla Selling,* New York: Mariner Books.

Marchetti, M. (2000). "Number 1 Sales Force: Cisco Systems," *Sales and Marketing Management,* 152(7), 60–61.

Morris, M. H., R. Avila, and E. Teeple (1990). "Sales Management as an Entrepreneurial Activity," *Journal of Personal Selling & Sales Management,* 10(2), 1–15.

Morris, M. H., R. LaForge, and T. Ingram (1994). "Entrepreneurship and the Sales Function," in G. Hills (ed.), *Marketing and Entrepreneurship,* Westport, CT: Quorum Books, 189–206.

Morris, M. H. and D. Kuratko (2002). *Corporate Entrepreneurship,* Fort Worth, TX: Harcourt College Publishers.

Morris, M. H., M. Schindehutte, and R. LaForge (2002). "Entrepreneurial Marketing: A Construct for Integrating Emerging Entrepreneurship and Marketing Perspectives," *Journal of Marketing Theory and Practice,* 10(4), 1–19.

Spoelstra, J. (2001). *Marketing Outrageously,* Austin, TX: Bard Press.

Stevenson, H. H., M. J. Roberts, H. I. Grousbeck, and A. Bhide (1999). *New Business Ventures and the Entrepreneur,* Homewood, IL: Irwin.

Strout, E. (2003). "Blue Skies Ahead," *Sales and Marketing Management,* 155(3), 24–30.

CHAPTER 3

ACHIEVING PEAK SALES ORGANIZATION PERFORMANCE

Introduction

Chapter 1 and Chapter 2 present insights into major changes required in sales organizations and the need for developing an entrepreneurial orientation within sales organizations. The remainder of the book focuses on specific topics in strategic sales leadership. Each chapter addresses an important topic with an emphasis on how sales organizations can identify and make needed changes and become more entrepreneurial.

The purpose of this chapter is to begin this journey. The objective is to help sales organizations achieve peak performance by highlighting the critical role played by field sales managers. Field sales managers must translate strategic and leadership decisions made at higher organizational levels into action by salespeople in the field. The chapter discusses ways sales managers can improve the knowledge, skills, and abilities needed to do their job in an efficient, effective, and profitable way. The transition from being a salesperson to being a sales manager is addressed. Needed skills and potential pitfalls are explored and discussed. The competitive benefits of linking sales to the internal business strategy are presented. At the same time, having an externally targeted, market focused, and customer-focused approach is emphasized. The advantages of improvement methods such as coaching, assessment tools, and contributory training systems are examined. The chapter ends with a look at models, templates, and sales improvement processes that can be key components of a winning sales approach. This discussion is written to benefit practicing field sales managers, however also to give insights into the field sales manager's job for those who manage and lead them.

The Transition to Field Sales Management

Field sales managers typically are promoted from salesperson positions, come from other business functions within the firm, or are hired from field sales management positions in other firms. Although there are similarities in the challenges, the transition also presents some differences for each group.

BREAK BOX: Becoming Aware

Step one in the BREAK process involves activating self-awareness of personal and collective behavior. The sales manager is responsible for his/her personal behaviors as well as the shared set of behaviors and beliefs that comprise an organization's culture. The following questions are designed to help the reader assess both the personal and collective behaviors that are impacting the sales unit and/or the firm.

A. Do you currently have a vision for your organization and has it been communicated, is it understood, and does the sales force buy into it?

1. Have a solid vision that has been communicated, is understood, and bought into.
2.
3.
4. Have a vision, however it has not been well communicated, lacks understanding and buy-in.
5.
6.
7. Have not communicated a vision.

Comments regarding vision:

_____

_____

_____

_____

B. Do you have a written sales manager action plan for your activity over the next year, is it understood, and is there buy-in?

1. There is a written sales manager action plan, it is understood, and there is buy-in.
2.
3.
4. There is a written sales manager action plan, however it hasn't been presented for understanding and buy-in.
5.
6.
7. There is no written sales manager action plan.

Continued

Comments regarding a sales manager action plan:

_____

_____

_____

_____

C. Does your sales force understand clearly what is expected of them?

1. The sales force has a clear understanding of what is expected of them.
2.
3.
4. The sales force has some understanding of what is expected of them.
5.
6.
7. The sales force does not understand what is expected of them.

Comments regarding the sales force understanding of what is expected of them:

_____

_____

_____

_____

D. Do you have a prioritized plan for improving your sales management skills?

1. There is a prioritized plan for improving sales management skills.
2.
3.
4. There has been some planning for improving sales management skills.
5.
6.
7. There is no plan for improving sales management skills.

Continued

Comments regarding a plan for improving sales management skills:

_____

_____

_____

_____

E. Do you currently use assessment tools, training reinforcement systems, competency stages, and/or development plans for your sales force?

1. We currently use assessment tools, training reinforcement systems, competency stages, and development plans for the sales force.

2.

3.

4. We have moderate use of assessment tools, training reinforcement systems, competency stages, and/or development plans for the sales force.

5.

6.

7. We do not use assessment tools, training reinforcement systems, competency stages, or development plans for the sales force.

Comments regarding the use of assessment tools, training reinforcement systems, competency stages, and development plans for the sales force.

_____

_____

_____

_____

Since most sales managers come from the ranks of salespeople, they must make the transition from doing the selling job to managing the sales process. It is a tough transition for most. The job is different. It is hard to give up what the new sales manager has been doing as a successful salesperson and to start the march toward being a successful sales manager. There is a tendency to "over manage." When on a sales call, the new sales manager tends to jump into and sometimes take over the call from the salesperson. Or they may try to mold those reporting to them into doing exactly what they would have done. Entrepreneurship can be stifled. Styles differ. People differ. Customers differ. The key at this point is observation. The new manager should get an understanding of what the new job is all about and learn all that can be learned to lead to success. A new sales manager must realize the role is new and different. They now need to get the job done through others. They need to develop their organization.

The situation of new sales managers coming from another function also presents a difficult transition that can have an even steeper learning curve. The same principles apply to become successful. In this situation, the new managers still need to first observe and then develop a good understanding of what the job is about. They need to learn what BREAKthrough concepts will lead to success in managing sales.

Another possibility for entering the ranks of sales management is the sales manager who has entered the company from a similar job in another firm. This would seem to be an easier transition, however the new person has to learn the product line, the new company, the people, the customers, the politics, the culture, and what processes are used in the new organization. Again, observe, listen, and get a good understanding of what the job in the new company is all about and then learn, gain experience, and learn some more to ensure success.

Finally, for those who already may be in the job of sales manager, a transition still could be necessary. It is necessary to get even better at doing the job. Most managers can benefit from a new look at improving themselves and their organization. The BREAK process can be the foundation for a step change in a sales manager's performance whether they be new to the job or an experienced hand.

So what can be done to learn all that one needs to know to be successful? Observe and listen. Learn what the job of sales management is all about. Learn from the salespeople in the organization. Learn from other sales managers in the company. Read more books about sales management. Attend training courses. Join non-competitive, multi-company sales manager networks. Benchmark. Pick a coach and a mentor. Develop the ability through on-the-job experience, hard work, and study.

The Field Sales Management Job

The job of a field sales manager is to ensure that the marketing strategy is profitably implemented at the customer interface. The marketing strategy should be linked to the overall business mission and strategy.

To accomplish the job, the sales manager needs to know the business strategy and the marketing strategy. He/she also has to ensure that the sales team not only understands the strategies, but also understands how their jobs link to these strategies. As mentioned in Chapter 2, four variables should be a key part of the sales manager's focus. They are structure, controls, human resource policies, and culture.

The job also includes making sure that the organization has the right people doing the right things. The sales manager needs to have confidence that the salespeople will do what is right. Don't strive to be looked at as a manager; however, aim to be considered by the sales team as a facilitator. What is needed is to act the same way with the sales force as one would act with a customer. Sales managers need to ask for the group's ideas and involvement. Enlightened delegation and empowerment is needed (Chapter 1). The trend is for salespersons to be more and more her/his own sales manager. Sales forces are sharing a leadership role. One of the sales manager's jobs is to align salespeople who are independent entrepreneurs. If the sales force is successful, the sales manager will be successful.

Another aspect of the job is to decide how the team will be organized and the number of people needed to do the job. The sales manager also needs to determine the job the sales force will do, then analyze the job being done, and provide regular, motivational, encouraging feedback.

An additional responsibility is to set a budget and to live within the budget. This is especially true in these days of downsizing, restructuring, and cost cutting. Look carefully at administrative expenses as well as sales expenses. If unforeseen circumstances happen, the job will include looking for and selling the need for additional funds. These funds could come from unused budgets in other parts of the organization. Forecasting is also a challenge, one that is very important to the organization for business planning. The forecast needs to be as accurate as possible with some stretch included. A hockey stick curve will have people questioning the sales manager's credibility. Be sure that the numbers are what are truly expected before submitting such a forecast to management.

A further aspect of the job is to ensure that the group is acting in a legal manner. Know the parameters of the Robinson-Patman Act and the Sherman Anti-Trust Act to keep the team out of legal trouble. Exhibit 3.1 lists some legal reminders for sales managers and salespeople.

Business ethics has been in the news a lot lately. A good piece of advice is to never do anything that would embarrass oneself, one's family or one's company if what one did appeared in the headlines of the local paper.

Exhibit 3.1   Legal Reminders

For Salespeople and Field Sales Managers:

1. Use factual data rather than general statements and avoid misrepresentation.
2. Thoroughly educate customers before the sale on the product's specifications, capabilities, and limitations.
3. Do not overstep authority as one's actions can be binding to the firm.
4. Do not discuss these topics with competitors: prices, profit margins, discounts, terms of sale, bids or intent to bid, sales territories or markets to be served, rejection or termination of customers.
5. Do not use one product for bait for selling another product.
6. Do not try to force the customer to buy only from your organization.
7. Offer the same price and support to buyers who purchase under the same set of circumstances.
8. Do not tamper with a competitor's product
9. Do not disparage a competitor's product without specific evidence of your contentions.
10. Avoid promises that will be difficult or impossible to honor.
11. Review sales presentations and claims for possible legal problems.
12. For technical products and services, make sure the sales presentation fully explains the capabilities and dangers of the products and service.

For Field Sales Managers:

1. Make the salesforce aware of potential conflicts with the law.
2. Carefully screen any independent sales agents used by the organization to ensure they are operating in a legal manner.

© Thomson

A sales manager needs to help salespeople develop ideas for helping customers succeed. One key to sales success is innovative and creative sales managers and salespersons. The customers must be able to see positive results from dealing with the sales team. The trust of the customers must be ensured so that it is never lost. If that respect is lost, it will probably never be regained. The sales manager has to obtain cooperation from and the respect of customers by being genuinely interested in their problems and needs and helping salespeople find solutions for them.

It is the job of a sales manager to help build the competency of the organization. Competency depends on being effective, efficient, and productive. Effectiveness depends on choices that are made, strategies that are implemented, priorities that are set, and the planning that is done. Efficiency depends on how motivated the organization is, the behavior that is demonstrated, the knowledge, skills and abilities of the sales force, as well as the processes chosen for use. Productivity depends on what is measured, how satisfied the customers are, and how well the organization works as individuals and as a team. It also depends upon whether sales people are getting what they want and need. The sales manager needs to help and support the sales team if requested or if the need is perceived.

Allow mistakes to happen. This is how people learn. Coach and praise. Teach, don't intimidate. Sales management plays a critical role in salesperson development. Keep people involved and excited. Help customers be satisfied. Set a vision and develop a plan. Be organized to make selling efficient and profitable. Set goals that force the individual to stretch, but are still obtainable. Invest time in the people working on the sales team. Encourage creativity. Build the organization's esteem. Have some fun. Be flexible.

There is a lot to do as a sales manager and it is no easy task. However, it is doable. It has been said that the capabilities and attitudes of sales management within a company show what the future is for that company. Sales management plays a crucial role in business success. The job is to deliver business results.

The Business Strategy

A field sales manager needs to have an understanding of the business strategy. There is a need to know the market environment, the value chain (the flow of goods from suppliers to the producer to the final user), value chain drivers (the key players), critical success factors, business financial targets, and the overall strategy. Also needed is a good understanding of the marketing strategy. The marketplace needs to be understood. In some cases when the search is on for this strategic information, it may become evident that there's not a clear direction for the business. If the business needs to develop a business strategy, this fact should be brought to management's attention. This is true also if the business has a strategy but there are holes in it that need to be filled. The same is true for the marketing strategy. If there isn't a target for what the business expects to accomplish, then the business will be less productive and the chance of sales success will be decreased.

A major Fortune 500 company in the Northeast has implemented a process to review and upgrade business, marketing, and sales strategies. The process showed that the linkage among the strategies had been weak. In addition, many times the process yielded one or more key strategies that had not been previously discovered. The goal was to understand and link the flow of the strategies leading to advantage in the marketplace.

The Vision

Strong leaders have a vision of what they want and where they want to take their organization. To be a successful field sales manager, it is imperative to have a vision and to describe where the organization has been and where it is going. What should the sales organization accomplish? How should they do it? The objective is to have an imaginary videotape running in the sales manager's mind that visualizes what she/he wants to happen and how it can be made to happen. A mental game plan is needed. In addition to business leaders, star athletes have proven that the concept of visualization has led to success time and time again.

So, what to do? Peter Drucker said, "The best way to predict the future is to create it." The question a sales manager has to ask himself/herself is "what does one want the future to look like for the organization?" The vision is based on the business and marketing strategy, and the inputs received from customers, the sales manager's manager, and the sales team. It takes thinking, planning, and preparation time. The sales manager constantly has to be thinking of new ways to stay ahead of the competition, and can go a long way toward creating the future by picturing it in her/his mind.

The following questions should be asked. What is to be accomplished? How should it be done? Why should it be done that way? What is the impact of implementing the vision on the company, the company's customers, and the sales group? If the action were done, what would the results be? What are other options for accomplishing what is to be accomplished? What seems to be the best option? Then play the tape. How does it look? What changes need to be made? The sales manager should rehearse the vision over and over in his/her mind. It is best to keep in mind that an entrepreneurial approach, as discussed in Chapter 2, is being suggested. Such an approach is more likely when jobs are designed broadly with less constraint and structure.

Now it is time to implement. Communicate the vision to management and to the team. Get their input. Change the vision as necessary. Focus on the vision. This focus helps to simplify time management as the team concentrates on doing the things that help to get the organization to its objectives. As the organization moves forward, better ideas will come, but the organization will occasionally stumble. Make the changes necessary and move on. Lead toward the vision by example. Solicit the support needed to ensure the vision is reached. The sales manager needs to support the team in any way he/she can to make sure the vision is accomplished. The vision should drive the sales manager and the team.

There is a way to test how the vision is being heard and received by the organization. Ask a random sampling of the group if the organization has a vision. Ask them what it is. Ask them what it means to them. It will be quickly learned if the vision has been communicated effectively and if it is meaningful to the team.

The Plan

Now that field sales managers know in their minds where they are taking the organization, it is time to have a plan. The plan doesn't have to be complicated and doesn't have to take a long time to prepare. Most managers usually think it will be a daunting task. If the plan is too long, it is going to end up in a file unread. It should be short and to the point. A friend of the author, a graduate of the Naval Academy, told the story about having to put plans on one sheet of paper for a high-ranking official. He said it was difficult to do, but he was finally able to accomplish the task. After getting the knack of writing one-page plans, it was no longer a burden to write them. More importantly, the plans were read. The plans do not necessarily have to be on one page, however it is being suggested that the information on the plan be pertinent and succinct. Interestingly, a number of key Fortune 500 firms have adopted the single page executive summary. The plan should be a working document. The plan should specify what is going to be accomplished, who has the responsibility to get it done, and when the action will be completed. Isn't it amazing how things tend to get done when someone has his/her name on a piece of paper and others know when an action is supposed to be completed?

When the author has asked groups how important it is to plan, almost all participants agree it is very important. When asked to see their plans, it is astounding the number of times no plan can be produced. In some development programs led by the author, planning is explored. As an exercise to prove a point, groups have been given a case study to read. The participants have then been put into groups of 4 to 6 to make a plan for this business case. In one and one half to two hours they return with a plan that most say is better than their own business plans. And this is for a business that they knew nothing about before reading the case. The exercise points out to them that plans are important and don't take long to produce. It is necessary that all functions with pertinent information important to the plan (manufacturing, research, product groups, etc.) are included in developing the plan.

A sales manager's strategic plan should include the following areas at a minimum:

1. The Marketplace
   - Assumptions
   - Trends

2. Key Customers
   - Segments
   - Targets
   - Buying processes
   - Items important for success

3. Competitors
   - Key competitive customer interactions
   - Offerings
   - Selling methods
   - Strengths/Weaknesses
   - Threats/Opportunities
   - Competitor strategy
   - Probable results

4. Sales Strategy
   - Customer relationship strategy (Chapter 4)
   - Human Resource strategy (Chapter 7)
   - Training strategy
   - Process strategy
   - Information needs strategy
   - Financial goals
   - Audit methods

5. Action (Who, what, and when)

The sales manager doesn't just write the plan and then walk away, but needs to revisit and update the plan on a regular basis. A plan can be used in many ways. In addition to a planning tool, it can be used as an audit tool, a sales tool with management, a communications tool, and a management tool. Now that the plan has been written, is the organization supporting the plan and supporting the sales force? What is the level of customer satisfaction as the plan is implemented?

Organization Support for the Sales Effort

Be well aware of complaints being registered by customers. Address the problem areas in the organization so it is easy for customers to do business with one's company. Put decision making as close to the customer as possible. Another way to tell if the organization is focused on the customer is to test the customer interface system. In retailing, the concept of a "secret shopper" has been around for a long time. A person is hired by the retail organization to visit stores to check how well customers are treated. The same concept applies to business-to-business sales. Have someone who has been primed with various customer interaction situations call with an order, or a complaint, or a problem that needs to be resolved. See how the organization responds. Tend to the problems that surface. All customers have probably been shocked, at one time or another, at being treated poorly. They wonder how such things could happen. Make sure this lack of customer focus isn't happening within one's company.

Addressing Marketplace Needs Through Organizational Design and Strategy

Another important aspect of organization is how the marketplace is being addressed. Are the appropriate customer relationship strategies in place? Is it best for the organization and customers to be interfacing with the market place the way it is being done? Some use a geographical approach. Others organize along product lines. Or is an industry or a market-focused approach the right way to go? Should new market development be separate from sales or combined with sales? Research says new market development should be separate from sales if at all possible. If not, the sales force tends to focus on the short-term needs of the marketplace and new market development is given little effort. What is the most effective, efficient, profitable, and customer friendly approach? Should all customers receive the same approach? Most often that is not the case. There are also many ways to reach a customer. What is best for the business (Chapter 4 on customer relationship strategies)? Should strategic account managers be used? Should the company call directly on customers using a sales force? What about using an inside salesperson in support of an outside salesperson? Would the Internet be the way to go? Direct mail? Team selling? Tele-sales? Distributors? Dealers? There is no easy answer. It is situational. It is not one size fits all, and maybe a combination is best. The best thing to do is to know the market, know the customers, weigh the options, and test the options. Just like test markets, the new approach can be tested in various regions to compare results before implementing an approach across the board.

Make it easy for the customer to do business. Make it efficient and effective for the organization. Talk to the customer about how he/she would like to do business. Do some market research. Implement a plan that is in line with the vision and in line with the customer's desires. As corporate customer satisfaction ratings are declining in general, keeping customers satisfied becomes a rich area for obtaining a competitive advantage.

The Customers

It is a known fact that profitable, satisfied, repeat customers are the lifeblood of an organization. However, they're not always treated that way. A colleague described a situation involving an airline ticket agent that had impressed him. The planes were delayed and customers were getting irate. The friend was impressed about how one particular agent handled the ire of the customers lined up in front of him. The colleague asked the agent what it was that helped him get through such a bad day so admirably while facing so many fuming customers. The agent didn't hesitate. He reached into his back pocket and pulled out his billfold. As he opened the billfold, he extracted the money that was there. He showed the money and said, "Do you see this? These are dollars that came from my customers in the form of a paycheck from my company. Each one of our customers needs to be treated with care and respect."

The business universe revolves around these customers. They should be the focus and the center of attention. It is the job of sales managers to make sure that the company has an external rather than an internal focus. It is important that customer focus is part of the sales force's vision and the vision of the entire organization.

The Expectations

It is beneficial to set high sales expectations for the sales force. Stretch goals are a good thing to have as long as there is a reasonable possibility that they can be met. If there is no way they can be met, the salespeople will lose their motivation to get to the goal. If the goals require minimal or an average amount of effort, people tend to slack off when they know they'll make the target. Minimal goals are a disincentive to work harder.

Interestingly, goals don't increase stress, but tend to lower it. The reduction in stress is due to goal setting providing needed direction for one's effort. With stated goals, the person knows where she/he is trying to go. If goals are not set, it is hard for salespeople to figure out if they are getting the job done or if they are doing what they should be doing. Having goals leads to productive salespeople with drive and energy.

When setting goals as a field sales manager, make sure that the goals will help to meet the targets that are expected by the organization. Generally speaking, sales forecasts are optimistic. However, sales attrition is greater than is forecast due to unexpected sales losses during the year. This leaves a growth gap between sales forecasts and actual sales that requires innovative thinking to close. New market development is generally more productive than new product development. It can help close the growth gap left by attrition. The product already exists. Therefore the company does not have to wait for an invention. What the sales team has to do is find new markets where the current products can be used. There are a wide variety of innovative and creative brainstorming techniques that can help to identify new opportunities. What follows is a discussion of improving sales management skills. Unfortunately most companies don't maximize the potential of their sales managers and salespeople (Chapter 1).

BREAK BOX: Reviewing and Relating

The second step in the BREAK process is to review the material and to identify specific ideas that relate to your sales organization. The following questions are designed to assist you in determining relevant ideas for your organization:

1. Does your strategic sales plan support your organization's business and marketing strategies or is some revision needed?
2. Is your company truly market- and customer-focused or are some changes needed, and if so, where?
3. Based on what you learned about visioning, do you feel your vision for the sales organization can be improved? Could the vision be communicated in a better way? Is your vision understood and supported?
4. Based on what you read about the importance of setting expectations, do you feel the sales force is clear regarding your expectations? Are there any opportunities for improvement?
5. Based on Exhibit 3.1, do you have any concerns about any legal aspects of your organization's selling activity?

Improving Field Sales Management Skills

Core skills that a field sales manager needs to have include understanding the selling process, effective communication, the ability to train, being a motivator, coaching, the ability to run a good meeting, budget development, functional interaction, and an ability to make decisions. Sales managers must also be able to interact well with other business functions and be aware of the pitfalls involved in the job.

Understand the Selling Process

One of the key skills necessary to be a good field sales manager is a thorough understanding of the selling process. What step-by-step sales approach is needed for sales success for the organization's customer markets? This step-by-step approach becomes the basis for coaching the sales team. The process should be used with consistency if it has been found to yield success. However, allow for individual personalities to shine through. Use the process as a skeleton around which the sales offering is presented. In other words, the process flow of planning, opening, questioning, presentation, and commitment should be consistent. However, individualism and innovation can be used within each part of the process to complement the salesperson's style.

Effective Communication

Another critical skill for field sales management is effective communication. Communication skills are important in all aspects of life. Sales management is no exception. A key to good communication and rapport with the sales team and management is listening. Involved and proactive listening consists of giving feedback to the speaker that shows that the listener has heard what has been said. When speaking, it is good to be succinct, to the point, and to illustrate key points with examples. Keep the message that is being conveyed simple to understand.

Being able to build relationships is important whether it is with the sales team or with other managers in the business. Don't dominate the conversation or the meeting, but stay involved, be interested, and contribute.

Training

The ability to train is another skill found in exceptional field sales managers. The fact that the process is known well enough for the sales manager to be able to teach the concept will be encouragement to the team to use the process, and help the sales manager build respect. For a sales manager to improve his/her ability to be a trainer, the results wanted must be determined and objectives set to meet those results. Then develop the content and decide on the best way to convey it. An interactive style is usually best. Make the learning experience fun. Select the best way to convey the material and the tools and equipment needed. Use easily learned steps, challenge the group with questions and encourage their questions. Then follow-up to ensure the training is being implemented.

Motivating

Another skill needed is to be a motivator. People are motivated by the culture of the business and the team, the ability to develop their skills, and the building of their self-esteem. If the job can be designed to cater to a salesperson's strengths and minimize her/his weaknesses, it is motivational. Rewards and recognition also play a big part in motivation. Different people are motivated by different needs. Therefore, offer a variety of rewards. There should be a link between job effort and performance, as well as performance and some form of recognition. It is important that recognition be considered fair (Chapter 6). Most people like to get recognition. Look for things that people are doing right and recognize them for their actions.

Coaching

Coaching ability is a necessary skill. Sales professionals need reinforcement of what they have been taught so they can effectively learn. Traveling with salespersons is a good way to see their strengths and where they need improvement. Role-playing is another excellent, and often underused, tool. Find out what salespeople think they are doing well and where they think improvement is needed. Ask them what they think they could do to improve. Reinforce their findings with improvement options. Encourage them to practice their improvement ideas.

Another talent is being able to appraise a person's performance in a way that will inspire, rather than cause defensiveness and hard feelings. Feedback should be given on a regular basis in an encouraging way. Again, it is better to have the salespersons talk about what they see as their strengths and areas for improvement. If they recognize areas for improvement themselves, they will have greater buy-in for improving these skills. All informal feedback should be positive and uplifting. High performance sales managers deliver negative feedback only in a scheduled, formal session.

Sales Meetings

As a field sales manager, it is important to be able to run a good sales meeting. Sales meetings serve a number of purposes. They are a place to reinforce the vision, review the business and marketing strategies, train, plan, and problem solve. Meetings offer an opportunity for all to swap ideas about what is working and what isn't. It is important that the sales team plays an active role in the meeting and that they feel part of it. The meeting should be well planned to make it effective. More and more companies use a design team to plan the meeting. They plan what they want to accomplish, how they plan to accomplish the objective, and the result they expect to get out of the meeting. This information leads to the meeting agenda and a meeting process.

Budgeting

Another important skill is the ability to develop a budget and then to be able to live within the budget. Everyone needs to know how the group is doing regarding the budget and adjustments should be made accordingly. It is best not to wait until the 4th quarter to adjust the budget, although this seems to be the norm in many companies.

To help in planning an organized approach to improving the sales management skills, sales managers can develop a competency template and a development template as it applies to them. These templates as applied to salespersons are conceptually shown in an abbreviated form in Exhibits 3.4 and 3.5.

Interactions Needed

Field sales managers have myriad interactions to maintain and strengthen. There is a need to interact with the sales team to keep abreast of how they are doing, what challenges they face, and what needs they have. Interaction is needed with the management team so that they know what is being accomplished and how they can help to overcome barriers. The management team is needed for support. This support can come by getting management involved to kick off meetings, to help get needed resources, both human and funding, and to be a "bounce-off" for the challenges that the business faces. Interaction is needed with customers at their place of work, in visits with their sale's organization, at visits to their manufacturing plants, and at entertainment events. An objective should be set for each of these interactions.

Operating at the customer interface the customer service team can make or break the organization. The team can provide customer information, fix problems, facilitate logistics, and build customer relationships. Customer service is a vital part of the organization and one that deserves a lot of credit and recognition for the customers being satisfied. It is imperative to build a good rapport with this group.

It is important that the manufacturing team and its capabilities are known. The team can help the company to be seen as heroes or as goats by customers. The sales manager needs to be in touch with the marketing team to exchange ideas and get agreement on approaches. The information systems team is important as reports are adjusted, new reports are requested, or adjustments need to be made. Legal counsel is needed. The kind of legal counsel that searches for options of how something can be done, rather than why it can't be done, is most advantageous. Sales managers should interact with the marketplace at trade shows and pertinent association meetings. Networking should be done with other sales managers in the company to share ideas.

The sales manager has limited time and a multiplicity of interactions to manage. Therefore, the interactions have to be managed on a systematic basis. If not managed, managers will find they are only reacting to problems. So schedule the needed interactions through breakfasts, luncheons, meetings, and by joining teams and networks.

Making Decisions

To be a high performance field sales manager, one needs to have a good decision-making process. Decisions are needed in a multitude of areas. A list of some key decision areas follows:

- Customer interface strategies
- Selling process
- Support processes needed
- System choices
- Information needed by sales management and by field sales
- Personnel selection and de-selection
- Training
- Ways to motivate
- Performance measurements
- Sales meeting content
- Where to spend time

- Vision
- What to delegate
- Recognition
- Rewards
- Compensation
- Competitor's strategies defined
- Territory organization
- Territory assignments
- Channel selection
- Elements of the customer offering

Who said the job would be easy? The point is that a good decision-making process won't make the job easy, just easier. Decisions need to be made and the organization needs to move on. Elements of a good decision-making process are shown in Exhibit 3.2.

Pitfalls

There are potential pitfalls lurking in the life of a field sales manager. The pitfalls sit in the background and if ignored can bring the sales manager down quickly. The first is not having a vision for the organization. When people don't know where they are going, any road will take them there. The manager's boss might not like where the organization landed. The organization will flounder without direction. The direction must be clear and must be something that people in the sales group can buy and support.

Exhibit 3.2   Decision-Making Process

1. Define the situation
2. Define the result wanted
3. Create options
4. Get input from those that will be affected by the decision (Involvement helps to get acceptance and ownership)
5. Develop the decision
6. Announce the decision
7. Ensure the decision is working beneficially
8. If not, make needed changes

© Thomson

Another potential pitfall is not getting people involved in the decision-making processes. There are two aspects to this, management and the sales team. If management is ignored, the sales manager will most likely not get the support needed. Management needs to be kept in the loop. Create the vision with them. Incorporate their upgrades or suggestions. Get to a mutually agreeable vision with management. During management interactions, don't overlook their interest in the bottom line. If management is not kept informed and if they don't know what the sales manager is trying to accomplish, the vision and the plan are in peril.

The other side of this is to get the sales team involved in a participative process to get its buy in and support for where the organization is going. It is important that they buy in. Then necessary support will be there. If the sales force is ignored and not involved, the chance of success is minimized. Listen and listen well to what the sales team has to say.

Get to know the lifeblood of the business. Visit with customers. However, when traveling with a salesperson, do not take over the call. Direct the discussion back to the salesperson whenever possible. Keep the salesperson in the driver's seat in the eyes of the customer. Don't let customers bypass one's salespeople to get to a manager. That isn't good for the sales manager and it isn't good for the organization. If a call is received from a customer about a problem, tell the customer you'll discuss it with their salesperson and that he/she will be back to them soon with some options for solving the problem. A sales manager's territory visit checklist is shown in Exhibit 3.3.

Don't act like the person with all the answers because, truth be known, that probably isn't the case. If a sales manager acts "too big for his/her britches", the manager may get sabotaged or have people in the organization talking to one's detriment. Ask questions, listen and learn. Avoid over control. There is a tendency to micromanage the salesperson and this should be avoided.

Don't be too critical of personnel. Doing so will put them on the defensive. Be positive, have details of performance and acknowledge positive actions and their results. Encourage them to be retrospective and share how they plan to continue to improve their performance in the future. Then suggestions can be added in a positive manner and with the recipient's well being at heart. However, be careful not to mistake activity for accomplishment.

Finally, as discussed in Chapter 2, controls can be beneficial to prevent chaos and waste, however they can be taken to the extreme. Controls may slow down the organization and could make it almost impossible to implement anything new or different. A simultaneous loose-tight entrepreneurial approach was suggested. This approach gives up some control to gain control.

Exhibit 3.3   Field Sales Manager's Territory Visit Checklist

---

1. Field Sales Manager/Salesperson Communication Meeting

   A. Review current status of the business
   B. Review key programs
   C. Review progress of salesperson's accomplishments vs. objectives
   D. Review policy changes
   E. Discuss any other topics of interest to the salesperson
   F. Plan any necessary follow-up from this meeting

2. Planning

   A. Is there a plan for key account coverage on a regular, timely basis?
   B. Are appointments being used?
   C. Is unavoidable "dead time" utilized in a productive manner?
   D. Are planning activities designed to maximize accomplishment of objectives?

3. The Sales Call

   A. Does the salesperson have an objective for each call?
   B. Did the salesperson bring the proper tools for making the call?
   C. Does the salesperson use the sales process satisfactorily?
   D. Is product knowledge sufficient?
   E. Is creativity and innovation used to address customer needs and solve problems?
   F. Does the salesperson reflect a professional image?
   G. Is key information recorded immediately following the call?
   H. Is necessary follow-up action taken or planned immediately after the call?
   I. Does the salesperson review the call by reflecting on the call planned, the call made, and the call she/he wishes were made to capture learnings that can lead to improved performance?

4. Administration

   A. Does the salesperson have all necessary tools to run the territory efficiently?
   B. Are phone calls well planned and efficiently handled?

© Thomson

BREAK BOX: Reviewing and Relating

The second step in the BREAK process is to review the material and to identify specific ideas that relate to your sales organization. The following questions are designed to assist you in determining relevant ideas for your organization.

1. Based on a review of the knowledge, skills, and abilities needed by field sales managers, are there any opportunities for improvement?
2. Reviewing the interaction segment, have the appropriate interactions been cultivated with the pertinent supporting organizations in your company? Do any of these interactions need to be strengthened?
3. Is your process for making decisions effective or does it need to be improved?
4. Reflecting back on the discussion of potential pitfalls, do any need your attention?

Improving the Organization

Now that improving a field sales manager's skills has been discussed, it is time to address improving the organization. As a sales leader it is beneficial to look at the total offering concept which can bear fruit in added sales and profits. Other possible improvement ideas include mapping, a customer-focused approach, personnel development, assessment tools, and training reinforcement systems. These ideas will be explored in this section.

Defining the Offering

The offering should not be looked at only as the product. The focus should be on the total offering, which includes all the services that can be beneficially provided. In addition to the product, the offering *could* include such things as technical support, reliable customer-focused customer service, entertainment, problem solving, quality, on-time delivery, research, new products, consultation, co-op advertising and warehousing. The salesperson can also be a differentiating factor as no two salespersons are exactly the same. Therefore, no two offerings are ever the same, even if the perception is that the offerings are equal. To share information as part of the offering is even more important today than it was in the past as the information often is viewed as a competitive advantage.

Mapping or Blueprinting

There is a technique called mapping (also referred to as blueprinting) that allows one to follow each step in a process to see where the bottlenecks and redundancies are. This step-by-step flow of the process involves identifying all visible and invisible parts of the sales/service process no matter how many twists and turns it takes. Mapping the processes that interface with customers can be eye opening. Adjustments can make the customer interface processes much more efficient and reduce the chance for error. For instance, what happens from the time an order is placed until the customer receives the order? As the flow is followed, do activities flow smoothly, overlap, or appear unnecessary. Are there ways to minimize errors? Can technology be improved? Can the process be made more efficient? If the organization hasn't done this exercise lately, it is highly recommended. A fibers division business unit of a Fortune 500 company used mapping and uncovered 32 areas that were negatively affecting their customer interface transactions. These were addressed leading to a much more efficient and effective customer approach. Customer satisfaction surveys showed the excellent progress that was being made as seen through the customer's eyes.

The Focus

As a business organization the focus is on profit. If the organization doesn't continually earn money it obviously won't be around for the long term. It is also true, that if the business doesn't have any customers, a profit can't be generated and the company certainly won't be around for the long run. To ensure a successful future, it is proposed therefore that the key focus of the business should be the customers. So many times it is easy to slip into the trap of being internally focused rather than externally focused. This does not serve the business well. If the customers are going to be well served and profits are going to be maximized, it is imperative that the salespeople are well trained for success.

Preparing the Organization's Greatest Assets

The field sales manager's greatest assets are the selling team and those that support the team. Are those assets being given their greatest chance for success? When a person thinks about the greatest professional athletes in the world, it must be admitted they are an elite group. These best players make up a very, very slim percentage of the total population. For instance in professional football in the United States, each year there are only about 1,700 athletes that get a chance to play in the National Football League. And what do these very best football players in the world do prior to each season? They go to training camp to hone their skills. It raises the question whether most businesses offer continuous training for their sales people to try to make them the best in the world?

Many companies don't take advantage of the many opportunities to offer their sales teams the chance for continuous improvement by using the wide variety of training mechanisms available to them. Included are:

- Books
- In-house sales training
- Open enrollment sales training
- TV remote training
- Correspondence courses
- Internet courses
- Salesperson and sales management assessment programs
- Role-playing
- Case studies
- Videotapes
- DVDs
- Speakers
- Outside sales coaches

Role-plays are simple and still offer one of the best learning experiences available. The role-play can be video taped to allow the participants to see themselves in action. Real life experiences that are common to the business can be simulated. It is a good way to assess areas of strength and areas for improvement. Others can observe the role-play so they can internalize what they would or wouldn't do, can help coach the "seller", and can learn from other's comments. Role-playing can be an excellent sales meeting activity as it helps identify areas for improvement and can lead to improved selling skills.

Assessment Tools

Many companies offer a salesperson assessment program. These are normally 360-degree feedback reports from a number of customers, peers, and management. The companies provide worksheets, which the recipients anonymously fill out and return to the company managing the assessment. The recipients anonymously fill out the form and return it to the company managing the assessment. That company then produces a summary form that is sent to the salesperson and his/her management. The report identifies strengths and areas for improvement as identified by each group contacted. Such assessments are valuable tools for sales managers as they target areas for BREAKthrough gains.

Assessment programs are also available for field sales managers. These programs provide a good way to get input on performance from management, peers, customers, and the sales team. This information helps to identify target areas for personal improvement as a sales manager.

Training Reinforcement Systems

To be effective, the key learnings from training programs have to be retained and implemented. Studies show that the information retention rate after people leave a training program can have a rapid decline. To make training programs more valuable, a number of companies have developed ways to ensure what is taught is remembered and implemented.

As an example, one company that has such a training follow-through solution is the Fort Hill Company of Wilmington, Delaware. They build expectations for post-training follow-through into the training program. They tie course learnings to priority work once the participant returns to the job. This creates a history of individual and group progress in implementing what they learned that engages the training leaders, participants, and managers. Their "Friday 5s" system provides program participants with three months of post-course, structured, web-based follow-through.

Training disconnects in the past:

- There has been no system to track and document the impact of training programs
- Training objectives have seldom been linked to priority work
- The training does not translate into business results
- Opportunities for post-training collaboration among colleagues have been missed
- There has been a void of accountability for participants attending the program

Organizations are looking more and more to try to pin down the value of training. These training reinforcement systems are enabling this to be done.

BREAK BOX: Reviewing and Relating

The second step in the BREAK process is to review the material and to identify specific ideas that relate to your sales organization. The following questions are designed to assist you in determining relevant ideas for your organization.

1. How could your total offering be expanded and improved to give your organization more of a competitive advantage and increased profit?
2. Are adequate development tools being provided to help the sales team continuously improve their abilities? Would other tools be beneficial and affordable?
3. Are assessment tools being utilized for the sales force and sales management? If not, would 360-degree feedback be effective and worth the effort?
4. Is training producing an adequate return on investment? Would a system aimed at helping to ensure implementation of new ideas learned pay off?

Corporate Insights

A natural flow from thinking about improving the organization is to look at some corporate examples also aiming at business improvement. These examples include competency and development templates, and sales improvement and sales effectiveness models. These templates and models offer further ideas for making a sales organization more competitive in the marketplace.

Competency Template

A number of companies have built competency templates for their organizations. Competency templates tie levels of development to selected performance criteria for the job (Exhibit 3.4). A category one performer would be someone new to the job. A category two performer would be someone who has mastered the basic elements of the job. A category three performer would be one who does work above and beyond expectations in a number of categories. A category four performer would be one that is proficient in all the success criteria for the job.

Exhibit 3.4 Salesperson's Competency Template (Conceptual Example)

Skill	Category 1	Category 2	Category 3	Category 4
Understands and uses the selling process	Is learning the selling process	Understands and uses the selling process	Among the best in the group in using the selling process	Understands and uses the selling process as well as teaches and coaches others in the selling process
Understands and uses the negotiation process	Is learning the negotiation process	Understands and uses the negotiation process	Among the best in the group at negotiating	Uses, teaches, and coaches the negotia-tion process

© Thomson

To develop a competency template the sales manager needs to identify the critical success factors for the job. This can be done by assessing what the best performers in each stage of development say are the factors critical to their being successful. What does a person have to master to be successful as a salesperson in the company? Then look at the various stages of development and write what the expectations would be for someone in that phase of their development. A modified example of the competency template is shown in Exhibit 3.5.

Development Template

Development templates are built off of competency templates. This process shows what training, reading, videotapes, and other developmental ideas are appropriate to help prepare sales personnel for the next phase in their ongoing development (Exhibit 3.5). The template is similar to the "Competency Template." The template shows four categories of performance on the horizontal axis as noted above. The vertical axis is the same as above showing the same critical success factors (knowledge, skills, and abilities). The part that changes is what is in the blanks on the templates. Each square should be filled in with specific development ideas that would help move a person from where he/she is up to the next category of performance.

Exhibit 3.5   Salesperson's Development Template (Conceptual Example)

Skill	Category 1	Category 2	Category 3	Category 4
Understands and uses the selling process	Books Training Videotapes Other Developmental Ideas	More sophisticated: Books, Training, Tapes, Other Developmental Ideas	Most sophisticated: Books, Training, Tapes	Teaches and coaches selling process Researches and refines the selling process
Understands and uses the negotiation process	Books Training Videotapes Other Dev. Ideas	More sophisticated: Books, Training, Tapes, Other Dev. Ideas	Most sophisticated: Books, Training, Tapes	Teaches and coaches negotiation skills

© Thomson

The Sales Improvement Model

The sales improvement model is focused on the customer. The process revolves around the customer interface strategies that are chosen (Chapter 4). The first question that should be asked is "What roles are needed in the organization?" Based on the customer interface strategies that the organization is implementing, what is the ideal candidate profile that should be used to identify the right people to use, hire, or transfer into the organization to fill these roles? The ideal candidate profile is covered in more depth in Chapter 7. This selection should be based on the knowledge, skills, abilities, and behaviors that are needed for each role.

The next question to ask is "How will the needed knowledge, skills, abilities (KSAs), and behaviors continue to be developed in the people in the organization?" What training is needed? How will the training be done? How will it be determined that the training is effective? How will the organization be tested regarding the needed KSAs? What reading should be done? What experiences would be beneficial for the development of employees? Studies have shown that sales ability levels out without continued training. Investment in the selling skills of the sales force is money well spent. The salespersons themselves should take much of the responsibility to improve themselves in the areas critical to their success.

Most organizations do not have a way to communicate key sales learnings throughout their organizations. One technique that is effective is to let experienced salespersons travel with each other on occasion so they can learn from each other. A quarterly newsletter of tips from field salespersons facilitates the sharing of ideas and often benefits the entire organization. The AT&T example in Chapter 2 regarding the management tool called "Deal-maker" is another situation where an organization shared learnings broadly. In this case the learning pertained to negotiating tactics and successes.

In this information age, it is important to know what information will be of benefit to customers and to the internal organization. The sales interface with customers is one of the best ways to get competitive information. What information is needed that could lead to competitive advantage? How is this information being obtained? Is the way information is gathered the most efficient way to get it? Is the information necessary? Is the type of information gathered the type that adds value? What would be the best way to get and disseminate information in the future? What actions need to be taken today to get started toward where the organization should be tomorrow? Does the organization have product or service information that can be sold as part of the company's total offering? Is the information that should be shared with the rest of the organization being captured, and is there an effective way of sharing the information? Many companies are now using a novel approach to getting better customer information. They have formed customer advisory teams, made up of customer representatives, that provide information on how a company is doing in serving customer needs and what can be done to better serve the customer's needs in the future. Information can help the organization or bog it down. It is important to make sure the information is helping customer and company decision-making ability, leads to a competitive advantage, and provides an opportunity to share key learnings with the people that can benefit from it.

Another key to sales success is to motivate the sales force to do what is necessary to get the job done. Set expectations up front. Let the organization know what is considered good and bad behavior. Also key to motivation is corporate culture. Corporate culture was addressed in Chapter 2. Being offered the right training at the right time can also motivate sales personnel. Building confidence is important and certainly helps in customer interactions. It is best to praise the good things that people are doing rather than criticize them and cut them down. Then offer the organization appropriate awards. People have needs such as respect from those higher in the organization, respect from peers, a feeling of being part of a team, and a feeling that what they do is important. They also need to feel that they have growth opportunities available to them. People also have a desire to receive increased rewards for improved performance. So if performance is linked to rewards they are motivated to perform. If job effort is then linked to job performance, they will expend effort. If they understand their role and have the ability to perform, they will perform. If the employees feel that their performance is rewarded equitably, they will have job satisfaction.

A final key aspect that spurs sales improvement is measuring sales force performance. As a field sales manager, define what actions, behaviors, and results are expected. Coaching and performance reviews should be based on the criteria set. It has been proven many times that what gets evaluated gets done. A salesperson should not be rated on areas over which he/she has no control. It is also best to mutually set the goals with the salesperson's involvement. Key actions that support the actual face-to-face selling activity also need to be evaluated to ensure they are supportive of success.

Salesperson capabilities are based on the following three areas. How effective are the salespeople? Effectiveness can be determined by assessing what the salespeople choose to do with time available. What priorities are set, what choices are made, and are the salespeople implementing their plans? The second area is how well the salespersons do their jobs. How motivated are they, what actions do they take, and what skills, knowledge and abilities do they employ? The third area, and most important for evaluating entrepreneurial salespersons, is what results have the salespersons accomplished?

The Sales Effectiveness Model

An effectiveness model for sales is a valuable tool for sales managers to know how to implement. To be most successful, an organization needs effective customer interface processes and systems (Chapter 4). The model guides one to look at how the sales organization hires, develops KSAs, implements processes and uses them (Chapter 7), utilizes information to their advantage, and motivates the organization (Chapter 2).

Then take a look at the people in the sales organization. How well do they implement their customer interactions, what customer interface processes do they use, and do they focus on the business and marketing strategies. The model also pays attention to salespeople's non-selling behaviors such as their ability to gather pertinent information, to disseminate the information effectively, and their ability to network and be a team player (Chapter 8).

BREAK BOX: Reviewing and Relating

The second step in the BREAK process is to review the material and to identify specific ideas that relate to your sales organization. The following questions are designed to assist you in determining relevant ideas for your organization:

1. Consider the concept of templates for development. Would such a system help your organization become more self-managed in the area of development?
2. Reviewing the sales improvement model, what specific improvements would be most beneficial to your organization?
3. Reviewing the sales effectiveness model, what specific elements of the model, if any, need attention in your organization?

When all of this happens in an effective and efficient manner, the result is better business performance. Sales, market share, profitability and customer satisfaction continues to improve leading to sustainable business results.

Conclusions and BREAKthrough Directions

As a summary and review, the job of field sales management is to implement the marketing strategy at the customer interface. The transition to the sales management job was explored. No matter what avenue gets a person to the sales management position, there is always a transition to the new job. Some transitions are more difficult than others. It was also noted that a transition awaits those currently doing the job of sales management. As many current managers might be set in their ways, this could be the toughest transition of all as new ideas and skills are tested and applied.

The importance of having a vision was explored. A sales manager needs to invent the future by deciding what she/he wants the future to look like and then drive toward that vision. It is recommended that the vision include an entrepreneurial approach for the sales force. The vision needs to be well communicated and understood throughout the organization.

The job consists of aligning salespeople who are independent entrepreneurs. It is also having the right people doing the right things. Other aspects of the job include setting and meeting goals, budgeting, knowing legal aspects, being ethical, gaining respect, building competency, interacting with upper management and cross-functional personnel, and coaching. It is a supported fact that sales management plays a crucial role in business success.

Job elements such as planning, setting expectations, ensuring customer focus, developing customer relationship strategies, setting structure, and planning new market development were noted. The bottom line is to make it easy for the customer to do business. The customer is the lifeblood of any business.

Sales management skills and ways to improve them were discussed. It is key to have an understanding of the selling process and to be able to teach and coach the elements of the process. The ability to build relationships, both internally and externally, and the ability to motivate are important to success. Sales meeting content and possibilities were reviewed. It is important to have goals that are aligned with and support business, marketing, and sales strategies. Key elements of a good decision-making process were detailed.

An awareness of potential pitfalls and roadblocks is important to the sales manager. Clear direction, management involvement, sales team involvement, attitude, and performance assessment all play a critical role in sales management success or failure. The advantages of broadening the offering were discussed. BREAKthrough thinking, mapping, development assessment tools, and training reinforcement systems were shown as ways to gain sustainable competitive advantage.

To conclude the chapter, tools were introduced to help increase a sales manager's success. These included the use of competency templates, development templates, customer interface strategies, the sales improvement model, and the sales effectiveness model.

The BREAK process comes into play in achieving peak sales organization performance. As field sales managers *become aware* of what the job is all about, understand the business and marketing strategy, and get to know the customers, they set the foundation for achieving peak sales performance. By *reviewing and relating* to the knowledge available for improving sales management skills, and for improving the organization, the sales managers can compare these aspects to what is going on in their organization. This leads to *envisioning and creating* new ways of thinking and new business practices to improve business results. *Applying and systematizing* key learnings within the sales manager's organization will help to ensure that the methods will be adopted, maintained, and improved.

Kicking results to the next level is up to sales managers, as they think about their businesses in a different light. First, reviewing the ideas presented to improve sales management skills and to improve the organization. Then they

---

BREAK BOX: Envisioning and Creating

The third step in the BREAK process is to envision how applying key ideas from this section to your sales organization might be accomplished and then to create the basic steps to make this improvement happen. Identify key priorities for action and list the general steps needed to make the change happen in your organization.

1. What opportunities have you identified from this section that would yield the greatest benefit to your organization? (Name up to three impact ideas).

2. For each opportunity identified, what key steps would be needed to successfully implement sustained change to your organization?

---

should implement what seems best for their organization through BREAK-through thinking to lead to BREAKthrough results.

Visit The Sales Educators Web site for further BREAK process materials on this chapter's topics. www.TheSalesEducators.com

---

References and Suggested Readings

Alessandra, T., Cathcart, J. and Monoky, J. (1990), *Be Your Own Sales Manager,* New York, NY: Simon & Schuster.

Alessandra, T. and Monoky, J. (1996), *The Sales Manager's Idea-A-Day Guide,* Chicago, IL: The Dartnell Corporation.

Bauer, G., Baunchalk, M., Ingram, T. and LaForge, R. (1998), *Emerging Trends in Sales Thought and Practice,* Westpoint, CT: Quorum Books.

Bosworth, M. (1995), *Solution Selling, Creating Buyers in Difficult Selling Markets,* New York, NY: McGraw-Hill.

Miller, W. (2001), *Proactive Sales Management: How to Lead, Motivate, and Stay Ahead of the Game,* New York, NY: American Management Association.

Wilner, J. (1997), *Seven Secrets to Successful Sales Management: The Sales Manager's Manual,* Boca Raton, FL: St. Lucie Press.

CHAPTER 4

DEVELOPING CUSTOMER RELATIONSHIP STRATEGIES

Introduction

The objective of this chapter is to identify ways in which the sales organization can forge strategic, profitable relationships with key customers. The goal is to articulate an enterprise-level perspective on the firm's strategic customer relationship choices and practices in achieving a sustainable competitive advantage leading to world-class sales performance. This chapter will begin with an overview of the concept of market-orientation in its role of driving marketing/sales strategy and practice. Drawing on the notion that market-oriented firms develop competitive advantage by selecting their customers wisely and focusing their core competencies on serving these strategically relevant customers exceptionally well, the notions of customer relationship strategy and management are developed in sales force terms. In this regard, particularly important topics include selection criteria for strategic accounts, selection criteria for strategic account managers, approaches for identifying and leveraging customer lifetime value, and the role of customer relationship management processes and technology in enabling effective strategic account planning and practices.

Building a Market-Oriented Organizational Culture to Support Strategic Customers

The competitive environment of the new millennium is intense and global. Salespeople are increasingly at risk of losing key customers due to limitations in their knowledge of how to truly empathize with and serve their customers. Often, enterprise-level strategic choices, resources, and linkages influence salesperson performance. One very important concept that has emerged from recent research is *market orientation,* defined as the organization-wide generation and dissemination of customer information and the specification of appropriate responses related to current and future customer needs and preferences. Simply stated, market orientation is the firm's ability to better satisfy its target customers, because of its enhanced "sensing and responding" capabilities concerning market opportunities and requirements.

Market orientation positions an organization for better performance because its sales executives and managers benefit from a more sophisticated understanding of its customers' concerns and needs, its relative competitive position in relating to these customers, and the enhanced ability to develop strategies and plans to achieve superior customer satisfaction. However, market orientation also requires significant investments to realize its fullest benefits. Thus, it is encouraging that market-oriented organizations have been found to achieve higher levels of sales and profitability growth, market share, new product success, and customer satisfaction. As one CEO put it, "Customers having increasing expectations means that a faster response is needed from selling companies, and sellers must provide increasing value over time. Companies must incorporate changes (e.g., technological, more sophisticated selling, etc.) on the fly—at rapid speed." *Paul Sarvadi, CEO of Administaff*

Market Orientation and Customer Relationship Management

To become market-driven and enable a market orientation, your company needs to develop a customer relationship strategy, supported by CRM processes and, quite possibly, the adoption of a sophisticated CRM technology solution provided by a leading firm such as SAP, Siebel, Microsoft CRM, Oracle, or Salesforce.com. It is critical to note that Customer Relationship Management is not simply a technology (which most people think of when they hear CRM). In fact, in their advertising, CRM sellers emphasize the need to establish close, and often personal, relationships with key customers. For example, the metaphors of the local barber and the watchmaker appear prominently in Siebel's advertising. Customer knowledge and intimacy is what matters most in CRM. And Edward Jones, one of the most successful brokers over the past ten years, has been careful in its CRM model to keep the account executive at the center of its CRM strategy and implementation plan.

Successful practitioners of CRM recognize this multi-layered aspect of CRM and, hence, consider CRM to be a general business philosophy that encompasses an integrated plan involving thoughtful customer-oriented strategies, cross-functional business processes, and enabling tools (i.e., technology) which foster a spirit of customer-centricity—putting your customers at the center of all company activities. However, they also recognize that close relationships with customers often place a significant premium on the role of the sales force. In these cases, sales leadership must successfully negotiate a CRM strategy and implementation plan that integrates the talent of the sales force and the leverage and scalability of CRM technology.

Customer Relationship Strategy and Management

Market-driven firms systematically segment their markets and customers in terms of how various firms prefer to buy and relate to their suppliers. Their goal is to understand the market at two levels: 1) the general market spaces and segments available and the competitive capabilities required for success; 2) the specific characteristics and requirements of the particular customers that occupy these market spaces. These firms realize that market segments are clusters of customers who share common business concerns, strategies, or operational challenges. Perhaps more importantly, these firms recognize that a single customer may represent a market segment in and of itself—due to either its financial size or sales potential or its longer term strategic fit with the selling firm's competitive position (i.e., its relevance in new technology development or end-user channel access). Hence, they often seek to develop customer intimacy, or a "one-to-one" relationship, with a key customer, or set of such customers. For example, Nokia's market space is defined princi-pally by its relationships with a set of four customers who provide access to over 80% of the end users of cell phones.

CRM: What is it?

Customer relationship management is the set of business strategies and prac-tices tied to the creation and leveraging of the linkages and relationships of the firm to its external stakeholders; in our case the channel customers and end users who provide the opportunity to build competitive advantage and superior profitability. More formal definitions of CRM are provided by many sources, academics and CRM solution marketers in particular. These defini-tions vary considerably depending on: 1) whether a strategic or tactical per-spective on CRM is taken; 2) the organizational role of the individual pro-viding the definition (i.e., marketing, sales, production, or logistics); and 3) cynically, in the case of CRM solutions providers, the nature of the solu-tion that they have to offer, usually an enterprise suite or a "best of breed" solution in a specific functional domain (e-marketing, call center solution, sales force automation or analytic package). For purposes of this chapter, two CRM definitions, one at the strategic level and the other more reflective of

Exhibit 4.1 Core Business Processes in Creating Customer Value

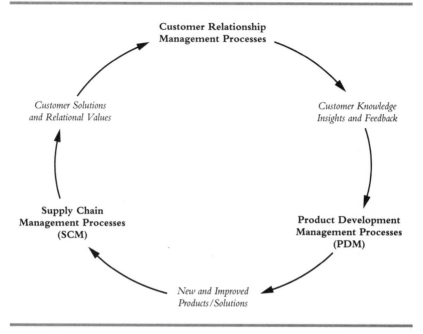

© Thomson

organizational structure and cross-functional processes, provide an appropriate perspective from a sales management point of view.

CRM: A Strategic View

From a *strategic* perspective (i.e., the top management's perspective), CRM is one of three core customer value creation processes that drive the financial performance of the firm (see Exhibit 4.1):

- CRM is the process that identifies customers, creates customer knowledge, builds customer relationships, and shapes customers' perceptions of the firm and its products/solutions.
- PDM, or new product [management]development, is the process of creating solutions that customers need and want.
- SCM, or supply chain management, is the process that incorporates the acquisition of all physical and informational inputs, and the effectiveness and efficiency with which these resources are translated into customer solutions.

This eagle-eye perspective emphasizes that customer value creation, and hence a firm's competitive position in its desired market spaces, depends critically on its ability to: 1) define a distinctive customer-centric perspective on what drives demand in its markets; and, 2) translate this customer-related knowledge into customer-valued solutions that can be produced and sold, profitably. From this strategic perspective, it is clear that CRM is potentially a core capability of the firm.

Why is this strategic perspective on CRM important to sales executives? The role of the sales leaders, sales managers, and key account managers is likely to be radically changed when CRM strategies, processes, and results capture the attention of top management. In fact, for strategic accounts, top management may play a direct, proactive role in account strategy development and relationship management. For example, it is widely reported that John Chambers of Cisco made weekly contact with the firm's strategic customers. Also, Procter & Gamble signals the strategic importance of its relationship with Wal-Mart by appointing a president of this account. Hence, from one perspective, these senior executive roles in customer contact and relationships provide both visibility and opportunity for sales executives. In the first place, the strategic emphasis on customers promises the attention of corporate executives to sales and channel issues and strategies. In the past, many companies treated sales and channel issues tactically. For example, in the case of a leading health insurance firm, this tactical perspective caused a serious disconnect between the firm's intended strategic direction and the realities of customer needs and preferences. Significant strategic and new product development decisions affecting customers were made in the absence of customer, field sales, and channel partner input. In fact, the once-per-year visit to key customers by the SVP, Corporate Strategy and Planning was treated derisively by the field sales force.

To the extent that the CRM strategy is an enterprise-level strategy, then customer value creation, sales force models, and channel partner relationships should be part and parcel of the corporate strategic planning process itself. Hence, CRM-related decisions should better reflect market and customer realities. Of course, sales executives, including sales managers and key account managers, must be well-versed in the corporate strategic thinking process and how to best articulate "local" market and customer information to shape these customer, sales, and channel strategic choices.

In the second place, CRM investments will be assessed in terms of their market-based asset valuation (see Exhibit 4.2). Brand equity has long been considered to be a market-based asset by senior-level marketing and finance

Exhibit 4.2   Assessing Financial Payback on CRM in Sales Intense Contexts

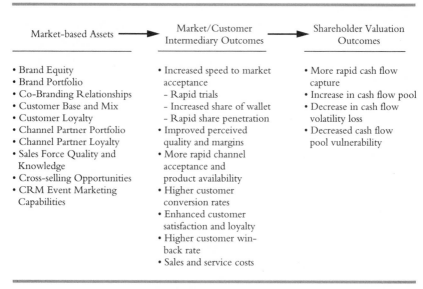

Market-based Assets	Market/Customer Intermediary Outcomes	Shareholder Valuation Outcomes

• Brand Equity
• Brand Portfolio
• Co-Branding Relationships
• Customer Base and Mix
• Customer Loyalty
• Channel Partner Portfolio
• Channel Partner Loyalty
• Sales Force Quality and Knowledge
• Cross-selling Opportunities
• CRM Event Marketing Capabilities
	• Increased speed to market acceptance
	  – Rapid trials
	  – Increased share of wallet
	  – Rapid share penetration
	• Improved perceived quality and margins
	• More rapid channel acceptance and product availability
	• Higher customer conversion rates
	• Enhanced customer satisfaction and loyalty
	• Higher customer win-back rate
	• Sales and service costs
		• More rapid cash flow capture
		• Increase in cash flow pool
		• Decrease in cash flow volatility loss
		• Decreased cash flow pool vulnerability

© Thomson

executives. These executives stress that brands represent a consumer franchise that can be leveraged for future market and financial purposes. For example, new products introduced as brand extensions are presumed to benefit in terms of image transfer from the parent brand. Brand equity may also be an asset in the sense that less marketing and advertising effort is required to build market share.

In contrast, sales force and channel expenditures have historically been evaluated as direct costs of generating sales. CRM thinking is changing this perspective. More attention is now paid to customer valuation and customer life cycle perspectives on CRM expenditures. In this point of view, customers are assets of the firm. Thus, the customer installed base and the "quality" of this customer base, customer loyalty, and channel loyalty are market-based assets that may be leveraged for future share, profit, or role flow. Hence, CRM investments should be evaluated according to the strategic options they provide over the lifetime of a given customer, or a set of similar customers. In this light, expenditures to build sales force size; enhance sales force quality, knowledge, and relationships; adopt account management strategies; and retain sales personnel should be evaluated in terms of their longer term profit.

In the third place, given this new strategic emphasis on the customer, sales force, and channel issues in establishing corporate strategies and resource investments, sales executives and managers must expect to be held accountable to a more diverse and enterprise-level set of performance scorecard objectives and results (see Exhibit 4.2, column 2). In addition to the traditional revenue generation targets, sales executives and managers can be expected to face a scorecard that examines the nature and quality of the revenue and profitability in specific customer-related terms. For example, assessments may examine such market/customer outcomes as speed to market acceptance, share of customer category expenditures (or share of wallet), perceived product and/or service quality, product availability in key channels, in-store merchandising acceptance and positioning, customer satisfaction and retention rates, customer win-back rates, and product and sales/service costs and margins. However, as will be discussed later, the changing role of the salesperson as account manager may involve additional scorecard evaluations in terms of customer learning and knowledge, cross-functional relationships, and new product involvement and profit.

Finally, sales executives and managers will likely be asked to justify customer, sales force, and channel partner investments in terms that relate to the shareholder value. An enterprise-view on CRM strategy and practices brings into play the CFO's perspective on the financial valuation methods for assessing the return on whatever CRM investments are indicated. Sales executives and managers seeking to apply a CRM strategy, such as increasing customer acquisition, enhancing customer loyalty, or building closer relationships with channel partners, will likely have to compete for financial resources at the corporate level. Hence, these sales executives will need to be able to translate these customer-level, intermediate outcomes into financial consequences relevant to the firm, including return on investment (ROI), economic value added (EVA), incremental shareholder market value (SHV), and net present value (NPV).

The challenge for sales executives and managers is to develop more sophistication in their "mental models" concerning how sales and channel capabilities are built, how they can be valued as corporate assets, and how they can be leveraged to achieve important customer-related outcomes. This is not to imply that sales leaders must immediately enroll in a night or weekend MBA program to earn a finance specialization. However, they will need to recognize that the visibility and opportunity to participate in strategy-making processes involving sales and channel issues comes with being able to more precisely, and usually quantitatively, articulate sales and channel plans and justify required investments in terms of their NPV implications. Hence, as many academics have noted, the cross-functional relationships among sales and financial executives will need to be leveraged to ensure the provision of customer value to strategically important customers at a viable rate of return; in NPV terms, for the firm.

The first steps in building this sales-finance bridge will likely involve the adoption of cash flow, rather than revenue, cost, and profitability as a criterion for evaluating the success of sales and channel strategies and programs. In Exhibit 4.2 (see column 3), four cash flow outcomes relevant to how sales and channel strategies might be assessed are identified. Sales executives can think in terms of these four general NPV outcomes when asked the ultimate CFO question: "bottom-line, how does your CRM proposal drive shareholder value?"

Exhibit 4.2 provides guidance on how CRM outcomes might relate to cash flow outcomes. For example, investments in building closer relationships with key customers may provide the marketing advantage of more rapid adoption of new products and solutions among highly visible customers who can provide prestige and referrals, as well as case-based evidence, to support the marketing programs. In turn, more rapid adoption accelerates cash flow and, given that "time is money", enhances the NPV of the cash flow realized. For example, a leading provider of CRM software solutions purposely adopted a lead-user strategy across a variety of key market segments with an eye to leveraging the reputation and visibility impact of these lead customers in maximizing "first mover" advantage.

Similarly, CRM investments in closer customer relationships may be investigated for their links to increasing the cash flow from the existing customer pool through their influences on: 1) higher average margins; 2) increased cross-selling of collateral products and services; 3) reduced service, inventory, receivables costs; or, 4) reduced sales force investments and direct selling costs. For example, a national accounts program at a leading electronics distributor was able to simultaneously enhance customer value, largely through supply chain management initiatives (reduced acquisition and inventory costs) and the provision of new value-added services (electronic catalogs, a wireless ordering system, a procurement forecasting and management system, and a new product alert system), while still enhancing cash flow through increased margins as its own SCM, service, and sales costs decreased. These results could only be achieved through true partnerships with a limited set of strategic customers.

Finally, since the rate of return on cash flow is a risk-adjusted estimate, any CRM initiative that reduces cash flow volatility over time, or its absolute vulnerability of permanent loss, enhances shareholder value (and

BREAK BOX: Becoming Aware

The first step in the BREAK process is becoming aware of your firm's current customer relationship strategy, customer-facing business processes, and the role of technology in handling customer relationships. Every firm has a customer relationship strategy, although it may not always be explicitly defined and shared across the organization. Hence, it is important for sales executives to access their firm's current customer relationship strategy and practices. The following questions are designed to guide you in the assessment process.

A) To what degree is your firm market-oriented—that is, is the organization-wide generation, dissemination, and use of customer information considered a strategic driver of your firm's performance?

1) Strongly agree
2)
3)
4)
5)
6)
7) Strongly disagree

Briefly describe the key aspects that led to your assessment on this CRM strategy assessment item.

_____
_____
_____
_____
_____

B) To what degree is your firm's customer relationship strategy explicitly defined and communicated cross-functionally, in terms of desirable target market segments and specific customers in these segments?

1) Strongly agree
2)
3)
4)

Continued

5)

6)

7) Strongly disagree

Briefly describe the key aspects that led to your assessment on this CRM strategy assessment item.

_____

_____

_____

_____

_____

C) To what degree do senior executives place a strategic emphasis on customer value creation, sales force strategy, and channel relationships in corporate strategic planning?

1) Strongly agree

2)

3)

4)

5)

6)

7) Strongly disagree

Briefly describe the key aspects that led to your assessment on this CRM strategy assessment item.

_____

_____

_____

_____

_____

_____

D) To what degree are customer valuation and customer lifetime value considered to be important in assessing the potential financial payback on customer relationship, sales force, and channel partner expenditures?

1) Strongly agree

2)

3)

Continued

4)

5)

6)

7) Strongly disagree

Briefly describe the key aspects that led to your assessment on this CRM strategy assessment item.

_____

_____

_____

_____

E) To what degree is your firm's success or failure judged in terms of customer-oriented performance metrics such as customer satisfaction, customer retention and loyalty, and customer profitability?

1) Strongly agree

2)

3)

4)

5)

6)

7) Strongly disagree

Briefly describe the key aspects that led to your assessment on this CRM strategy assessment item.

_____

_____

_____

_____

_____

F) To what degree are sales executives asked to articulate their perspectives on how customer relationships, sales force, and channel capabilities are best developed, managed, and leveraged?

1) Strongly agree

2)

3)

Continued

4)
5)
6)
7) Strongly disagree

Briefly describe the key aspects that led to your assessment on this CRM strategy assessment item.

_____

_____

_____

_____

_____

Please calculate your total score across the six CRM Strategy Assessment questions.

TOTAL SCORE _____

How would you access your firm's score relative to the leaders in your industry? Is your firm a leader in strategic thinking about customers? Or, are you a follower? Please comment briefly below:

_____

_____

_____

_____

_____

_____

CFO comfort levels). For example, investments in building closer relationships with strategic and key accounts may increase customer loyalty and retention and thereby reduce fluctuations in purchases at a given account, and/or vulnerability to customer loss (and the attendant need for customer "win-back" or new customer acquisition investments to replace lost sales volume).

CRM: An Organizational View

An enterprise-level CRM strategy adopts a customer-centric perspective that fundamentally changes the role of marketing and sales in the organization.

Successful CRM models make a holistic- or single-company view of the customer the centerpiece of company strategy. The sales force often agreeably responds to this notion of "becoming customer-oriented." Sales personnel see themselves as the only ones who regularly interact with the customer and, hence, truly understand customers. Sales personnel often express frustration with marketing's new products because of their lack of application to their specific customers. They also express chagrin with marketing as a "black hole" for salesperson-generated ideas and intelligence. Finally, sales personnel are often frustrated at lost sales opportunities or dissatisfied customers due to the unwillingness, or inability, of internal departments to respond in a timely or supportive fashion. Sales personnel see themselves having a "one-to-one" relationship with the customer. But what is needed in CRM is for the *selling company* to operate on a one-to-one basis. As one consultant notes, one-to-one relationships occur "whenever the customer tells you something . . . and you change your behavior with respect to this individual based on this interaction."

In B2B contexts, where large customers are readily identified for their market potential, account managers are likely to respond to a CRM initiative with a yawn, and to some degree they are correct. That is, to the degree that an account manager has been able to bring organizational resources to bear on critical customer needs, then a one-to-one relationship with the customer has been successfully implemented. However, it is important to note that these wins depend on the sheer talent, will, and influence of the account manager. The goal of CRM is to adopt an organizational model of CRM by systematically selecting the right target customers, from a strategic fit perspective, and then designing a cost-effective strategy, organizational structure, business model and processes, human resource, and technology strategy to serve these customers profitably. Technology is a major innovation, through integrated databases, networking, and analytical models, for enabling companies to relate more closely to high priority customers.

Given a corporate-level strategy that emphasizes the value of building and investing in customer relationships, an organization view can be articulated. Ideally, the enterprise view can be defined as follows

". . . A cross-functional process for achieving a continuing dialogue with customers, across all of their contact and access points, with personalized treatment of the most valuable customers, to increase customer retention and the effectiveness of marketing initiatives."

A well-defined and established CRM model can develop a distinctive competency in the process of market-relating to the degree that a firm can develop three cross-functional capabilities: knowledge acquisition, knowledge utilization, and organizational alignment. This is consistent with the view that learning organizations must collect, share, analyze, and act on information to develop a knowledge-based competitive advantage.

To review this organizational learning literature is beyond the scope of this CRM overview. The main point is that an enterprise-level perspective on CRM requires the generation of a cross-functional dialogue with customers that yields usable customer information that: (1) can be captured in a database; (2) can be shared and analyzed by corporate and functional level executives for its customer relationship intelligence and insights; and (3) can be translated into customer value through products, solutions, and services.

To capture an organizational perspective on the enterprise-level CRM model and the role of the sales force as a customer access and interaction strategy, two concepts, analytical CRM and operational CRM, are developed in Exhibit 4.3. *Analytical CRM* is analysis of customer-level data and more general market intelligence information to provide strategic and tactical customer and market insights. In Exhibit 4.3, the analytical CRM processes include the specifics of the analytical methods and tools used to provide strategic insights that drive the firm's choices in four general, interlinked strategy arenas: marketing strategy, customer relationship strategy, services delivery strategy, and go-to-market strategy. Executive-level decisions in each of these strategic domains directly affect customer value creation, the relative price/value tradeoff customers face, and the relative ease and convenience of the customers' interactions with the selling firm. Two critical analytic processes relevant to "go-to-market" strategy and the CRM strategic objectives and model employed are those involved in developing a coherent definition of the customer relationship typology (or competitive playing field) the firm faces and the specification of the customer relationship strategies that might best suit each potential customer market segment targeted.

Operational CRM involves translating the core marketing strategies, in particular the go-to-market strategy, developed in the analytical CRM phase, into a coherent and replicable customer access model and interaction strategy (see Exhibit 4.3, bottom half). The fundamental objective is to generate the customer demand targeted in the analytical CRM phase, among the desired customers, and employing the core marketing-related strategies chosen to offer customer value. This is the implementation phase of the right

Exhibit 4.3 Enterprise-level CRM Model and Processes

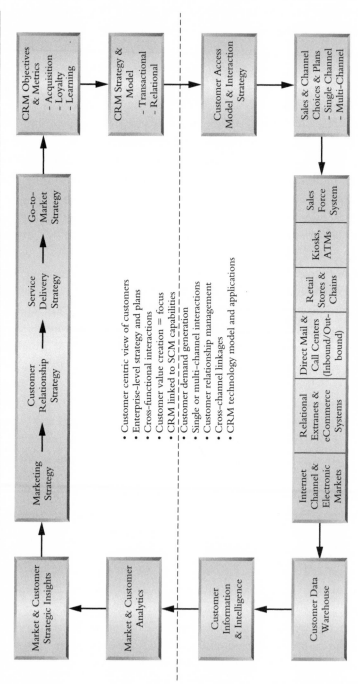

© Thomson

104

customer → right strategy → right organization → right processes → right systems → right people → right rewards success cycle that was designed to deliver customer value at a profit to the selling firm.

Historically, these operational CRM issues were considered tactical and were most often implemented through a sales force organization. That is, the field sales force implemented the CRM plan as they called on key customers, delivered sales messages, and closed business. Usually, the sales force was incentivized on achieving sales revenue targets, although more sophisticated firms often added product-related sales, cost control, and margin targets as well. Sales personnel were not usually privy to the particulars of the firm's marketing-related strategies, often in the belief that these proprietary issues should be shared only on a need-to-know basis. A natural consequence of this marketing-sales disconnect was the view that marketing was perceived to be strategic (i.e., focused on the larger-term competitive horizon) and sales was tactical (i.e., focused on the immediate customer transaction). This marketing and sales disconnect compromised customer value creation and often customer satisfaction, as promises were made in the heat of the sale that ultimately were not deliverable by the firm.

Adopting a CRM perspective on the customer alters this sales implementation model in several ways in order to better link marketing and sales and provide a clearer focus on customer value creation. In the first place, customer relationship and go-to-market strategy are now more clearly integrated with the traditional marketing strategies at the analytical CRM and planning phases. In other words, the customer relationship typology and intended customer relationship strategy are more clearly defined in terms of: 1) targeted segments and customers; and, 2) the intended customer value creation model and selling requirements. Hence, the potential customer value contributions of the alternate channels and the sales organizations are more clearly and explicitly specified, and openly communicated, to all "customer-facing" employees, including the sales force.

In the second place, the intended CRM strategy and model is more readily translated into operational CRM strategy focused on the most desirable strategic approaches for customer access and engagement. This is the operational CRM link to the customer's preferred buying approach in channel access terms. In terms of the operational CRM decisions, the firm must select the most appropriate customer access and interaction channels. This is a more complex strategy today because there are now a variety of possible conduits to reach desired customers, and customers are increasingly more discriminating and demanding in how they prefer to interact with a selling firm. In Exhibit 4.3, the set of alternate customer access channels, or "touch-points," includes the sales force system (both direct and indirect), ATMs and kiosks, retail stores and chains, direct mail and call centers, relational extranets, and eCommerce platforms, Internet channels (wholly-owned or indirect), and eBusiness electronic marketplaces. Hence, at one level, the firm must carefully identify the alternate channels that may be employed to provide customer access and select the ones that best fit the selling firm's customer demand generation, control, and profitability goals and terms. The traditional field sales organization is but one choice among a set of alternate channels.

On a second level, customers are increasingly sophisticated in their use of available channel systems. For example, a direct field-based sales force, a local distributor, or a local retailer may be highly valued by customers for its local convenience, product trend and application expertise, and personalized style of conducting business. A call center or Internet solution may be valued for the help its customer service representatives and technical service experts may provide. An extranet or dedicated eBusiness application may be valued because it simplifies standardized buying processes and cuts costs. And, finally a dedicated-account manager, or customer-focused team, may be valued for its relationship qualities, including value chain solutions, customer business acumen, and customer-specific business process knowledge. In many cases, buyers prefer a multi-channel approach, perhaps favoring a direct sales force for purchases where expertise matters, an indirect distributor channel for emergency purchases or inventory minimization, and a call center or an Internet for its easy access and timeliness. Hence, the capability to provide integrated multi-channel approaches, supported by indirect channel partnerships and sophisticated CRM and PRM technology applications, is increasingly a source of competitive advantage.

A final issue in operational CRM is customer learning. A centerpiece in an enterprise CRM approach is a centralized data warehouse that has the potential to capture, integrate, and share data from all "points of contact" with the customer, including the sales force system. Thus, it is critical that the firm defines a "closed loop" learning system that includes customer feedback for use in the CRM analytical process. In many cases this involves the acquisition of explicit customer information, such as hits to a Web site, call center contacts, requests for quotes (RFQs) posted, purchases made, or complaints registered. This explicit knowledge about customers is readily managed using technology solutions. However, implicit (or tacit) knowledge, such as sales call dialogues, which are personal and context specific, also is

BREAK BOX: Becoming Aware

The second stage of the BREAK process is becoming aware of your firm's current practices, processes, and systems for complementing CRM across the organization. The following questions are designed to guide you in assessing the degree to which your firm has successfully achieved an organizational CRM model and implementation.

A) To what degree does your firm systematically and selectively identify potential customers and classify them according to a rigorous value assessment process?

1. Strongly agree
2.
3.
4.
5.
6.
7. Strongly disagree

Briefly describe the key aspects that led to your assessment on this CRM strategy assessment item.

_____

_____

_____

_____

_____

B) To what degree does your firm systematically and consistently assess the relative value of its current customers, the costs of winning a customer back or retaining them, and a cutoff criterion for walking away from less attractive customers?

1. Strongly agree
2.
3.
4.
5.
6.
7. Strongly disagree

Continued

Briefly describe the key aspects that led to your assessment on this CRM strategy assessment item.

_____

_____

_____

_____

_____

C) To what degree are target market segments and specific customer priorities developed at the analytical CRM stage by marketing executives shared with sales and channel executives (the operational CRM level)?

1. Strongly agree
2.
3.
4.
5.
6.
7. Strongly disagree

Briefly describe the key aspects that led to your assessment on this CRM strategy assessment item.

_____

_____

_____

_____

_____

D) To what degree has your firm systematically defined and distinguished the customer access model and interaction strategy according to the customer's preferred buying approach?

1. Strongly agree
2.
3.
4.
5.
6.
7. Strongly disagree

Continued

Briefly describe the key aspects that led to your assessment on this CRM strategy assessment item.

_____

_____

_____

_____

_____

E) To what degree does your firm successfully employ multiple sales models and strategies, such as sales force, the internet, an extranet, call centers, and distributors?

1. Strongly agree
2.
3.
4.
5.
6.
7. Strongly disagree

Briefly describe the key aspects that led to your assessment on this CRM strategy assessment item.

_____

_____

_____

_____

_____

F) To what degree is your firm able to provide an integrated, multi-channel approach for customers who prefer to buy differently depending on the purchasing context?

1. Strongly agree
2.
3.
4.
5.
6.
7. Strongly disagree

Continued

Briefly describe the key aspects that led to your assessment on this CRM strategy assessment item.

_____

_____

_____

_____

_____

G) To what degree is your firm able to capture, integrate, and share customer data from all "touch points" with the customer, including the sales force system?

1. Strongly agree
2.
3.
4.
5.
6.
7. Strongly disagree

Briefly describe the key aspects that led to your assessment on this CRM strategy assessment item.

_____

_____

_____

_____

_____

H) To what degree has your firm been able to successfully implement a "closed loop" learning process that links the analytical and procedural CRM processes?

1. Strongly agree
2.
3.
4.
5.
6.
7. Strongly disagree

Continued

Briefly describe the key aspects that led to your assessment on this CRM strategy assessment item.

_____

_____

_____

_____

_____

I) To what degree is the role of the sales force in demand generation (the agentic role) and customer learning (the learning role) clearly defined, measured, and rewarded?

1. Strongly agree
2.
3.
4.
5.
6.
7. Strongly disagree

Briefly describe the key aspects that led to your assessment on this CRM strategy assessment item.

_____

_____

_____

_____

_____

J) To what degree has your firm been successful in employing eBusiness applications that meet customer buying and interaction preferences, while supporting the intended role of the sales force in generating demand and informing the customer learning system?

1. Strongly agree
2.
3.
4.
5.
6.
7. Strongly disagree

Continued

Briefly describe the key aspects that contributed to your assessment on this CRM assessment item.

_____

_____

_____

_____

K) To what degree are customer-based metrics, relative to sales revenue generation, employed in the sales force and channel performance evaluation system?

1. Strongly agree
2.
3.
4.
5.
6.
7. Strongly disagree

Briefly describe the key aspects that led to your assessment on this CRM strategy assessment item.

_____

_____

_____

_____

_____

Please calculate your total score across the eleven (A thru K) CRM Strategy Assessment questions.

TOTAL SCORE _____

How would you assess your firm's score relative to the leaders in your industry? Is your firm a leader in strategic thinking about customers? Or, are you a follower? Please comment briefly below:

_____

_____

_____

_____

critical. For example, sales personnel learn through customer dialogues, shared experiences, stories, and plant visitations. Sales personnel may also provide customer intelligence and insights based on their own implicit experiences and judgments. Hence, operational CRM systems must engage sales personnel in the customer feedback and learning process. This is no small task, especially if an antagonistic relationship between marketing and sales is part of the firm's culture.

Developing a Customer Relationship Model

As indicated above, developing an enterprise-level customer relationship strategy requires the firm to: 1) develop a clear definition of the customer relationship typology, or set of possible customer segments, the firm faces; 2) specify the scope of its intended customer relationship strategy in terms of a set of desirable target customer segments. Given these two elements of the CRM puzzle, the firm can then proceed to develop a leading-edge customer relationship and go-to-market strategy to serve each distinct segment targeted. Particularly important from our perspective is the role that the sales force and eBusiness applications play in implementing the firm's intended customer access and interaction model. The remainder of this chapter will outline the decision processes involved in defining a customer relationship typology, a customer relationship strategy, and the role of the sales force and eBusiness in implementing the resulting CRM model.

Customer Relationship Typology

Building close customer relationships with *all* customers is not feasible or necessary. For example, the loss of a significant key account was noted for a corrugated box company when it recommended the purchase of corrugated box rejects to cut the customer's purchasing costs. Customers should be arrayed along a customer relationship continuum ranging from pure transactional to pure collaborative exchanges. Although consultants in CRM and sales emphasize that environmental changes such as trends toward global exchanges, intense competitive rivalry, rapid technology change, increased customer sophistication, and emphases on total supply chain effectiveness and efficiency are fueling a shift to relationship buying, it is still true that sizable market potential is accounted for by transactional customers. Hence, market-oriented and market-driven firms must seek to understand their markets in terms of a customer relationship typology; or a competitive playing field that defines the general set of customer segments, and specific customers defining a given market; along with the attendant business marketing, selling, and servicing models necessary to build a competitive advantage in each.

The simplest customer relationship typology is to analyze customers in terms of their propensity to be transactional or relational in their buying approaches. Many observers opine that a sea of change has occurred in fundamental buying models from the "old economy" transactional model, with its emphasis on product-based, adversarial exchange and negotiation, to the "new economy" relational model, with its emphasis on customer solutions embedded in "best-in-class" supplier relationship and strategic partnerships. In reality, both models apply and may be employed successfully depending on industry competitive conditions.

More sophisticated expositions of these transactional versus relational distinctions in buying are articulated in the purchasing literature. For purposes of exposition, these distinctions are summarized in Exhibit 4.4. The primary point is that defining the customer's relationship typology requires a fine grain investigation of how customers buy that may yield a range of customer models along the transactional to relational continuum. The particular typology presented in Exhibit 4.4 provides guidance for this investigation process. However, as noted later, a leading healthcare firm identified five customer segments in its customer relationship typology.

Why is this customer relationship typology (CRT) important? The CRT defines the competitive playing field facing the selling firm. The strategic choice facing the firm is to define the breadth and depth in its customer relationship strategy, or the set of targeted customer segments it intends to pursue, realizing that each segment will require a distinct business model, including selling and servicing models. These customer relationship strategy issues are discussed below. However, it is important to note here that delimiting the scope of the intended customer relationship strategy is a challenge that many firms are unwilling to face. In our experience, too many firms are unwilling to walk away from less desirable customer segments. Rather, they attempt to serve all customer segments due to fears of passing up potential future profits, allowing an opening for a competitive inroad by a competitor, mitigating risks of customer demand changes, or uncritical thinking concerning the resource and management demands involved in employing multiple business and selling models. As

Exhibit 4.4   Customer Relationship Typology Schema

Transactional		Relational	
Discrete Transaction	**Solution Transaction**	**Relationship Partner**	**Collaborative Partner**
Buy product at best price	Bring solution to a business application problem	Build relationship based on value chain synergies	Joint strategic collaboration targeting end-users
Discrete transaction	Solution life cycle trans-action	Open-ended relationship	Partnership presumed (strategic soul mate)
Always open to buy	Open to switch	Open to suggestions to improve the relationship	Open-ended "Green" agreements and contract"
Classic adver-sarial buying process	Reasoned bargaining (Asymmetric)	Open nego-tiation of relational agreement	Collaborative political exchange model
Win-Lose on purchase price	Win-Lose on relative power	Win-Win through relational qualities	Win-Win through joint problem solving
Product quality only	Product and service value-in-use	Best-in-class supplier qualities	TQM leader-ship through collaboration
Resolute and distant	Respect and satisfaction	Trust and re-sponsiveness	Reciprocity and trust

© Thomson

Chapter 5 will cover in more depth, employing two distinct selling models, one for transactional segments and one for relational segments, requires very distinct sales force organizational and human resource approaches and capabilities, namely a traditional sales territory model and a strategic account management model. In general, a more focused customer relationship model is advisable.

Customer Relationship Strategy

A selling firm may choose to specialize, for example, focusing only on either transactional customers or strategic partnership customers. This narrow focus allows the firm to specialize its resource deployments to best fit the indicated buying preference of the targeted segment. For example, a specialty chemical company identified six customer segments in its boating manufacturer CRT, with one firm considered a transactional segment in and of itself due to its large volume. After considerable deliberation, the selling firm decided to walk away from this major account in order to rationalize its resource deployments on the more sophisticated brand-oriented manufacturers and a set of firms that, while lacking engineering expertise, nevertheless sought to compete on a new product and brand name basis. This relatively selective customer relationship strategy allowed the firm to specialize its engineering, sales, and service resources and capabilities to focus on these segments.

On the other hand, a firm may decide to compete in several or all of the customer segments available. For example, a leading healthcare firm decided to compete in all five customer segments in its customer relationship typology. As a consequence, it found it necessary to develop several distinct business models, including a traditional field sales force, an account management system, a customer-focused team model, local distributor relationships, and an online/call center ordering system. Needless to say, this firm faced many challenges as it sought to simultaneously develop a strategic account model for its high-end customers, while maintaining its traditional sales territory and distribution model. Hence, a firm's customer relationship strategy choices have significant impact on its necessary go-to-market and CRM strategy, including the very nature of the firm's customer access and customer interaction requirements.

The Role of the Sales Force in a CRM System

The role of the sales force in a CRM model depends on how the firm decides it can most effectively and efficiently manage its dialogue with desired customers and channels. As noted earlier, the firm's choices concerning its customer relationship strategy determine its indicated requirements for its customer access and interaction. The good old days of using the traditional geographically organized sales force, in which a salesperson is implicitly responsible for all customers, all products, and all services, may no longer necessarily be cost-effective in light of the specialized expertise required for the more relational customers, and the availability of lower cost (and perhaps equally effective) channels such as the Internet, call centers, direct mail, and extranets. Literally, the use of a direct sales force should not be presumed for all customer segments. Sales force investments must be justified on a cash flow and NPV basis, relative to alternate ways to access the customer and manage customer relationships.

In thinking about the role of the sales force, customer demand generation is a fundamental CRM process (revisit Exhibit 4.3). This is the *agentic role,* or the involvement of the direct sales organization of some type as a sales agent in generating and managing customer demand according to the selling firm's intended customer relationship objectives, strategy, and metrics. However, adopting a CRM model raises the value of customer information and knowledge, and hence makes customer learning a fundamental CRM process as well. Hence, the *learning role* of the sales force must be clearly delineated as well. Thus, firms must reframe the sales force role to include an appropriate balance among the agentic and learning requirements of the enterprise CRM model.

In establishing the role of the direct sales force, four selling models are important. These four models will be overviewed here. They will be more completely discussed in Chapter 5, with particular attention paid to strategic account management approaches. In the first place, the agentic role may be implemented using a primarily talent-based model in which the direct sales force, perhaps supplemented by sales force automation tools, fully manages the customer demand generation process. In practice, this selling approach is commonly used when the customer prefers to buy transactionally. The traditional sales territory model best fits this sales context. Literally, the salesperson manages the demand generation process for all customers in the sales territory. Hence, the salesperson sets customer priorities, a customer coverage strategy, intended selling approaches and messages, and a strategy for managing future transactions. Thus, this is a decentralized and talent-based model, which stresses achieving sales productivity over customer learning. A fundamental challenge, from an enterprise CRM perspective, is the relative difficulty of engaging the field sales force in completing the learning loop in the CRM model.

A second alternative that has received considerable play, in light of new channel and technology options, is to either outsource (a bad word in many organizations today) or disintermediate (another bad word today) the direct field sales organization. The most common form of outsourcing is to use an indirect channel, such as a distributor or an Internet marketplace. The presumption is that the customer demand generation process may be effectively managed by a third-party partner at a lower total cost including investment considerations. Since direct control by the revenue firm is lessened, a common requirement for the selling firm is to work closely with the indirect channel to insure that the demand generation and management process is fully implemented. This selling model is decentralized and talent-based, with typical compromises in agent control, customer learning, and customer relationship management.

Disintermediating the sales force (or for that matter indirect channels) is often referred to as the Dell model. In Dell's case, the demand generation and customer management process is largely handled through the Internet and call centers (although account management models are also employed). That is, customers often do not require, or prefer, a sales interaction with a direct or indirect field sales force (as an intermediary). Hence, the name disintermediation, commonly thought of as "bypassing the middleman" to deal directly with the customer. For rapidly changing markets, sophisticated customers, or commoditized products, the fundamental notion is that the selling firm can substitute more technology driven and lower cost selling models for the services of a talent-based field sales system.

As implied above, Dell actually employs an integrated multi-channel sales model. Customers are provided a set of channel choices, including Internet, call center, retail, account manager, and collaborative partner models. Transaction customers tend to use the Internet and call centers; relational customers prefer account manager or collaborative partner models. However, larger B2B firms often buy using more than one selling model in order to manage the total costs of an integrated information system solution.

A third selling model is the account manager model, usually employed when the demand generation process targets longer-term, relationship-oriented customers. As discussed in Chapter 5, these customers are often defined as either strategic accounts or strategic partner accounts. In either case, the salesperson is assigned a specific customer, or a set of customers, as target accounts. Serving in an account manager role, he/she is assigned the task of generating a relationship with the account based on the notion of establishing a preferred, or possibly sole supplier, position over an extended time frame. The account manager is the face of the selling firm to the buyer. However, an integrated multi-channel model, including even indirect channels, may be used to supplement (not disintermediate) the account manager's efforts. Hence, this selling model is both talent and technology based and is centralized to achieve tighter control over selling efforts.

A final selling model is that of the dedicated customer-focused team for a specific customer (or CFT). In this selling approach, an organization-to-organization relationship is established to build and manage a long-term, usually sole supplier, relationship with a strategic partner customer. As will be discussed in Chapter 5, the strategic partner account manager actually manages the partnership as a distinct business enterprise with joint goals and metrics. This selling model centralizes the selling process in order to provide an enterprise-level specialization on the strategic partner relationship. CFT managers require a sophisticated set of talent-based skills, along with an enterprise-level CRM process supported by technology and eBusiness solutions.

The Role of eBusiness Applications in Customer Relationship Strategy

The establishment of trust-based relationships with customers, whether collaborative or not, provides excellent opportunities to employ a variety of eBusiness systems and solutions for the customer and/or the partnership. Typically, these eBusiness approaches emphasize effectiveness or efficiency improvements along the supply chain. Many of these applications target sourcing-related issues that have previously been handled by account managers, field sales personnel, or customer service representatives. For example, sales personnel are expected to be informed about their firm's products, their attributes, and their application in use. Electronic catalogs can provide customers easy access to a larger set of suppliers (referred to as *market liquidity*), product-in-use application guidelines and references, and product comparison software or analytics. Sales personnel are also expected to be up-to-date and timely in their product availability and pricing knowledge. eBusiness applications can provide both the customer and the salesperson access to the most recent price or availability data. Sales personnel are often responsible for a variety of follow-up services, including delivery updates, new product announcements, warranty alerts and updates, product recalls and so forth. These information demands may be more readily managed, for both the salesperson's and the customer's benefit, through a customer portal. Finally, sales personnel are often responsible for contract management and usage issues, such as whether or not the local plants are buying on contract or using more expensive local suppliers. Again, these contract management issues may be streamlined using Internet-based solutions.

To exemplify how the Internet is being leveraged to systematize buyer-seller relationships, and leverage salesperson resources, the practices of several B2B leading firms are reviewed. For example, one of the top three largest wholesale electronics distributors implemented a national accounts management program targeting the large, sophisticated customers and offering guaranteed pricing and a variety of supply chain solutions designed to increase efficiency and cut costs. Essentially, it provided demand management and value-added services to buyers who indicated they were interested in the "one-stop shopping" convenience that a partnership provided. National account managers (NAMs) in this instance prospected for new national accounts, developed new relationships, managed established relationships, and worked with field sales personnel at the local plant level. Clearly, they were stretched to fulfill all of these time demands. To systematize these national account relationships, and provide value-added services to cement customer relationships, the firm invested in eCommerce solutions, including an online catalog, a wireless ordering system, product comparison analytics, a web-enabled inventory management system, direct links to a variety of external, or third-party, electronic marketplaces (or portals), and a financial management system. The firm has subsequently been recognized as the leader in its industry in eBusiness applications and performance.

A second eBusiness example involves one of the world's largest electronics distributors in the rapidly changing and risky computer industry. In this case, new product introductions and speed to market critically influenced the supplier's end-market success. Hence, the distributor's "value-add" for its strategic accounts lay largely in its ability to help these customers identify the latest trends and products, ameliorate its inventory obsolescence and pricing risks, and enhance supply chain efficiency. Hence, it invested in a variety of eBusiness applications to supplement its sales force's efforts, in particular to provide more time to work with field engineers in new product development consulting for select partner firms. These eBusiness solutions included an online product catalog, a product availability risk management system, an electronic contact system for announcing OEM product design changes, an electronic materials planning system, and a contract manager system to monitor forecasted versus actual purchases. These systems freed the strategic account managers and local sales and support personnel to spend more time working with strategic customers, especially at the home office, decision-making level.

BREAK BOX: Reviewing and Relating

Relating the ideas and concepts discussed so far to your firm's strategic account strategy and practices involves reviewing the material. The following questions are designed to guide you through this part of the process.

1. Consider your assessment of your firm's market orientation, as well as its clarity in defining and communicating its customer relationship strategy. A) What opportunities are there for improving your firm's market orientation? B) What opportunities are there for enhancing the managerial processes employed to define and relate its core target market segments and lead customer priorities?

2. Review the discussion of the role of customer value creation in defining and planning your firm's customer relationship, sales force, and channel strategies. A) What opportunities are there for enhancing the role of customer value creation in influencing the development of your firm's corporate strategies in general? In influencing your firm's sales force and channel strategy in particular? B) What communications opportunities are there for improving the firm's shared agreement on the firm's customer relationship model and strategies?

3. Consider the discussion of the strategic role of C-level sales executives in influencing your firm's definition of its customer relationship model and strategy. A) What opportunities are there for improving the influence of these key senior sales leaders in your firm's corporate strategic planning process? B) What opportunities are there for improving the articulation of your firm's finalized corporate CRM strategies to the sales organization and key managerial personnel?

4. Review the notions of customer valuation and customer lifetime value. A) What opportunities are there for enhancing the degree to which customer lifetime value is employed in defining CRM, sales force, and channel selection strategies? B) What ideas concerning customer lifetime value definition and measurement should be considered by your sales force in planning their customer contact priorities? The firm's selection of alternate sales channels to complement the customer value creating of the direct sales force? The firm's selection of alternate sales channels to replace the use of a direct sales force?

Continued

5. Review the discussion of the use of customer related metrics such as customer satisfaction, customer retention and customer profitability in defining your sales force and channel strategy. A) What opportunities are there for enhancing the role of these customer metrics in judging the success or failure of your firm in general? B) The sales organization in particular? C) The performance of alternate CRM and sales channel approaches?

6. Consider the notion of sales channels as customer touch points and the need to capture, integrate, and share all of the data gathered at these customer touch points to drive your firm's corporate strategic planning and valuation processes. A) What opportunities are there for streamlining and automating your firm's customer information collection and sharing processes from the direct sales force? From alternate sales channels? B) What opportunities are there for enhancing the availability and use of customer data available from alternate sales channels to enhance your sales forces' performance?

7. Review the ideas presented concerning the demand generation and customer learning roles of the sales organization. A) What opportunities are there at your firm to clarify and prioritize the role of the sales force in implementing these two, often conflicting, sales force responsibilities? B) What approaches are best advised to motivate the sales force to fully participate in the "closed loop" learning processes of the firm?

8. Consider the availability of new sales channels to better serve customers in terms of their preferred approaches to buying. Review the discussion of these eBusiness approaches and how they may enhance customer's buying processes, including information search and new product announcements, in ways that enhance the performance of the sales force. A) What opportunities are there for employing the use of eBusiness approaches to improve the effectiveness and/or efficiency of your firm's customers? Your firm's sales organization? B) What managerial approaches are needed to gain the acceptance and use of these eBusiness approaches by customers? By your firm's sales force?

The hospital supply business provides a variety of opportunities for eBusiness applications designed to support sales personnel and strategic partner relationships. One leading distributor converted its established EDI systems to a recognized "Best Practice" electronic portal model that supported a variety of value-added applications. Representative applications include: web-based decision support; medication management; ordering systems; automated medicine dispensing and tracking systems; "stockless" inventory management services; a complete medical materials catalog and pricing comparison system; a pharmacy inventory management system; a wireless, automated inventory system featuring radio frequency transmitters (or RFID); and an ATM system to enable patients to directly access health information and fill prescription needs. A competing hospital supply company was able to capture customer-level data on supply chain issues, package this information into customer intelligence solutions, and profitably sell these intelligence solutions back to its customers.

To summarize, sales personnel, key account managers and strategic partner managers increasingly must focus on broad gauge supply chain solutions as value-added services for their customers. The implication is that these account managers need to be conversant with supply chain issues from an account selling and managing point of view. Hence, sales managers and sales personnel will increasingly be involved in customer dialogues aimed at building complex electronic systems and web-based services, as customers seek to simplify their supply chains and improve their sourcing effectiveness and efficiency. From a sales manager's point of view, the opportunity is to identify eBusiness solutions that enhance the quality of the customer's experience and productivity, while leveraging the sales forces' performance.

Conclusions and BREAKthrough Directions

In this chapter, we discussed customer relationship strategy and management as a core capability of firms seeking to compete successfully in B2B market contexts. In particular, we noted that market-oriented firms systematically and thoughtfully segment their markets and choose their customers wisely. They choose to compete on a playing field that provides the opportunity for market leadership and market leading returns to capital. They value their customers as strategic assets and rationalize their customer relationship investments so as to realize the loyalty of these key customers. In sum, these firms seek to adopt a strategic perspective on CRM and seek to build a customer-centric organization to serve desirable customers.

BREAK BOX: Envisioning and Creating

Now think about ways of applying the key ideas in this chapter in your sales organization and creating the basic steps needed for this to happen. Identify a key priority for action in each of the following areas and the general steps that would be needed to make it happen in your sales organization:

1. Enhancing your firm's market orientation and aligning your sales organization with the strategic customer-oriented initiatives indicated as high priorities.
2. Generating a useful flow of sales organization information upwards to fuel senior management's attention to customer valuation, needs and requirements, as well as the interests of the sales organization, in your firm's strategic planning process.
3. Enhancing your sales organization's attention to customer valuation and customer lifetime value in designing and implementing your customer relationship strategy and sales plan.
4. Enhancing your firm's customer retention and "win-back" performance.
5. Employing multiple channels to better meet customer buying preferences, while enhancing or maintaining the performance of your sales organization.
6. Improving the attention of your sales organization to the customer learning requirements involved in fueling your firm's analytical CRM systems.
7. Designing appropriate eBusiness and CRM strategies and solutions to enhance the effectiveness and efficiency of your sales organization.
8. Improving your firm's performance evaluation and compensation system in light of the goal of enhancing attention to longer term customer relationship and customer valuation metrics.

In implementing a CRM organizational model we stressed the need for a closed loop learning model that systematically links the analytical and operational processes and practices driving market and customer intelligence, and customer value creation. We stressed the cross-functional nature of this customer-relating and interacting CRM process. In this model, a variety of go-to-market, customer relationship, and customer interaction strategies may be relevant depending on the customer's preferred way to buy. Thus, achieving an integrated go-to-market and CRM strategy is a senior-level and board-level topic for market-driven firms.

The BREAK process stressed becoming aware of a range of CRM strategy and organizational issues, reviewing and relating the concepts and ideas discussed in this chapter, and envisioning and creating the type of organization desired utilizing these concepts. In concert, the prior Becoming Aware exercises should have guided you in an audit of your organization's current understanding and implementation of CRM as an enterprise-level strategy for selecting and relating to your customers. In this final step, the Envisioning and Creating step, you are asked to revisit your BREAK process assessments and identify a set of strategic priorities that are central in advancing your firm to a leadership position in CRM in your industry. To simplify this you might first sort the items into three groups: 1) those that are immediately critical to correct on-going customer experience breakdowns that are significantly affecting your firm's performance; 2) those that are critical longer term to provide customer-based strategic options for your firm in moving to a leadership position in your industry; and, 3) those that sound nice, but must be put off until another day. Once you have identified a set of CRM strategic initiatives, then outline an action plan necessary to significantly improve your firm's performance on each strategic initiative. Make sure to identify the requirements for a CRM process champion, critical role-players who need to be sold on the CRM initiative and how they might be approached, and critical CRM-related investments, including human, financial, and technological resources and capabilities. GOOD luck in your quest!

Visit The Sales Educators Web site for further BREAK process materials on this chapter's topics. www.TheSalesEducators.com

References and Suggested Readings

Anderson, James C. and James A. Narus (1991), "Partnering as a Focused Market Strategy," *California Management Review*, 33 (3), 95-124.

Chrzanowski, Keith A. and Thomas W. Leigh (1990), "Customer Relationship Strategy and Customer-Focused Teams," in Bauer, Gerald J., Mark S. Baunchalk, Thomas N. Ingram, and Raymond W. LaForge, *Emerging Trends in Sales Thought and Practice*, Wesport, CT: Quoram Books, 51-80.

Day, George S. (2001), "Capabilities for Forging Customer Relationships," *MSI Report* # 00-118, 1-33, p. 4.

Peppers, Don and Martha Rogers (2001), *Managing Customer Relationships: A Strategic Framework*, p. 36.

Srivastava, Rajendra K., Tasadduq A. Shervani, and Liam Fahey (1998), "Market-based Assets and Shareholder Value: A Framework," *Journal of Marketing*, 62 (1), 2-18.

CHAPTER 5

LEVERAGING STRATEGIC ACCOUNT STRATEGIES

Introduction

Building on Chapter 1, the business landscape has changed such that selling firms can no longer afford to target the masses hoping for profitable business relationships; there must be more strategy involved in selecting those accounts that can support the specific goals of the selling firm. This chapter provides a framework for identifying strategic accounts and discusses tools and guidelines for working with these all-important accounts. The chapter includes a set of break exercises to guide the sales manager, working in conjunction with senior sales leadership, to assess the firm's current standing with its key customers, specifying an action plan for a suitable strategic account strategy.

Strategic Accounts Defined

More and more companies today are struggling with determining what makes an account particularly suited to become a *strategic* or *key* account. In general, the following elements define strategic accounts. First, these accounts are strategic with respect to revenues, profits, expansion, market share, fit and growth opportunities for the future. Second, they are strategic with respect to the nature of the relationship (partnership) between the seller and the buyer. Third, they are strategic with respect to the development of new products and services. In their book *Rethinking the Sales Force*, Neil Rackham and John DeVincentis describe strategic account selling as enterprise selling, which requires the alignment of strategic interests by the customer and supplier and significant value creation across a number of functions. The high cost and risk involved in initiating and maintaining the relationship means that enterprise selling is offered only to those customers who are extremely important with respect to the selling company's goals.

Strategic and Global Account Management as a Go-To-Market Strategy

The genesis of strategic account selling began in the 1960s out of the need for sellers to devote significant corporate resources to large, complex accounts having special requirements. Today, strategic account management is practiced on the national, regional, multinational and global levels according to the organizational characteristics and operational behavior of both the seller and buyer. The practice of strategic account management is becoming a science worthy of academic research and a subject that is also generating much interest from companies seeking new ways to thrive in highly competitive conditions, achieve competitive advantage and create future growth. Above all, companies are striving to preserve those customer relationships that are of strategic importance to their firm's future financial health.

Determining Key and Strategic Accounts

In determining which accounts should be strategic accounts, many factors must be taken into consideration. A strategic account is more than just a large customer. The high level of customer contact and the level of customer support required, along with the structure of the supplier's account team, may help to identify a strategic customer. Further, a strategic account may require more account penetration than nonstrategic accounts. Finally, the strategic account is far more complex in terms of planning and implementation issues.

Traditionally, the size of the account, its complexity in terms of multiple locations or plants, the complexity of the buying center, in terms of the involvement of top management, the number of departmental functions involved in the purchases, and oftentimes, the centralized nature of buying processes are common characteristics of strategic accounts. Customers who met the set of firm-level descriptive criteria were typically assigned a national account manager, or NAM. In many cases, the selling firm was explicitly recognizing its dependency on the customer and, hence, its willingness to invest in a NAM to provide the TLC essential to keep the customer happy (and supposedly loyal). NAM account investments were relatively expensive, thus minimum "hurdle" levels of sales volume, number of employees, or future sales potential were critical in the decision to make a NAM investment. In other cases, the NAM was established to recognize that specialized knowledge of the customer was required to properly sell and serve the customer, and thereby retain their loyalty.

Size of Account

Clearly, strategic accounts will likely be large accounts, with sales volume as the determinant of size. Some minimum volume requirements must be established, and existing and potential accounts that do not meet that minimum should not qualify for strategic account status. Following are some important questions to ask about strategic accounts:

1. What should be the minimum volume for strategic account status?
2. Should different minimum volumes be established for existing customers and potential customers?
3. What product/service mix will be needed to create a long-term relationship with the strategic customer?
4. What will be the return on investment (ROI) of resources?

Recent thinking suggests that firms use the profitability of each customer to determine whether the account qualifies for strategic account status. Often the largest account in terms of sales volume—even the most loyal account— is not the most profitable account. Because of the higher costs associated with servicing key accounts, only the most profitable accounts can justify the higher expenditure in resources dedicated to these partnerships.

Multiple Locations, Multiple Functions, Multiple Levels

Managers often feel that their firm's key account portfolio is homogeneous. Consequently, they prepare programs for their key accounts that all look the same. They tend to organize themselves on the same basis; for example, key account managers all have the same profile, are all recruited for the same functions, and all think of similar actions for their accounts.

In reality, the extreme importance of key accounts necessitates specific procedures and coordination. These accounts frequently have highly differentiated structures and complex behaviors; they may be geographically dispersed, have different buying procedures, or have negotiators at a high level in the customer organization.

Strategic accounts are, most often, those that have multiple buying locations, multiple functions involved in the buying decision (e.g., marketing, finance, and operations), and multiple levels influencing the final decision (e.g., senior managers, midlevel managers, and plant personnel). The existence of multiple locations requires coordinated support for those involved in purchasing decisions. When determining which accounts qualify for strategic account status, however, having multiple locations is not sufficient justification for elevation of an account to that level. Companies interested in partnering on a strategic level must employ a multi-location mind-set (e.g., each geographic location covered by the key account manager operates interdependently) and a strategic mind-set that realizes the buying synergies that can occur as a result of having a national or global scope.

Centralized Purchasing

Most strategic accounts have a centralized purchasing function, which means that buyers are located, typically, in a centralized facility (i.e., headquarter office) and are responsible for dispersing products to remote or satellite offices. Key account managers call on the headquarter offices of these buyers and communicate what is sold to account representatives in the field. The account representatives are then responsible for following through and implementing the approach agreed on by the key account manager and the buyer.

Other Considerations in Determining Strategic Accounts

Accounts are generally classified according to their potential value and the probability of achieving that potential, which is affected by several factors, including the following:

1. The propensity of the client to outsource and/or partner with suppliers. Clearly, companies seeking to partner with strategic accounts must obtain in-depth historical information concerning outsourcing and partnering activities of clients targeted for strategic account status. The strategic account may have a particular strategic focus (e.g., securing a particular account will help the seller to enter and penetrate other potential key accounts).

2. The supplier's current relationship with a client. This includes an assessment of the supplier's current sales programs, the recent history of those sales programs, level of contact with the client, and other signals from the client that might be pertinent to the decision to elevate the account to strategic account status.

3. The strength of competitors' positions and competitive offerings. In ascertaining competitive strength, salespeople must consider client needs being served and the number of organizations that are currently servicing those needs. Further, salespeople must examine the quality of competitive sales programs to identify recent successes and failures. The level of contact competitors have with clients is also an important consideration.

It is important to note that the strategic account selection criteria to this point have emphasized the selling firm's point of view. That is, implicit in this perspective is the customer's value to the selling firm. For example, the leading software firm in Exhibit 5.1 emphasizes corporate prospects

Exhibit 5.1   Sample Selection Criteria for Key and Strategic Accounts

Leading the Software Firm in Share Building Phase	Leading Electronics Innovator

Sales force size >250
Senior-level sponsorship
Multinational firms
Multi-channel firms
Industry leadership position
New industry to customer set
Facilitates development of
   technology roadmaps
	Should be likely to advance
	   technology roadmap by
	   providing access to lead
	   users
	Sales to partner firms will be
	   substantial (absolute or
	   potential revenue)
	Will allocate a significant (or
	   exclusive) share of processor
	   from seller (share of wallet)
	Accepts total cost orientation as
	   its business philosophy
	Willingness to put equal equity
	   (skin in the game) in the
	   partnership

© Thomson

that are large in sales force size, have executive sponsorship, compete in multi-national markets, use multiple channels, are industry leaders, and that offer the potential to advance the selling firm's technology roadmap. Similarly, the leading electronics firm in Exhibit 5.1 stresses customers who advance the seller's technology roadmap by providing channel access to lead-users, a dominant sales position with the customer (share of wallet), absolute sales potential (size of wallet), acceptance of a total cost orientation as its business philosophy, and is willing to put equity at stake (skin in the game).

The latter two of these criteria mention partnerships. However, the seller's strategy actually stresses the value of the product offering to the customer as its primary buying criterion. Furthermore, the seller will downgrade relationship customers who do not meet sales, profit, complimentary product purchase standards, or behave opportunistically. Hence, it appears that the seller's view is predominant, probably because of its innovation leadership and market-place dominance.

Determining Strategic Partnering Accounts

As firms become more market-oriented and market-driven, they seek to more precisely segment their markets and choose their customers more wisely. They recognize that the customer view is more critical to take into account, in particular the customer's preference as to how it prefers to buy and relate to its suppliers. Seller investments in building strategic partnerships necessitate deeper knowledge of the customer's business model and its sourcing processes.

Profiling Customer Buying Preferences

Once a selling firm has developed a CRM strategy involving strategic partnerships (as discussed in the previous chapter), it must profile potential customers according to their viability and interest in long-term relationships (see Exhibit 5.2). It is important to note that the selection criteria previously identified for profiling key and strategic accounts are necessary but not sufficient for selecting potential partners. In the first place, these criteria do not speak to the issue of how the firm prefers to buy. Such criteria as size, complexity, industry type or purchasing centralization provide little insight concerning *how* they buy. As Exhibit 5.3 indicates, these criteria are, in market segment terms, merely organizational demographics. To infer that a purchase, or purchasing approach, is a function of a buying firm's size or industry is a leap of faith. For example, a variety of companies across industries might be interested in buying a CRM or PRM system. Why? Because they share common end-user customer buying behavior, fundamental business processes, and cost pressures despite the fact that they compete in different industries. For example, the airline, banking, and retail industries all face buyer-seller requirements involving a large number of customer transactions which are relatively recurrent, urgent to fulfill in a timely fashion, and relatively expensive to process by hand. Hence, a CRM system, properly developed and implemented, might represent a solution that provides a cost-effective way to manage these exchanges. Thus, an initial step in screening candidate firms for strategic partnerships is to profile their business strategies, operating approaches, purchasing or sourcing policies, unique situational factors such as urgency or irregularity in purchases, and individual buyer characteristics (risk aversion, cost sensitivity).

Relationship Orientation

Relationship orientation is mentioned in Exhibit 5.3 as an individual buyer characteristic. Clearly, the relational orientation of a key buyer, in terms of a

Exhibit 5.2   Strategic Account Planning and Implementation Process

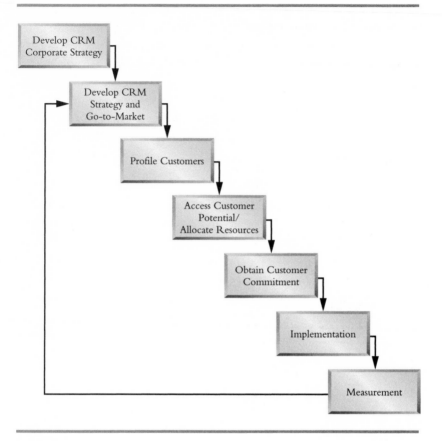

© Thomson

preference for transactional purchasing versus relationship sourcing is critical. A key buyer who believes in the need to at least periodically search the market for a better "deal" can interfere with an otherwise solid B2B relationship, perhaps turning it unprofitable, or ultimately undermining it. For example, an individual buyer for a product category at Wal-Mart might press for pricing concessions and command considerable attention from the relationship seller's management team. Moreover, the ascendancy of a transactionally-oriented buyer to a senior sourcing position can place strategic relationships in jeopardy. This actually happened at GM when José Ignacio Lopez de Arriortua reopened all "best in class" relationships with a demand for price concessions.

Strategic partnerships are organization-to-organization (or wall-to-wall) in nature (see Exhibit 5.5). Hence, the overriding selection criteria for

Exhibit 5.3   Organizational Segmentation

- Organizational Demographics
  Industry Category
  Organizational Size
  Organizational Location
  Purchasing Organizational
  Structure

  Purchase = f (Size; Industry
  Type)

- Organizational Operating Variables
  Process Technology
  Organizational Capabilities
  Organizational Economic
  Position
  Marketplace Strategic Position
  and Objectives
  Product or Brand Usage Status
  and Rate

  Purchase = f (Operating
  Variable; Capability; Strategy)

- Purchasing Approaches
  Purchasing Power Structures
  General Purchasing Policies
  Purchasing Criteria: Benefits and
  Attributes Sought
  Responsiveness to Marketing
  Mix Variables
  Source Loyalty Status

  Purchase = f (Purchasing
  Structure, Policies, Benefits)

- Situational Influences on the
  Purchase
  Urgency of Order Fulfillment
  Product Usage Application
  Size of the Order

  Purchase = f (Urgent Need,
  Time of Day)

- Individual Buyer's Personal
  Characteristics
  Risk Aversion
  Cost Sensitivity
  Search Meticulousness
  Relationship Orientation

  Purchase = f (Buyer's
  Preferences and Attitudes)

© Thomson

choosing strategic partner prospects are the existence of a compelling reason to partner. In general, a compelling reason to partner would involve an analysis of desired end-markets of mutual interest to both parties, and the recognition that joint strategic efforts might provide a distinct competitive advantage in these markets. For example, in the highly competitive auto-motive end-user market, Ford and GM are finding it tough to compete on a power/gas mileage basis with such competitors as Honda and Toyota. Either firm might decide to build in-house capabilities to attack this strate-gic problem. An alternative might be to develop a strategic partnership with a firm that can more cost effectively share this technological development burden. Ford's partnership with Eaton, the leading innovator in air flow systems, is an example of such a strategic partnership.

The Wal-Mart/P&G partnership may be another. In this latter case, the relationship evolved over time from a transactional to a relationship model, as the respective firms built trust and came to a realization that each could benefit from a joint focus on driving share in a mutually desirable end-user market, while at the same time, adopting a TQM focus on increased efficiency. In essence, a compelling reason to partner, trust and shared dialogue; and ultimately, mutual respect for business process capabilities, fueled the development of the partnership in terms of joint end-user mar-ket strategies, a joint enterprise vision, partnership operating principles, a shared TQM perspective, and ultimately a partnership intelligence and information-sharing model. Thus, candidates for strategic partnership may exist among the selling firm's present customer base; in particular, among relationship accounts. Hence, the deep knowledge of the customer, possessed by the account manager, is an asset that may be creatively and strategically leveraged.

Consideration of the above examples suggests a set of strategic partner-ship selection criteria with which to articulate a compelling reason to purchase, including: access to new markets, first mover possibilities in new markets, customer intelligence and tracking, access to technology, enhanced customer service, risk management reduction in terms of volatility and vulnerability, and enhanced efficiencies. In addition to these partnership opportunities or mutual interest criteria, a variety of mutual attributes related to the practicality of forming a partnership are critical. These include compatible corporate cultures and business philosophy; acceptance or inter-est in adopting business processes that may be leveraged through joint activ-ities; and trust, respect, and similarity in management style, practices, and language.

Importance of Industry Context

Profiling customers for strategic partnerships is a creative problem-solving process and should be recognized as such. Although the general set of partner selection criteria provide guidance in developing an analytical process for profiling customers, each industry context will have its own nuances, in terms of which criteria should be emphasized in profiling customers, their relative importance, and how each is defined and measured. Strategic partnerships are multi-functional in nature; hence the diagnostic process should reflect this fact. Several successful customer relationship typologies have been developed through a "bottom-up" segmentation approach employed by a cross-functional team in a week-long planning process. The outcome of this exercise is typically verified through more detailed field interviews and marketing research prior to implementation.

To illustrate the importance of industry context, three sets of strategic partnership profiling criteria are presented in Exhibit 5.4. In the case of a leading health care products distributor, the goal was to identify the hospitals that were candidates for varying relationship strategies ranging from transactional to partnering. An initial analysis isolated the more financially viable and usually urban hospitals. These hospitals were then profiled according to their degree of managed care sophistication, commitment, and capability; their leadership recognition for developing innovative, integrated health care systems; and the degree to which they accept and are interested in win-win partnerships, adopting a total cost orientation, and allocating a significant share of their business to the partner. All in all, five segments (or buckets) were identified with each ultimately receiving a unique sales approach. Strategic partners received a fully dedicated cross-functional team. Emerging and potential partners received account managers, and contract and transactional customers were allocated to a territory sales team, local distributors, or call centers. The remaining two examples in Exhibit 5.4 emphasize similar criteria, with industry nuances reflected.

Developing the Strategic Partnership Perspective

Simply put, a strategic partnership is an agreed-upon relationship between two or more parties who choose to cooperate in an enterprise and share its risks and rewards. From the perspective of strategic account management, partnering is more than the evolution of long-term contractual relationships. Partnering requires a degree of cooperation that transcends preferred supplier status. Thus, a partnership represents a relationship that is based on

Exhibit 5.4   Selection Criteria for Strategic Partner Accounts

Leading Health Care Distributor	Leading Electronic Distributor	Leading Computer Firm
• Degree of managed care sophistication, commitment, and capability • Degree to which they are leaders in developing integrated health care systems and processes • Degree to which they accept and understand partnerships (a win–win) as a supplier orientation • Willingness to adopt new buying and operating strategies, especially those related to adopting a total cost orientation to sourcing • Current share of business allocated to partnership • Financial viability in terms of share, profits, and financial viability	• Customer's orientation and sophistication in supply chain management and strategic sourcing • Customer's adoption of a total cost orientation to sourcing • Potential for partner to realize competitive advantage with its downstream customers • Senior management buy in—at the home office • Uniformity of operating policies and systems across plants • Local knowledge and relationships with plant executives • Evidence of prior experience with partnership relationships	• Compelling strategic reason to partner • Willingness to assign a dedicated partnership team • Willingness to invest significantly in the partnership • Willingness to share risks and gains • Willingness to share business plans • Early access to technology roadmap • Adoption of TQM model • Willingness to set shared metrics • Willingness to promote joint successes

© Thomson

trust, reciprocity, and collaborative "win-win" problem-solving to achieve intended end-user market outcomes. Clearly defined expectations and frequent communications are hallmarks of successful strategic partnerships. Strategic partners seek to avoid major threats to the partnership by identifying potential problems early and then negotiating solutions with an eye toward preserving the relationship. Therefore, key account managers must meet with their key account buyers frequently in order to reexamine the buyers' expectations with regard to the services the salesperson and the sales company are providing.

Successful partnerships evolve over time as the respective firms create a joint vision for the partnering enterprise, establish joint plans and operating practices, work on establishing shared business processes and systems, and develop trust and interpersonal relationships. In fact, according to Tom Muccio, retired P&G Vice-President of the P&G/Wal-Mart partnership, the development of a strategic partnership is a journey that often begins with a single multi-functional team objective such as increasing customer satisfaction, gaining share in a selected end-user market or product category, or cutting supply chain costs. More importantly, as the competitive environment continues to change, the strategic partners must be very careful to frame new strategies or emerging problems in terms of the strategic partnership. Clearly, this changes the role of the salesperson from transactional selling, or the salesperson-as-persuader role, to that of the salesperson-as-account manager role.

Traditional Interaction versus Partnership Interaction

Creating partnerships—the most sophisticated of buyer-seller relationships—requires new thinking. Traditional selling involves a salesperson contacting a purchaser from the buying organization, after which all communication between the buying and selling firm is routed through the direct relationship between salesperson and the buyer. In practice, this is often referred to as the "bow tie" model (see Exhibit 5.5). The salesperson is assigned the role of boundary-spanner, literally becoming the face of the selling firm to the buying firm. The buyer, usually a professional purchasing agent, is the supposed conduit for all salesperson contact within the buying firm. Often a game ensues as the salesperson attempts to find other "portals" to reach end-users and decision-makers.

Given its typical transactional focus, the boundary-spanning model can seriously impair relationship building and management. In complex, multidivisional firms such as Procter & Gamble, ConAgra, and Clorox in consumer

Exhibit 5.5   Traditional versus Partnership Interaction Models

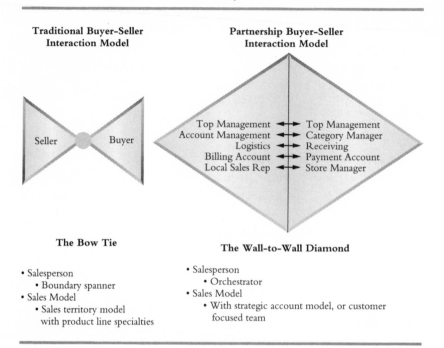

Traditional Buyer-Seller
Interaction Model

Partnership Buyer-Seller
Interaction Model

Seller   Buyer

Top Management ←→ Top Management
Account Management ←→ Category Manager
Logistics ←→ Receiving
Billing Account ←→ Payment Account
Local Sales Rep ←→ Store Manager

The Bow Tie

The Wall-to-Wall Diamond

- Salesperson
  - Boundary spanner
- Sales Model
  - Sales territory model
  with product line specialties

- Salesperson
  - Orchestrator
- Sales Model
  - With strategic account model, or customer
  focused team

© Thomson

packaged goods; or Pfizer, Abbott, and Cardinal Healthcare in the pharmaceutical industry, the "bow tie" model can result in conflicting competition among various divisions, brands, and sales personnel; a tactical focus on product sales; lack of attention to the significant drivers of supply chain inefficiency; functionally-defined expertise (on both sides); and, resource duplication. Strategic account selling is different in that it involves aligning the buying and selling firms organizationally so that decision-makers and functional specialists are matched between the two firms; thus enhancing the likelihood of establishing a shared strategy and the necessary communication flows to negotiate relationship adjustments over time. This is popularly viewed as aligning the firms in a "wall-to-wall" fashion (see Exhibit 5.5). The goal is to manage the joint enterprise of the relationship partners, as a unique enterprise, rather than simply a buyer and seller interaction. The P&G/Wal-Mart partnership is now organized in this fashion. In P&G's case, the partnership is treated as a distinct business with a senior executive at the helm. Similarly, Cardinal Healthcare has established customer-focused teams at hospitals such as those at Emory and Duke University, respectively. In this case, field-located account managers manage the partner relationships.

Team Selling

In recent years, there has been a growing trend toward large customers being served by teams of individuals whose members are matched up with specific individuals in customer organizations. Teams allow for the accessibility to pooled intelligence. Researchers have distinguished between Selling Teams and Selling Centers. The term selling team describes team selling as a combination of sales and support staff under the direction of a key account manager who sets strategy and coordinates information flows. The team can consist of anyone in the selling firm, such as top executives, engineers, or product planners, whose knowledge of a product, customer, or industry can be used to the seller's advantage. It forms a core group of people whose primary objective is to establish and maintain strong customer relationships with a strategic account. Thus, it is a formal, customer-focused group.

In contrast, the Selling Center is a transaction-focused group whose primary objective is successful completion of a specific sales opportunity. Team membership is more ad hoc and fluid than with the selling team. The team convenes to provide information and advice to other Selling Center members. Thus, the use of Selling Centers is more tactical in nature while a Selling Team is more strategic with the mission being to develop and implement the seller's marketing program for the buying organization to which the team is assigned.

Major Account Selling versus Smaller Account Selling

Many differences exist between the salesperson's role in key account selling and the role of the salesperson in selling to small accounts. For example, small account selling normally involves face-to-face meetings between just the salesperson and a prospect. In contrast, key account selling involves a series of meetings over an extended period of time with many different people who may influence the ultimate decision maker but may not make a purchase decision (e.g., buying center). Furthermore, the small account salesperson typically has no direct access to the ultimate decision maker, whereas in key account selling, the account manager works more closely with the ultimate decision maker. In key account selling, the size of the sale is larger than that of a smaller account, and the time horizon for purchasing also differs between large and small accounts.

In key account selling, the typical sales cycle is longer than with smaller ac-counts, and many more people are involved in the buying decision. Salespeople must, therefore, de-emphasize the "close" and place more emphasis on prepar-ing for the call and anticipating the account's needs. In key account selling, the emphasis is on completing transactions and partnering, not on "closing." Key account managers earn gradually increasing levels of commitments from their buyers rather than pushing the buyers to close transactions in short time frames. There are some exceptions, of course. For example, when a sales company is preparing to increase prices, key account managers often urge buyers to stock up before the prices increase. This is often referred to as forward buying.

Furthermore, the prospects/clients in large accounts are usually profes-sional buyers. This means that they are very aware of selling techniques and recognize them immediately. Salespeople should use alternate probing meth-ods that are more business-centered and bring longer-term results, and they should think more strategically about the questions they ask. Their questions must be more oriented toward a problem-solution focus and must be broader in nature than those used with small accounts.

The bottom line is that key account selling requires some different skills than those that are typically taught in most sales courses. Key account sales-people must:

- Know their clients' business by becoming part of their organization
- Consult with prospects to assist them in understanding or in seeing problems and potential solutions differently
- Think creatively about providing broader solutions
- Facilitate in order to make it easier for customers to understand and solve problems
- Work the strategic account at all levels of the organization
- Get senior executive commitment, since higher-level partnerships require senior-level executive commitment from both organizations
- Set up regular (e.g., annual, semiannual) top-to-top meetings with all stakeholders involved
- Build trust
- Be speedy and dependable in responding to problems
- Stay in frequent contact with the decision maker(s), penetrating the account, casting a wide net, and building relationships with many people in the strategic account
- Be honest and candid in their communications with buying center members
- Coordinate the members of the selling team

In their 1991 book *Managing Major Sales,* Neil Rackham and Richard Ruff state the following about selling to large accounts versus small accounts: (1) The skills that make salespeople successful in small account sales can sometimes be detrimental in larger account sales; (2) the closing techniques that are effective in smaller account sales can sometimes cost the salesperson business as the sale grows larger; (3) the classic questioning methods (e.g., SPIN) may suffice in smaller sales but may not be enough in larger account sales; (4) objection-handling skills contribute only marginally to sales success in key account sales, since effective key account salespeople focus on objection *prevention* rather than objection *handling;* and (5) in many traditional sales courses, the emphasis is on selling benefits rather than features, but some benefits that succeed in small account sales are counterproductive when used in key account sales. Thus, key account salespeople must have a level of sophistication not always found in those selling to smaller accounts.

Selection Criteria for Key Account Managers

Key account managers (KAMs) have many responsibilities in servicing strategic accounts. Therefore, proper selection of KAMs is critical to the success of a strategic account program. Leadership and communication, coaching and goal-setting, planning and organizing, and business and diplomacy skills are all very important to the role of a KAM. Some of the KAM's responsibilities include:

1. Setting the strategic direction for the account management team; this requires leadership and communication skills.
2. Monitoring investments in the key account on behalf of the selling firm and securing follow-through from operations personnel who deliver products and services to the key account, which requires coaching and goal-setting skills.
3. Ensuring that the strategic account receives quality service and products from the selling organization, which requires planning and organizing skills.
4. Assuming the executive role by initiating and maintaining high-level contacts in both the buying and selling firms; this requires business and diplomacy skills. The typical KAM . . .

   . . . is the empowered focal point for the entire customer service system.
   . . . is equipped with general business skills.
   . . . understands financial and information systems issues.
   . . . cannot rely on selling skills alone for excellence in performance.

... must have a broad experience base.

... has the confidence of top management in the selling organization.

... has the confidence of top management in the buying organization.

A more detailed discussion of the role of the direct sales force in strategic relationships, followed by an overview of technology-based applications in the area of partnership relationship management (or PRM) that may enhance the success of strategic partnerships, are discussed next.

The Role of the Direct Sales Force in Managing Strategic Accounts

The salesperson's role in the web of relationships developed in strategic account selling is to orchestrate all of the relationships by ensuring proper introductions and continuous contact. This is why selling organizations must be careful to promote only those salespeople who will ultimately be capable of taking responsibility for nurturing partnering relationships as key account managers. Note that in terms of contact frequency, the strategic account manager still has the highest contact frequency with the account personnel. Hence, the role of the account manager is customer linking, or to effectively and efficiently manage the ongoing dialogue between the customer and the selling organization so as to achieve mutually agreeable performance metrics.

The nature of customer linking and hence the nature of the buyer-seller dialogue managed by the account manager will vary depending on the degree to which the relationship involves strategic collaboration. A representative set of responsibilities relating to each of these sales models, referred to as the relationship selling and collaborative partner selling structure, is presented in Exhibit 5.6. A key distinction is the degree to which strategic account-relevant information is openly shared by the buying firm.

Salesperson as Account Manager

For the salesperson-as-account manager role, a diagnostic learning role is indicated. That is, an account manager selling to a new strategic account prospect (or target) must build a trust-based relationship with key decision influencers in order to initiate a strategic dialogue. In many cases, the account manager will need to manage a conversation focused on allowing the salesperson to diagnose the customer's "hot-buttons," including strategic direction and priorities, value chain and business process drivers and problems, and relationship expectations. In other cases, such as when the buying firm has identified the supplier as a "best in class" supplier, the firm may be relatively open concerning these meaningful strategic issues. The key point

Exhibit 5.6   Salesperson Role Responsibilities for Strategic Account

Relationship Selling Model	Collaborative Partner Selling
Salesperson-as-Account Manager Model	*Salesperson-as-Strategic Marketer Model*
• Base prospecting on strategic fit and relationship potential	• Build relationships with executive suite and all decision influences
• Identify key decision influences and build trust at many organizational levels (top to bottom)	• Collaborate with top management in strategic development process
• Diagnose customer strategic direction and value chain issues	• Identify partnership value proposition and supplier strategic role and capability
• Identify key value chain drivers and business processes that fit selling firm capabilities	• Identify supplier role in key business processes, capabilities, and systems at the buying firm
• Work jointly with buyer team to customize market offerings and solutions	• Develop relationship strategy, architecture, professional linkages, exchanges, and performance standards
• Work with supplier organization to extend relational bonds with buying firm	• Define administrative policies and procedures
• Verify mutual satisfaction with relationship	• Negotiate conflict resolution and feedback mechanisms
	• Monitor external market trends and partnership performance
	• Maintain close personal and organization relationships with buying center

© Thomson

is that the customer has *independently* established its business strategy and processes and, hence, the salesperson must be knowledgeable about how to employ organizational learning approaches to develop a meaningful dialogue with the customer. It is important to note that this learning role is not simply effectuated in terms of the explicit questioning formats commonly taught in strategic selling programs. Rather it involves a variety of

Exhibit 5.7   Fundamental Aspects of Wisdom in Relationship Selling

---

Wisdom as an Expert Knowledge System

- Rich declarative and procedural knowledge
- Life span contextualism

    - Personal and work contexts
    - Personal and organizational life dynamics
    - Life themes, life projects, life scripts
    - Work and personal role relationships

- Relativism: Knowledge about, and acceptance of, individual differences in values, goals, practices in life.
- Uncertainty: Knowledge about the uncertainties, indeterminacy, and vagaries of life and how to cope with them.

© Thomson

complex and tacit learning skills involved in everyday conversation (such as story-telling, brain-storming, analogical thinking, and commiserating). Since this is a business context, these conversational skills require both breadth and depth of experience in how businesses in general operate, as well as specific industry-level experience. Hence, successful account managers take time to develop and are to be valued as a company asset.

Beyond this breadth and depth of experience account managers must be wise. The role of wisdom as an expert knowledge capability in relationship selling content has not been adequately examined. The fundamental aspects of wisdom are presented in Exhibit 5.7. It is important to note that wisdom is a complex knowledge structure involving a solid base of declarative and procedural knowledge that is supplemented by a rich, experienced-based understanding of the nuances of every day and business life; an acceptance of the idea that each individual or corporate culture may be unique in its values, goals, and practices; and the recognition that change and its risks are fundamental to personal and business relationships. Hence, a minimum range and depth of experience is a likely requirement for the typical account manager.

The account manager plays several other roles in addition to the customer learning role. In the first place, the account manager must be *entrepreneurial*, in the sense of being able to think strategically about the customer's end-user markets and opportunities. In other words, the account manager must be creative in thinking about the customer's customers and how these end-user aspects might affect the customer's strategic options. This entrepreneurial role provides the substance of longer-term customer value. Secondly, account managers must be *intrapreneurial*, in the sense that they must be capable of successfully marshalling the organizational commitments and resources necessary to meet the customer's requirements. This intrapreneurial role is important because the account manager does not have dedicated organizational team resources focused on the customer. Hence, the account manager's skills at internal selling and relationship building at the selling firm are also critical. Finally, the account manager is placed in the role of *resource manager*, in the sense of balancing the selling firm's return on its resource investments with customer value creation and satisfaction. Account managers who request selling firm commitments for a particular account, such as a customer visit by a top management executive, an exceptional delivery time, or exceptional accounts receivable conditions, must consider the payback on these investments.

Salesperson as Strategic Marketer

For the salesperson-as-marketer, the preceding roles also apply to their strategic collaborative accounts. The keywords in the salesperson–as–strategic marketer world are collaborate and strategic. The strategic partner account manager (a) collaborates with the customer in identifying and developing joint strategic opportunities in end-user markets; (b) seeks to go beyond trust to build joint business processes, information systems, and a social architecture; (c) pursues deep understanding of the customer's organizational culture, decision-making process, and political agendas; (d) establishes and communicates the selling team's customer engagement model and metrics; and, (e) serves as the "single point of contact" for the customer in establishing and framing future partnership opportunities and resolving partner promise breakdowns.

In light of these strategic collaboration roles, it becomes clearer why firms in a variety of industries (e.g., consumer package goods; health care) operate their strategic partnerships as distinct business enterprises, with the account manager role defined accordingly in general business management terms. For example, a leading healthcare firm considers a range of general business management competencies for its customer-focused team managers, including business acumen, leadership skills, learning orientation, maturity and depth of experience in personal and business contexts; capability to work collaboratively and constructively with partners and team members; and commitment to collaborative efforts and joint results. At a somewhat more general level, a leading packaged goods firm looks for such typical senior management characteristics as creativity and curiosity, wisdom, diplomacy, political negotiation skills, and empathy (each clearly rooted in business contexts).

BREAK BOX: Becoming Aware

An early stage in becoming aware of your firm's strategic account strategy and practices involves an analysis of your firm's strategic account planning and managing approach. The following questions are designed to guide you through this assessment process.

A) To what degree are customer characteristics such as size of account, complexity in the buying process, and the use of centralized purchasing employed in classifying key and strategic accounts?

1. A very low degree
2.
3.
4.
5.
6.
7. A very high degree

Briefly describe the key aspects that led to your assessment on this strategic account strategy assessment item.

_____

_____

_____

_____

_____

B) To what degree are more strategic issues at the customer level such as the customer's relationship philosophy, use of total cost philosophy in purchasing, technological leadership, and industry leadership position employed in selecting key and strategic accounts?

1. A very low degree
2.
3.
4.
5.
6.
7. A very high degree

Continued

Briefly describe the key aspects that led to your assessment on this strategic account strategy assessment item.

_____

_____

_____

_____

_____

C) To what degree does your firm target customers who exhibit a "compelling strategic reason to partner" with your firm because of your firm's unique capabilities?

1. A very low degree
2.
3.
4.
5.
6.
7. A very high degree

Briefly describe the key aspects that led to your assessment on this strategic account strategy assessment item.

_____

_____

_____

_____

_____

D) To what degree has your firm moved beyond the "boundary spanning" (or bow tie) sales model to implement the collaborative partner (or wall-to-wall) sales model?

1. A very low degree
2.
3.
4.
5.
6.
7. A very high degree

Continued

Briefly describe the key aspects that led to your assessment on this strategic account strategy assessment item.

_____

_____

_____

_____

_____

E) To what degree is your firm able to successfully implement the collaborative partner sales model with strategic accounts that prefer this approach?

1. A very low degree
2.
3.
4.
5.
6.
7. A very high degree

Briefly describe the key aspects that led to your assessment on this strategic account strategy assessment item.

_____

_____

_____

_____

_____

F) To what degree is your firm able to attract, develop, and retain the "right" strategic account managers?

1. A very low degree
2.
3.
4.
5.
6.
7. A very high degree

Continued

Briefly describe the key aspects that led to your assessment on this strategic account strategy assessment item.

_____

_____

_____

_____

G) To what degree has your firm been able to successfully employ CRM and PRM technology to enable and enhance its competitive position with strategic accounts?

1. A very low degree
2.
3.
4.
5.
6.
7. A very high degree

Briefly describe the key aspects that led to your assessment on this strategic account strategy assessment item.

_____

_____

_____

_____

H) To what degree has your firm been able to successfully employ technology applications to enable and enhance its competitive position with strategic accounts?

1. A very low degree
2.
3.
4.
5.
6.
7. A very high degree

Continued

Briefly describe the key aspects that led to your assessment on this strategic account strategy assessment.

_____

_____

_____

_____

_____

Please calculate your total score across the six Strategic Account Strategy Assessment questions.

TOTAL SCORE _____

How would you access your firm's score relative to the leaders in your industry? In your candid opinion, is your firm a leader in strategic thinking about customers? Or, is your firm a follower? Please comment briefly below:

_____

_____

_____

_____

The Role of Technology in Managing Strategic Accounts and Partnerships

Partner relationship management, or PRM, is the analog of CRM systems applied to business partnerships. PRM solutions are useful in formalizing business relationships and partnerships. For strategic accounts involving complex channel systems and multiple points of contact, these PRM solutions provide the account manager many of the same functional benefits as CRM. For example, PRM functionalities include partner profiling, best practices and documentation, targeted and personalized partner communications, customer event and contract usage activity feedback, sales force automation (SFA), and a variety of eBusiness applications focused on demand management, order management, and risk management. The discussion that follows will highlight best practices in PRM and the benefits that are achievable through this tool.

PRM Applications

Partner relationship management (PRM) approaches and technology are commonly employed by firms that employ indirect channel relationships. When it comes to indirect channels, and even strategic accounts, selling firms are polygamous (for example, Intel, Siebel Systems, and IBM). That is, distinct indirect channels provide access to distinct target markets, add distinct products, services and applications, and allow the selling firm to offer distinct marketing, pricing, and promotional campaigns to each of these distinct customer segments. The complexity of channel choices and the various needs of alternate channel partners make PRM technologies increasingly attractive.

The goals and objective of adopting a PRM strategy mindset and technology involve a variety of revenue enhancing and cost-reducing outcomes. As Siebel Systems Inc. notes, successful PRM models are based on understanding how the ultimate customer prefers to buy and how your desired channel partners prefer to sell. Given this, a PRM solution can be designed to: (1) ensure that the seller's brand equity is appropriately managed through consistent messaging across channel partners; (2) increase the likelihood of partner "mindshare," or attention and effort, applied to the vendor's requirements; and, (3) increase both partner and end-user customer satisfaction and loyalty. Revenue enhancement improvements from PRM include: more rapid speed to market due to the increased market coverage and customer equity; more rapid partner learning and increased selling effectiveness; shorter sales cycles using demand generation tools; improved margins due to intelligent cross-selling programs; enhanced service response time and follow-up; increased control over marketing campaign implementation and effectiveness; and enhanced quality of the channel partner pool through the use of PRM analytics. Costs are potentially reduced by automating the partner lifecycle management process; providing partners with self-service and self-paced training packages; reducing product catalog and distribution costs using electronic applications; reducing service management costs using the web; and, reducing marketing campaign costs through automating promotional approaches and reimbursements, cutting hard copies of marketing materials, and so forth.

As with CRM, PRM approaches may be implemented using a talent-based model (i.e., a missionary salesperson to work closely with channel partners), a mixed talent/technology model (i.e., the salesperson supported with SFA technology functionality), or a technology-driven system (i.e., a PRM model applying ePartner applications). The talent-based approach, in effect, involves the use of two channels, a direct sales force whose role is usually focused on jointly working with the indirect channel partners to insure that their role in demand generation is fully executed and enabled. For example, selling firms (or vendors) will typically develop a number of partner-related strategies to support the channel partner's efforts at end-user customer demand generation, including "pull" promotion programs, cooperative advertising, promotional materials, and in-store salesperson training and incentive systems. Selling firms also provide a variety of services to their channel partners to facilitate their operating practices, including warranty and repair resources, technical assistance, and logistics systems. As discussed earlier, carefully selecting channel partners for their potential strategic contributions in demand generation, customer coverage, and customer support are critical in the success of the PRM program. No amount of channel partner support will drive the success of a lax or incompetent partner.

PRM approaches increasingly apply technology-based functionality, often referred to as ePartnering solutions. The ePartnering objective is to automate a variety of the management processes related to the various stages involved in partner relationship management. For example, PRM solutions typically include a partner profile database, partner certification status tracking systems, systems for managing partner incentives and records, partner performance scorecard signaling and monitoring systems, sales process tools to support demand generation and management (lead generation, lead distribution, product/solution configuration models, request for proposal (RFP) quote and proposal generators, order management catalogs and Internet applications), and personalized approaches to support accurate and timely partner communications.

A popular term in PRM is partner life cycle management. The focus here is on the development and implementation of an integrated PRM system to specifically enhance the likelihood of achieving close, long-term relationships with desirable channel partners. While many of the preceding tools are part and parcel in this partner relationship process, partner life cycle applications clearly define and support these relationships through goal-setting and reward status tools, individual level partner forecasting systems, reporting systems, and contract management tools.

Key aspects in PRM success include information, communications, and knowledge management. In using indirect channel partners, control and communication issues between the vendor and partner may place end-user market objectives at risk. Hence, communications, in the sense of sharing timely information about leads, products, and promotional deals, and intelligence, such as end-user pipeline information, forecasting, and customer pipeline management, are critical PRM functions. Specifics on PRM

BREAK BOX: Reviewing and Relating

Relating the ideas and concepts discussed so far to your firm's strategic account strategy and practices involves reviewing the material. The following questions are designed to guide you through this part of the process.

1. Consider the key and strategic accounts selection strategies discussed. Do the strategies suggest any new ideas about targeting specific customers in your sales organization?
2. Review the discussion and examples about the key and strategic accounts selection and targeting strategies. Are there opportunities for leveraging the strategies in your sales organization?
3. Think about your organization's unique capabilities. Could there be opportunities for more partnering with key and strategic accounts not thought about before reading this chapter?
4. Consider the discussion of the collaborative partner sales model. Did this material generate any ideas for your sales organization?
5. In your candid opinion, to what extent is your organization making full use of CRM and PRM technologies in leveraging the strategic account strategies discussed in this chapter? What changes would you suggest implementing in your sales organization?

---

functionality are readily available from supplier Web sites (see Siebel and SAP in particular) and consultants (see CRM.guru.com).

So far in this chapter, we have defined strategic accounts and emphasized the important resources needed for success in strategic account programs. We conclude this chapter with practical tools to use when allocating resources to strategic accounts.

Utilizing Customer Lifetime Value, Customer Relationship Management, and Strategic Account Planning

Sales organizations have come to realize that customers produce profits and are assets that need to be managed, and this realization has led many sales organizations to embrace Customer Lifetime Value (CLV) principles. When customers are viewed as assets, CLV concepts enable salespeople to estimate the monetary value of customers.

Today, the foundation for profitability and sales sustainability lies in the retention of customers, and many sales organizations have shifted their focus from customer acquisition to retention. One reason for this shift is that, in most cases, the average cost of servicing a customer declines as time passes and the number of retained customers increases. Put another way, it costs less to serve loyal customers than to acquire and serve new ones. A second reason is that the profitability of customers is related to the length of the relationship with those customers. These are the economic benefits of developing lifelong customer relationships. In addition, sales organizations which focus on retention of customers benefit from increased referrals, increased product penetration, and lower operating expenses, all of which contribute to the lifetime value of customers.

Customer lifetime value (CLV) is the net profit earned from sales to a given customer during the time that customer purchases from the sales organization. One goal of sales companies is to increase customer loyalty of those customers who have the biggest impact on their top line. At the same time, customers remain loyal only if they derive value from the relationship provided by the sales organization over time. So, key account managers *must* keep current on information concerning their strategic accounts and must also share that knowledge with their companies in order to maximize the selling effort. For example, some customers may have the potential to purchase more, but may have elected to purchase from several sellers/suppliers. Of course, information is also critical in this case, because selling companies can create value propositions that can motivate targeted strategic accounts to consolidate their purchases. Finally, there are always customers who simply want to engage in transactions either one time or sporadically and not engage in a business relationship, per se.

If key account managers take a lifetime view of their customers, then the time, effort, and resources spent on obtaining new customers and maintaining existing accounts can be viewed as investments that will pay back over the lifetime of relationships with those customers. Cost-to-serve issues cannot be ignored in key account management. By knowing the lifetime worth of their customers, key account managers put themselves in a better position to anticipate the resources needed to develop the strategic account and appropriately respond to customer requests. Knowing each strategic account's lifetime value helps KAMs:

1. Determine how much to spend to acquire a new customer.
2. Determine the level of customer service needed.

3. Determine how much focus should be placed on customer retention.

4. Shift their focus from one-time sales to the creation of closer relationships with customers.

5. Retain more customers than their competition, which may not use lifetime value concepts to guide sales strategies and tactics.

6. Keep their customers for longer periods of time.

7. Develop more profitable customers, as there is a positive relationship between length of relationship and profitability, in most cases.

8. Gain referrals from customers with whom solid relationships exist.

Lifetime value has become a highly useful method for directing marketing strategy. Before demonstrating how to use CLV analyses, we will define the components of such analyses.

Conceptualizing Customer Lifetime Value

Customer lifetime value includes the total financial contribution (e.g., revenues minus costs) of a customer over the lifetime of that customer's relationship with a sales company. Calculating a customer's lifetime value requires knowledge of the cost of acquiring the customer, computations of the stream of revenues forthcoming from the customer, and computations of the recurring costs of delivering service to that customer. Recurring costs and recurring revenues are compared to obtain a net margin, which is the difference between the selling price and the purchase price of an item after deducting all expenses; it is usually expressed as a percentage of the selling price (net profit divided by net revenues). Net margin, when calculated over the life span of the customer, allows for the calculation of a cumulative margin, which is the ongoing accrual of the net margin over time. Cumulative margin, when compared to the costs of acquiring the customer, results in an estimate of the lifetime value of a customer.

Customer retention occurs when salespeople make offers and customers accept those offers over the long term. A salesperson that focuses solely on ROI might stop calling on a prospect after several attempts. However, a salesperson with a CLV perspective would be more likely to continue calling on a high-value prospect to secure the initial sale, thereby beginning what could become a long-term, mutually profitable relationship.

It is important to appreciate and understand how CLV can be applied in the field of selling in order to understand the importance of learning how to calculate CLV. The next section describes what the "lifetime" part of CLV really means.

Understanding the "Value" Part of Customer Lifetime Value

Key account managers use CLV concepts to segment customers into groups based on revenues generated (including frequency of purchase and purchasing patterns) or costs incurred (products purchased, channels used, service levels). If customers can be grouped according to revenues and costs, salespeople will have a good idea about which of their customers are profitable and which are unprofitable. This information will help salespeople establish strategies for managing their relationships with their customers. It will also help salespeople know how to spend their time. According to one estimate, salespeople spend 600 hours per year in face-to-face contact with customers, so they must choose wisely when deciding who to contact.

As salespeople gain an understanding of their customer groups, they can attempt to create value (to produce importance or worth) in one of five ways:

1. *Acquire:* find new customers who are profitable by themselves or who contribute to spreading the selling organization's fixed costs over a wider base.
2. *Increase revenues:* stimulate the product/service consumption rates of existing customers in order to generate more revenues from them in each relevant time period.
3. *Retain:* increase customer loyalty in order to extend their individual lifetime with the selling company, thus extending the time period in which these customers contribute to the margins of the selling organization.
4. *Reduce recurring costs:* improve the efficiency of operations in order to reduce the cost of serving each customer.
5. *Reduce acquisition costs:* improve the efficiency with which customers are acquired by streamlining logistics or sales costs.

Retaining customers and reducing recurring costs can affect the profitability of both the sales organization and the customer, and thus affects the customer's overall value. Finally, as salespeople use company-provided data and become more proficient in estimating lifetime values of customers, they may make better resource allocation decisions. The reduction in acquisition costs from better prospecting also can affect the profitability of both the sales organization and its customers. Now that we understand the concept behind CLV and its importance to salespeople, we can learn how to calculate CLV. Increasingly sales organizations are using CLV as a way to predict the success or failure of various sales strategies.

Calculating Customer Lifetime Value

Calculating CLV requires that salespeople first determine how long a typical customer will do business with him/her. This may seem trivial, but consider this: The typical U.S. business loses 15–20 percent of its customers annually. A key component of calculating CLV is estimating customers' life cycles.

Customer life cycle is a term used to describe the series of steps customers go through when they consider purchasing, using, and maintaining loyalty to a product or service. Customer behavior changes over time, and salespeople must view these changes as insights into future customer behaviors. All these changes over time make up the customer life cycle. The customer life cycle approach has three main goals: (1) to attain new customers and increase the number of relationships; (2) to increase the profitability of those relationships by selling more products and services to existing customers; and (3) to increase the duration of profitable relationships by making sure that desirable customers continue doing business with the sales organization. The objective throughout the customer life cycle is to make the right offer at the right time to the right prospect.

Using Recency, Frequency, and Purchase Data

To create a life cycle for a customer, salespeople collect and analyze data such as purchase frequency, recency of purchases, average purchase size, and number of customer visits and contacts over time. Exhibit 5.8 is an example of developing a lifetime value table for business-to-business customers buying from ABC, a sales company.

Following is an explanation of the calculations; year 1 represents the year of acquiring 2000 business customers in this customer segment, and year 2 is everybody's second year with ABC. A year later, ABC has 2500 customers, but only 1500 of those who bought in year 1 are still buying (500 customers did not repurchase). That means that ABC's retention rate is 75%. Over time, the retention rate of the loyal ABC customers who are still buying increases. The average customer placed 1.5 orders in their year of acquisition, with an average order value of $6,250. As customers became more loyal, they placed more orders per year, of increasing size. The acquisition cost was $500 per customer. The cost of servicing the existing customers should decrease substantially after the first year of acquiring them. Again, this type of information is useful when making resource-allocation decisions.

Exhibit 5.8 A Lifetime Value Table

	Year 1	Year 2	Year 3
Number of Customers	2,000	2,500	3,300
Retention Rate	75.00%	80.00%	85.00%
Average Orders Per Year	1.5	1.75	1.8
Average Order Size	$6,250	$7,000	$7,500
Total Revenue	$18,750,000	$30,625,000	$44,550,000
Direct Cost %	75.00%	65.00%	60.00%
Costs	$14,062,500	$19,906,250	$26,730,000
Acquisition Cost			
($500 per customer)	$1,000,000	$500,000	$650,000
Total Costs	$15,062,500	$20,406,250	$27,380,000
Gross Profit	$3,687,500	$10,218,750	$17,170,000
Cumulative Gross Profit	$3,687,500	$13,906,250	$31,076,250
Customer Lifetime Value			
For This Customer Segment	$1,843.75	$4,087.5	$5,203.03

© Thomson

Conclusions and BREAKthrough Directions

This chapter makes an important distinction between accounts, or customers, in general and *strategic accounts*. In this day and age, with organizations more and more focused on improving bottom line financial performance, many firms are turning to sophisticated approaches to classifying customers based on how much return on investment in that customer may be forthcoming. This concept that "not all customers are created equally" certainly isn't new—however, it has garnered more attention recently than ever before largely because of increased competition for getting and keeping the best customers. Today, understanding and using the concept of customer lifetime value is central to business success.

Toward this end, this chapter provided you with a definitive set of criteria for determining which of your accounts are strategic accounts based on your own business model and goals. Especially, you learned of the critical nature of imbuing a culture for partnerships with strategic accounts such that decisions are made jointly, with shared resources and strongly aligned infrastructures and systems, toward win-win solutions for both parties. The salesperson's role

---

BREAK BOX: Envisioning and Creating

Now think about ways of applying the key ideas in this chapter in your sales organization and creating the basic steps needed for this to happen. Identify a key priority for action in each of the following areas and the general steps that would be needed to make it happen in your sales organization:

1. Using key and strategic account strategies to target specific customers and deploy the right resources.
2. Using the collaborative partner sales model with key and strategic accounts and the bow tie sales model with non-strategic accounts.
3. Leveraging CRM and PRM technologies in a more effective way throughout your sales organization.

---

changes dramatically under such a business philosophy—becoming that of a combined account manager and strategic marketer, with the capability and authority to gather and distribute resources toward building the business with the strategic account. Naturally, the shift toward implementing an effective strategic account model has been greatly enhanced by myriad modern technological improvements and tools that are available today for the sales force.

The BREAK box above provides you with some important next steps for applying what you have learned in this chapter to your own sales organization.

Visit The Sales Educators Web site for further BREAK process materials on this chapter's topics. www.TheSalesEducators.com

---

References and Suggested Readings

Lytle, Chris (2002), "The Secret to Winning Back Customers," http://sales.monster.com/articles/winningback/; http://sales.monster.com/articles/winningback.

Moon, Mark A. and Gary M. Armstrong (1994), "Selling Teams: A Conceptual Framework and Research Agenda," *Journal of Personal Selling & Sales Management,* Vol. 14, Number 1, 17–30.

Reinartz, Werner and V. Kumar (2002), "The Mismanagement of Customer Loyalty," *Harvard Business Review* (July), 86–97.

Shapiro, Benson P., and Thomas V. Bonoma (1984), "How to Segment Industrial Markets," *Harvard Business Review,* 62 (3), 104–110.

Chapter 6

Designing Strategic Sales Compensation Systems

Introduction

The focus in this chapter is on the design and implementation of sales compensation systems that balance the needs of the sales organization, salespeople, and customers. This requires a close correlation between the sales organization's strategic plan and the compensation system. The sales organization's strategic plan will encourage specific sales activities, and strong performance on those activities should be rewarded through the compensation system.

Among the myriad changes in the sales manager's work environment, three factors in particular have greatly impacted sales compensation systems. First, individual salesperson roles have become more complex. Second, team selling continues to grow in popularity. Selling roles for individual salespeople and selling teams have become complex in order to establish productive long-relationships with customers. Third, there has been a growing accountability in sales organizations from a financial perspective. The key question is: does the sales organization add appropriate customer value and return on investment to justify the cost of its compensation system?

Strategic Sales Compensation Systems: A Foundation

Optimal salesforce compensation systems are built on a solid foundation. Important elements of this foundation include an understanding of the role of compensation in motivating salespeople, best practices of optimal compensation plans, and selected motivational theories. A strong foundation also utilizes a minimum of four essential tools: the strategic plan; the sales forecast; sales jobs descriptions; and the profit-and-loss statement.

Motivating Salespeople

To understand the role of compensation in motivating salespeople, it is important to recognize that motivation is a multi-faceted variable that represents more than a salesperson's willingness to work hard. Motivation has three key dimensions: intensity, persistence, and direction. Intensity refers to

BREAK BOX: Becoming Aware

The first step in the BREAK process involves Becoming Aware of key factors related to the sales compensation system in your sales organization. The following questions are designed to help you assess your sales compensation situation:

A) Do your salespeople work sufficiently hard to get the job done?

1. Most definitely
2.
3.
4. Not Sure
5.
6.
7. Definitely not

Comments on how hard your salespeople work:

_____

_____

B) Are your salespeople sufficiently persistent over time, especially when facing adverse conditions?

1. Most definitely
2.
3.
4. Not sure
5.
6.
7. Definitely not

Comments about your salespeople's persistence levels:

_____

_____

_____

C) Are your salespeople sufficiently motivated to spend time on the right sales activities?

1. Most definitely
2.

Continued

3.

4. Not Sure

5.

6.

7. Definitely not

Comments on whether or not your salespeople spend time on the right sales activities:

_____

_____

_____

D) Which rewards are most important to your salespeople? List these rewards in order of their importance to your salespeople (as a group): pay; opportunity for advancement (promotion); formal recognition for accomplishments; personal growth opportunities; a sense of accomplishment; and a sense of being liked and respected.

1 Reward: _____

2 Reward: _____

3 Reward: _____

4 Reward: _____

5 Reward: _____

6 Reward: _____

7 Reward: _____

Comment on the adequacy of each reward:

_____

_____

_____

_____

_____

_____

---

the amount of physical and mental effort a salesperson is willing to expend. Persistence is willingness to sustain effort over an extended time period, especially when faced with adverse conditions. Direction recognizes that salespeople exercise some discretion about which activities they will pursue. All three elements of motivation should be addressed by the sales organization's compensation and reward system.

Traditionally, sales organizations placed too much relative emphasis on motivation as a determinant of salesperson performance. While it is indeed important to recognize motivation as a key determinant of performance, it is also important to recognize that other factors impact performance. For example, a salesperson's skill level and job-related aptitude directly impact performance. Other factors beyond the control of salespeople, such as company policies and strategy, also impact sales performance. The important point here is that a high motivation level is a necessary, but insufficient, condition for achieving high performance. In the absence of a sound sales strategy, a solid training program and an enlightened approach to the full range of sales management activities, the world's most motivated sales force will not likely succeed.

Contrary to conventional wisdom, salespeople are not solely motivated by money. Yes, money is the generally the most sought-after reward. But younger salespeople are often more motivated by the opportunity to move up in the organization, which may or may not bring a substantial short-run financial reward. Research also indicates that salespeople can be motivated by a sense of accomplishment and the opportunity to experience personal growth through their job experiences. Salespeople tend to have healthy egos, and are also motivated by formal and informal recognition for a job well done.

Best Practices: Optimal Compensation Plans

Optimal sales compensation plans meet these objectives:

1. balance the needs of the sales organization, salespeople, and customers.
2. achieve acceptable ratios of costs compared to financial outcomes such as sales volume, gross margin, and contribution margin.
3. encourage specific sales activities in support of the organization's overall, marketing, and sales force strategies, goals, and objectives.
4. attract and retain highly-productive salespeople, while encouraging less productive salespeople to leave the organization.
5. reward performance based on measurable criteria that salespeople can easily understand.
6. Allow adjustments that can be implemented with a reasonable expenditure of time and money.

Balance

Optimizing the sales compensation system is not an easy task, and one of the most problematic areas is trying to balance the needs of the company with those of salespeople and customers. For example, some financial services and insurance companies recruit inexperienced salespeople who are paid on a straight commission basis. During the first year of their employment, many of these new hires struggle to make ends meet, often living off savings and increasing personal debt. First-year turnover rates are high in these companies, as more than a few salespeople become discouraged and seek employment elsewhere. In this situation, one has to wonder if such a compensation program meets the needs of employees and customers. Presumably, customers for insurance and financial services would like to have a long-term relationship with their sales representative as well as the company. In another situation, a major energy company paid its salespeople very respectable salaries, but no incentives (bonus or commission). Ultimately, the sales force was not motivated to aggressively seek new customers and the company's lack of growth in key markets created a significant corporate problem.

Financially Sound

Achieving targeted financial outcomes at a reasonable cost must be a goal of the sales compensation system. In effect, company sales forces are comparable to channel intermediaries, or middlemen, in moving products and services through the channel or supply chain. Like middlemen, sales organizations must justify their value-add or else they become candidates for elimination. In keeping with this thinking, the ultimate justification for a sales organization is to deliver value equal to or greater than the costs of doing so. It is essential that an organization maintain a competitive cost structure, and sales compensation is a major cost to most companies. A major Wall Street brokerage was paying its brokers on a straight commission with a fairly low minimum required sales volume expectation. The rationale was "if they don't sell it, we don't pay it." Then the brokerage took a hard look at its real cost of sales and instituted a new minimum to cover fixed costs and a portion of variable costs allocated on per salesperson basis. The result was that 15 percent of the brokers were terminated, with almost all departures being replaced by a productive replacement.

Encouraging Specific Activities

A sales compensation plan should be capable of directing sales activity to the right products, services, and markets in support of organizational priorities. These priorities should be spelled out in the firm's strategic plan and relevant strategic plans at the business unit level and the sales organization level. A compensation plan heavily weighted toward total dollar sales, for example, may not direct behavior toward new product introductions, selling longer-cycle but higher-margin items, or maintaining appropriate margins.

Attract and Retain Top Performers

The best sales compensation plans will attract and help retain the best sales talent. They should also encourage turnover among non-productive salespeople. To achieve these dual goals, sales compensation must be tied closely to sales performance. Salespeople are fairly savvy about determining what they are worth in the marketplace, and opportunities are abundant for top producers. A company can expect that competitors will seek out top performers, and quite often customers will attempt to hire top producers. Thus, compensation systems must provide significant income to top producers, though not necessarily unlimited income opportunities. On the other hand, poor performers should not be able to achieve incomes beyond their worth. To allow this is to perpetuate a mediocre sales force which will not meet company nor customer expectations.

Easily Understood

It is important to have a compensation plan that salespeople easily understand. For decades, a major computer company was renowned for its complex system of awarding variable points for certain types of products sold. In addition there was a complicated method for paying commissions over the life of a leased system, with penalties for termination of the lease regardless of the reason for the cancellation. There was a widespread mistrust of the compensation system among the sales force, and monthly paychecks were often big surprises—in positive and negative ways. The company overhauled its compensations system, thereby eliminating a major source of job dissatisfaction and increasing sales force motivation. Further, it was no coincidence that the company reversed several years of lackluster performance, returning to a leadership position in its markets.

Reasonably Flexible

Optimal compensation plans are not set in stone. They can be adjusted as conditions change. Market conditions are now more frequently characterized by change than by maintenance of the status quo. Opportunities may quickly arise and then just as quickly disappear. Compensation plans that can flex within reason to capture these opportunities are preferred to those that cannot. Inflexible plans can also overpay and underpay sales people to the extreme. For example, during the oil embargo of the 1970s, petroleum-based products quickly came into a period of short supply. Scores of companies were paying their salespeople commissions and bonuses based on dollar sales volume. Prices shot through the stratosphere, and thousands of salespeople enjoyed huge windfalls. Heading into the next annual cycle, many of these same companies did not change their compensation systems. Supply lines were reopened with the easing of the embargo, inventories were adjusted, and suddenly there was a glut in the market, leading to huge price cuts. Salespeople in these companies went from feast to famine, creating morale problems amidst real financial problems. Other companies adjusted their compensation plans heading into year two of the oil shortage, basing compensation on a weighted average of unit sales and dollar sales, with unit sales being far more heavily weighted. Unit sales for the year were down slightly, but nowhere nearly as far down as dollar sales, thus salespeople in these companies were paid fairly for what they accomplished during the year.

A general assessment of compensation plans drawn from industry surveys and trade publications indicate that a substantial improvement is needed in many organizations in order to optimize sales compensation systems. From an administrative perspective, managing sales compensation is often time and labor intensive, and many plans are not responsive to changes in the marketplace. From a sales force motivation perspective, salespeople often mistrust more complicated systems and spend valuable time double-checking their records to ensure fair payment. To move toward an optimal sales compensation system, sales managers and executives can benefit from a foundation that is both humanistic and economically sound. The humanistic element can be better understood by using behavioral theories in an applied management approach, while the basic profit and loss statement provides the key tool for achieving a sound economic foundation for the sales compensation system.

Motivational Theories as Part of the Foundation

While social scientists have on occasion argued that theory can be useful to business practitioners, there are skeptics in the sales management community. Motivational theories are not intended to provide simple answers to complex questions, nor are they intended to provide broad brush prescriptions for motivating a sales force. Rather, motivational theories provide useful insights into understanding human behavior in the sales job context. Theories may be classified into two categories: those that guide the discovery of new knowledge, and those that facilitate performance improvement.

BREAK BOX: Reviewing and Relating

The second step in the BREAK process is to review the material and to identify specific ideas that relate to your sales organization. The following questions are designed to assist you in determining relevant ideas and action items for your organization.

1. Does your compensation system balance the needs of your organization, your customers, and your salespeople?
2. Is the cost of your compensation system acceptable?
3. Does your compensation system encourage specific sales activities that contribute to strategic plans at different levels in your organization?
4. Does your compensation system help attract and retain productive salespeople?
5. Are your salespeople paid on measurable criteria that are easily understood?
6. Can your compensation system be adjusted without creating major problems?

In this section, we will focus on the latter category. Exhibit 6.1 summarizes some the key sales motivation implications generated by these theories.

One set of theories that can provide useful insights for sales executives and sales managers are those that describe the types of needs that people have and ultimately which rewards they seek. These theories include Maslow's need-hierarchy theory and Alderfer's ERG (Existence, Relatedness, and Growth) theory, and McClelland's learned-needs theory. These theories, while different, propose that human behavior is driven by the desire to satisfy a variety of needs in different circumstances.

Maslow's Need Hierarchy

Maslow's need-hierarchy has endured for well over six decades as a popular way to study sales force motivation. According to Maslow, basic human needs are arranged in a hierarchy ranging from lower-order needs such as physiological, safety, and security needs to higher order needs such as the need for self fulfillment. In the mid-range of the hierarchy, social needs include love and belongingness and those related to self-respect and respect by others. The key concept is that once lower-order needs are satisfied,

Exhibit 6.1   Sales Management Implications of Motivation Theories

Theory	Sales Management Implications
Maslow's need hierarchy theory	Consider individual needs when designing motivational programs; offer a variety of rewards if individual needs cannot be considered.
Alderfer's ERG theory	Salespeople may become frustrated if they cannot satisfy higher-order needs (e.g. esteem need fulfilled by promotion) and seek instead to maximize a lower-order reward (e.g. income) related to lower-order need fulfillment.
McClelland's learned-needs theory	It may be worthwhile to attempt to increase a salesperson's need for achievement through training or coaching; teach salespeople to exercise self-control and demonstrate maturity to balance their need for power when dealing with customers.
Expectancy theory	Clearly communicate the linkages between (1) job effort and performance and (2) performance and rewards.
Equity theory	Offer rewards valued by the salesforce; reward each salesperson on an equitable basis compared with other salespeople.
Attribution theory	Ensure that salespeople understand the cause-and-effect relationships between their behavior and performance; consider the importance of direction of effort along with intensity and persistence of effort.
Reinforcement theory	Consistently reinforce desired behavior and discourage undesirable behavior

© Thomson

higher order needs will become most important to the individual. Once higher-order needs are met, their importance to the person intensifies. The key contributions of Maslow's thinking to sales force motivation is a recognition that individual needs vary and should be taken into account when designing compensation and reward programs. If it is not feasible to consider individual needs, Maslow's theory suggests that offering a variety of rewards can have a positive impact on sales force motivation.

Alderfer's ERG Theory

Alderfer's ERG theory is similar to Maslow's theory with one notable exception. According to Alderfer's theory, salespeople may become frustrated if they cannot achieve higher-order needs and drop back down the hierarchy and attempt to maximize a lower-order reward rather than continue to seek the higher-order reward. For example, a career salesperson may have unmet self-fulfillment needs as a result of having been passed over for a promotion into sales management. Maslow would argue that this person would continue to strive for the promotion, while Alderfer offers an alternative: this person might give up on the promotion and try instead to maximize a lower-order reward such as pay. Surveys that indicate pay as the most sought reward among older salespeople add some support for Alderfer's position.

McClelland's Learned-Needs Theory

McClelland's learned-needs theory says that people learn to strive for achievement, affiliation with others, and power. Salespeople who have a strong need for achievement may prefer higher-order rewards such as opportunities for growth and advancement and feelings of accomplishment. Those with high affiliation needs want to be a part of a team, or might build strong relationships with their customers—whether or not they have strong ties to their own company. Some salespeople covet power and the ability to influence others, and this can be a positive characteristic for those seeking a promotion into sales management if properly directed.

Another set of relevant theories delve into the mental processes people engage in as they decide on alternative courses of action and how much effort to expend. These theories include expectancy theory, equity theory, attribution theory, and reinforcement theory. According to proponents of expectancy theory, salespeople are maximally motivated if they see a strong linkage between their efforts and job performance, and have strong belief that their efforts will bring rewards that are highly valued. For example, straight commission salespeople who are highly motivated by money will expend a lot of effort if they truly believe there is a strong correlation between their efforts and job performance. Thus it is extremely important to clearly communicate the linkages between job effort, performance, and rewards.

Equity Theory

Equity theory holds that salespeople will compare their treatment in comparison to relevant others in the organization (typically other salespeople), and motivation will be positively or negatively affected by this comparison. The theory suggests that individuals will make this comparison using input/output ratios, where inputs might be educational level, effort expended, or job experience and expertise. Outputs typically would include pay, promotion opportunities, and other rewards. A salesperson sensitive to equity issues might say, "I don't mind making less than Susan, because she has great experience, but I resent making less than Joe, because he really doesn't work very hard compared to how I work." Equity theory reminds us of the need to be fair in designing compensation and reward systems, and to build a strong link between pay and performance.

Attribution Theory

Attribution theory is based on observations that people are interested not only in *how* they are performing, but also *why* they are performing at a given level. This calls attention to the important interaction between coaching, mentoring, and providing feedback with motivation. Attribution theory also reminds us that maximum motivation is not achieved simply because a salesperson is working hard and willing to persevere in the face of adversity. Their efforts must be properly directed as well. For example, Doris, a sales representative for a hospital supply company, was having a hard time landing a big account. She felt that the answer was simply to spend more time getting to know the needs of all of the key personnel who would affect the buying decision. After making a joint call with Doris, her sales manager Rebecca counseled her to change her strategy and to concentrate on the key decision maker, which resulted in a new contract within two weeks. Had Doris continued to attribute her failure to a lack of effort rather than to following the wrong strategy, her motivation level could have suffered along with her performance level.

Reinforcement Theory

Reinforcement theory proposes that specific behaviors can be encouraged, modified, or eliminated through positive or negative reinforcement, punishment, or simply by withholding positive reinforcement. Compensation and reward systems that feature a variety of rewards such as a salary component, bonuses, and commissions have an opportunity to reinforce a wide variety of behaviors. On the other hand, compensation systems that rely totally on incentive pay on a single dimension, e.g., total sales volume, will likely have a difficult time reinforcing behaviors not directly related to generating sales volume.

Essential Tools for Building the Compensation Foundation

There are four essential tools for building a solid foundation for the sales compensation system: the strategic plan; the sales forecast, job descriptions; and the profit-and-loss statement (P&L). Without a thorough working knowledge of how to use these tools as related to the compensation system, sales executives and sales managers have little chance at designing and implementing a productive compensation plan. These tools must be used in an integrated manner, such that the requirements and metrics from each are consistent with the other three.

Strategic Plan

Here we will assume that sales managers and sales executives at all levels in the organization have a significant hand in developing the strategic plan (refer to Chapter 3 for the contents of a sales manager's strategic plan) for their operating unit. We will also assume that these sales managers and executives must craft a strategic plan in the context of a corporate strategic plan or perhaps a business unit strategic plan. In the case of small businesses, the context is typically shaped by the key strategic priorities and resources of the company. The key point is that a strategic plan must be in place before sales compensation can be designed or significantly modified.

Sales managers and sales executives must understand how changes in corporate priorities can impact the salesforce and how changes in the strategic plan can impact sales compensation. It is a common occurrence for corporate priorities in one area to impact operations in another area. These impacts are not always synergistic, and sometimes can be detrimental to sales forces and customers. For example, consider how a stated corporate priority of improving profitability through cost reduction can produce suboptimal salesforce results. Under this scenario, the production department of a plastic bag manufacturer decides to cut costs in a variety of ways, including reducing the cost of raw materials. Ultimately, the bags are produced thinner and routinely fall below the industry standard for plus-or-minus three percent deviation in thickness. Early on, the customers do not notice, but eventually they discover the thin bags and the manufacturer loses several key accounts. Not only has the salesforce and the company been hurt, but salespeople's compensation has also been reduced through lost customers and lower-than expected sales as measured in pounds. Rewind to when the cost-cutting initiative was enacted. Savvy sales managers and executives would have taken all possible steps to ensure that cost-cutting would not extend to any practice that would diminish product quality. The summary here is that sales executives must carefully examine corporate strategic plans and initiatives to ensure consistency with the sales organization's strategic plan to ensure compatibility up, down, and across the organization. A failure to do so can wreak havoc on customer relations, prevent accomplishment of key sales objectives, and negatively impact salesforce motivation through the compensation plan.

Sales Forecast

The sales forecast, or expected sales for a given time period under a given strategic plan, is one of the most critical documents produced by a sales leader. Forecasts are used as an input into practically everything a company does, from planning capital expenditures to determining staffing levels and scheduling production. The forecast is also a critical part of the foundation for sales compensation. In compensation systems featuring incentive pay for sales volume and/or sales growth, the forecast is crucial to rewarding salespeople fairly for their accomplishments. If the forecast is too low, salespeople are rewarded at inappropriately high levels; if it is too high, salespeople do not make their numbers and earnings can be discouragingly low. The message here is that sales managers and executives cannot rely on others to crank out the forecast. They must become experts at forecasting, rely on multiple methods to arrive at an acceptable forecast, and be prepared to defend their forecast with others in the organization (including their own salespeople). The correct forecast is one that is always carefully calculated, usually with some input from salespeople and perhaps key customers. The right forecast is also quite often a negotiated forecast between sales managers and upper management. Sales compensation is far too important to base it, even in part, on a poorly constructed forecast.

Job Descriptions

For compensation planning and implementation, it is imperative that the salespeople's key roles and expectations as spelled out in their job descriptions are tied to the strategic plan. Job descriptions may also make explicit mention of achieving volume-based sales targets or quotas. If so, once again, the importance of producing an acceptable sales forecast is reinforced. There is also the possibility that job descriptions mention other financial expectations of salespeople, such achieving certain margin or profitability goals as discussed in the following section.

Profit and Loss Statement

Understanding the profit and loss statement (P&L) is a key piece for all sales managers and executives. Even if the major components of the sales compensation system are fixed and not subject to change during a given time period, the P&L can still be used to drive particular initiatives and objectives developed with salespeople in a management by objective (MBO) system.

To consider the P&L as a planning tool, refer to Exhibit 6.2. Many sales organizations contribute to the bottom line by producing a healthy top line on the P&L—overall sales volume. If the sales organization has a sole

Exhibit 6.2   The Profit and Loss Statement as a Compensation Planning Tool

Moving down the P&L statement from total sales volume to contribution margin as a basis for salesperson compensation, salespeople are directed to influence a growing number of variables.

Performance Metric/Basis for Compensation	Variables Impacted by Salespeople
1. Total Sales Volume	Total sales volume
Total Sales Volume (less discounts, freight, and returns) = 2. Net Sales	Total sales volume, plus discounts, freight, and returns.
Net Sales (less cost of goods) = 3. Gross Margin	Total sales volume, discounts, freight, returns, product mix sold, and pricing.
Gross Margin (less other costs) = 4. Contribution (to Profit) Margin	Total sales volume, discounts, freight, returns, product mix sold, pricing, selling expenses.

© Thomson

BREAK BOX: Reviewing and Relating

The second step in the BREAK process is to review the material and to identify specific ideas that relate to your sales organization. The following questions are designed to assist you in determining relevant ideas and action items for your organization.

1. Does your sales organization have a strategic plan? If not, do not make major changes in the compensation system before developing one.
2. Have problematic initiatives in other portions of the corporate strategic plan been identified and dealt with prior to implementing the sales organization's strategic plan? This should be done to ensure that salespeople's compensation is not unfairly impacted.
3. Does the sales forecast impact salesforce compensation? If so, has the forecast been carefully prepared with input from salespeople and perhaps key customers?
4. Is the forecast acceptable to upper management?
5. Is the forecast attainable yet a challenge?
6. Is the P&L statement used to guide compensation decisions? Are P&L-based incentives for salespeople consistent with the strategic plan, the forecast, and job descriptions?

---

responsibility of achieving sales growth, it is highly likely that the appropriate compensation plan will stress incentive pay on total sales volume. In many cases, however, this singular orientation is not always the full sum of what is expected of a sales organization. For example, if we pay salespeople on net sales rather than total sales volume, what are we asking the salespeople to do in addition to generating significant volume? We are motivating them, through the compensation plan, to also control for returns, discounts, and applicable freight costs. If we move the compensation basis from net sales to gross margin, we are asking salespeople to manage several additional factors including selling price and mix of products sold. Taking it one step further, if we base compensation on contribution to profit or contribution margin, the incremental expectation is that salespeople will now also control their direct selling expenses.

Designing and Implementing Sales Compensation Plans

There are six steps in designing and implementing sales compensation plans:

1. Defining the job: roles, expected outcomes, and/or behaviors.
2. Defining appropriate pay levels.
3. Determining the compensation mix: salary, commission, and bonus.
4. Implementing the plan.
5. Evaluating the plan.
6. Making adjustments to the plan.

Defining Sales Job Roles

Across many industries, professional selling has changed dramatically over the past decade, with salespeople taking on important roles beyond the generation of sales volume. Today's salespeople are more focused on adding customer value by facilitating the customer's strategic priorities and marshalling the resources of the selling organizations to offer ongoing problem solution and opportunity provision to their customers. Even industries that have been traditionally slow to change the selling function now expect more from salespeople than in the past. For example, it is not uncommon to find today's automobile salespeople charged not only with selling units, but also for achieving customer satisfaction goals.

The correlation between job definition and sales compensation boils down to a single question: "What do we want our salespeople to do?" The answer to this question will feed directly into the next step in sales compensation design, determining pay levels. In answering the "what do we want our salespeople to do" question, consider these examples of common sales roles:

1. New business: Commonly referred to as pioneers, order-getters, market makers, and hunters, these salespeople specialize in securing new business and building market share.
2. Customer retention: These salespeople focus on holding market share and share of customer by maintaining business from year to year with existing customers. Salespeople fulfilling this role are sometimes referred to as order-takers and farmers, with the latter referring to ongoing care of the "cash crop."
3. Sales support: This category includes technical specialists and salespeople who promote products, but do not make the actual sale. This latter group includes detailers in the pharmaceutical industry who call on physicians, merchandisers in retail stores, and

missionaries who "spread the gospel" at the grassroots level, including trade shows and promotional events.

4. Combinations of new business, customer retention, and sales support: Many large sales organizations have salespeople who are responsible for all of these roles. Salespeople who sell to distributors often combine these roles, serving as a working partner with distributor salespeople to pull product through the channel and making solo end-user calls to further support sales through the distributor.

5. Key account and systems salespeople: These salespeople are usually key players on cross-functional teams dealing with large-scale, complex sales situations. National account representatives and supply-chain facilitators fall into this category.

These are only a few of the common roles of salespeople. It should be clear that with the wide range of roles available to salespeople, it is important to carefully define these roles and capture them in a job description as a prelude to designing the compensation level and compensation mix. As roles are defined, the necessary skills and qualifications for salespeople should also be defined. These skills and qualifications will impact subsequent pay levels.

Defining Appropriate Pay Levels

Defining appropriate pay levels will depend on how various sales positions have been defined and what is expected from the salespeople in these positions. It also requires knowledge about competitive salaries and what it will take to attract and retain productive salespeople. Benchmarking earnings levels for salespeople can be accomplished through a variety of methods, including: reviewing trade publications; using general and customized sales compensation surveys; scouring Internet sites such as monster.com and salary.com; and using placement firms and employment agents.

In general, more complicated sales positions that require a wider range of skills will call for higher compensation levels than simpler sales positions. For example, there is a long-standing tradition that sales positions in consumer goods companies pay less than those involving technical sales in business-to-business settings. In the marketing of consumer goods, other forms of marketing communications such as advertising and sales promotion play a more important role than for most technical B2B products, where personal selling is usually the most important part of the marketing communications mix. Even in consumer goods sales positions, some companies are defining the role of the salesforce in ways that change the tradition of consumer goods salespeople receiving less pay than B2B salespeople. A leading food company, for example, utilizes their salespeople more as localized marketing managers than as pure salespeople. Salespeople work with retail accounts to determine promotional messages, make media decisions, and a host of other marketing strategy decisions.

While it is difficult to generalize about what constitutes appropriate pay levels, we can say that higher levels are typically associated with:

1. Job experience, as most senior salespeople have built a record of success. Without a record of success, salespeople are likely to find another way to earn a living.
2. The importance of personal selling in the overall marketing effort.
3. The extent to which there is an expectation that salespeople sell new products into new markets. They deserve to be paid more than those who primarily service existing customers, fulfilling more of an order-taker status.
4. Higher skill levels, especially those that call for creativity and problem-solving.
5. Responsibility for major accounts, where there is a high expectation that salespeople add considerable value for the customer.
6. Highly competitive markets where an intense personal selling effort is important for customer retention and growth.

Determining Compensation Mix

The basic alternatives for sales compensation are salary, commission, and combination pay plans. The advantages and disadvantages of each type are summarized in Exhibit 6.3.

Straight Salary

Straight salary plans are rare in sales settings, and are typically used for sales trainees and sales support personnel. Such plans do allow the organization to direct the behavior of salespeople, and are easy to administer. Straight salary plans give salespeople a stable income, which can lead to increased loyalty. With such plans, reassigning territories is a simple administrative task with minimal impact on the salesforce. However, the lack of incentive pay and tendency to reward seniority rather than merit limits the usefulness of straight salary plans. Further, straight salary plans are not conducive to retaining highly productive salespeople who often seek incentive pay.

Exhibit 6.3   Summary of Sales Compensation Plans

Plan Type	Advantages	Disadvantages	Common Uses
Salary	Simple administration: planned earnings facilitates budgeting; more control of non-selling activities; stable income can increase salesperson loyalty; reassigning sales territories not a problem	Lack of incentive to improve performance; pay often based on seniority, not merit; may not retain high performers; fixed costs may be a burden	Sales trainees; sales support personnel
Commission	Direct link of income and results; strong incentive to improve performance; costs reduced during downturns; less operating capital	Less control of nonselling activity; reassigning customers and sales territories can be a problem; salesforce turnover may be a problem during downturns	Real estate, insurance; wholesaling; securities; automobiles
Combination: salary plus commission, bonus	More flexible in providing incentives for a variety of desired sales outcomes and behaviors	Complex to administer; may encourage too many objectives, especially crisis-oriented objectives	Widely-used, most popular type of sales compensation plan

© Thomson

Straight Commission

Straight commission plans are often found in real estate, financial services, wholesaling and automobile sales. These plans directly link income to results, and thus provide a strong incentive to improve results. Capital requirements for the organization are lessened, and variable sales costs are reduced during downturns. On the other hand, straight commission plans based solely on sales volume gives the organization less flexibility in directing sales behavior, which sometimes leads to neglect of non-selling activities such as servicing existing customers. Reassigning customers and sales territories is often problematic with straight commission plans. Salespeople will have a tendency to sell those products that most easily enable high commission earnings, sometimes focusing more on short term sales than on long term customer relationships. Finally, when market downturns occur, turnover in the salesforce may become a problem.

Although commission plans are typically straightforward, sales organizations must make several decisions when using such plans. Will the commission be based on total sales volume, net sales, or on profitability-oriented targets such as gross margin and contribution margin? Despite the growth of profitability-oriented commission plans, most commission plans are based on sales volume. Will the commission rate remain constant, or will it increase or decrease at pre-specified sales levels? Increasing commission rates, or progressive commissions, provide additional incentive to salespeople, but higher sales costs for the organization. Decreasing rates, or regressive commissions, might be appropriate when it is difficult to secure accounts, but once they are secured, reorders become routine. The issue of splitting commissions when two or more salespeople work together to make the sale is another decision area for sales organizations. Commission plans need not be complicated, but they are usually more complicated than salary-only pay plans.

Combination Plans

The limitations of straight salary and straight commission plans have led to widespread popularity of combination plans, which feature a base salary plus commissions and/or bonuses. Bonuses are paid to individuals or teams for performance, such as achieving sales targets and opening new accounts. Though combination programs are more complicated than salary or commission compensation plans and may encourage too many sales objectives, they afford the organization more flexibility in establishing salesperson objectives across a wide range of activities. With markets in a constant state of change, the flexibility of combination plans to strategically adapt is a real plus.

With forethought, combination plans need not be overly complicated. Combination plans can be quite simple and yet powerful in motivating salespeople toward achieving key objectives. For example, take a mature industry such as institutional food. Manufacturers typically sell through wholesalers to the restaurant, hotel, school, employee cafeteria, and government markets. Retention of these wholesalers is crucial to annual success, since the market growth is limited from year to year. Competition among manufacturers is intense as most seek to grow faster than the market. The challenge is to retain key customers, gain new distribution or an increasing share of market with current distributors, establish a significant number of new products each year, and maintain a balance between volume and profitability since margins are under pressure.

Given this scenario, one alternative among combination plans that is simple but yet powerful could have these elements:

1. A salary component that provides 70–80 percent of the salesperson's expected annual income. This allows the company to direct the salesforce toward longer term objectives such as maintaining current customers and establishing new products in a highly competitive marketplace. The significant salary base also facilitates the assignment of developmental objectives, such as having salespeople conduct market analyses to prepare them for future management assignments.

2. An annual bonus of 10 percent if the salesperson achieves 100 percent of a dollar sales volume target. This is a simple, easy to understand component that relies on a pre-established forecast and resulting sales target. This bonus also establishes a basis for recognition programs and a reasonable level of peer pressure.

3. An additional annual bonus tied to two factors: achieving more than 100 percent of the sales volume target, and company profitability. The additional bonus is paid on sales up to 25 percent over the volume target. If the company makes its profit plan, the salesperson could earn an additional bonus point for every point over the target (maximum 25 percent); if the company does not meet its profit goal, then the salesperson is paid one-half of a bonus point for every point over the target (maximum 12.5 percent). This component not only encourages sales volume, but profitable sales volume. Granted, salespeople in this scenario do not control company profitability, but

their actions can increase or diminish company profitability. For example, salespeople are motivated to control their expenses and be judicious in offering concessions such as price discounts.

4. Sales contests are used sparingly during the year to direct sales activities into priority areas. These allow additional financial rewards, but costs versus results are carefully monitored.

This combination plan is not overly complex, yet offers a fair amount of flexibility in directing salespeople's behaviors. The manufacturer in this case controls pricing and thus targeted margins. Salespeople are given some leeway in deviating from list prices depending upon their demonstrated understanding of the market and the impact of lowering prices on profitability, but pricing is ultimately administered jointly by product managers and sales managers.

Implementing the Compensation Plan

The implementation of the compensation plan in a new sales organization is fairly straightforward. There should be a master document that clearly spells out the details of the plan. The master document can be edited for recruiting and employee orientation purposes. As recruiting commences, the sales organization will get a quick read on whether the compensation plan is successful in terms of attracting suitable candidates. If this is not the case, tweaking may be necessary to assemble the inaugural salesforce. If the organization is modifying its existing plan, the implementation process is more complex. This topic will be covered in a subsequent section, "Making Adjustments to the Plan."

Evaluating the Plan

Compensation plans should be monitored closely during the first six to twelve months after implementation. Beyond this initial period, evaluation should be continual on at least an annual basis. Criteria for evaluating the plan should tie closely to the criteria for optimal compensation systems introduced early in this chapter. Is the plan meeting the needs of the sales organization, its customers, and the salesforce? A major software supplier changed its commission structure after finding that it was not meeting the needs of its customers. The commission plan featured accelerators, or higher commission rates for sales made during the closing days of each business quarter to support the company's push to achieve quarterly earnings forecasts. The accelerators caused salespeople to push customers for sales late in the quarter, which in many cases was resented by customers who planned to buy at a later date. The CEO of the company noted that the commission accelerators not only led to pushy sales tactics, but also to over promising and steep discounting rather than selling according to what was best for the customer and, in the long run, the sales organization. The CEO ultimately declared the accelerators "perverse" and abolished them.

Compensation plans should evaluated against their costs, with an eye toward being competitive in the employee earnings market while maintaining an acceptable costs versus sales or profitability ratios. Just as is the case with any cost component in the P&L, only organizations that command a premium price can afford a higher cost of doing business. Further, the fact that most products and services eventually become commodities in highly price sensitive markets adds to the importance of maintaining a reasonable cost structure for the sales compensation system.

Strategic alignment is an important factor when evaluating sales compensation systems. Is the compensation system truly supporting the sales organization's strategies, goals, and objectives? Too often sales organizations are found exhorting their salespeople to build long-term customer relationships, yet providing incentives only for short-term sales volume.

Is the compensation system helping to retain highly-productive salespeople? Do the salespeople easily understand how they are paid? If less than productive salespeople are departing because of dissatisfaction with the pay plan, no problem. If high performers are departing, there is obviously a big problem. Salespeople usually communicate quite candidly when departing for a better earnings opportunity, so this problem is easily detected. In the most progressive sales organizations, management has their early warning detectors on alert and tries to eliminate the problem before it demands attention.

Making Adjustments

Adjustments to sales compensation plans are not uncommon. Major changes are typically greeted with skepticism by the salesforce, and their number one concern is that they will make less money. Number two is that they will have to work a lot harder to sustain current income levels. A sales compensation change that results in lower earnings for top producers is the worst case scenario and will only happen if compensation levels have grown beyond the financial value it produces for the organization. In such cases, a major rebuilding effort will be required to replace a large number of departing salespeople.

In most cases requiring a compensation system change, sales management must sell the salesforce on the change. It will be important to show salespeople how they can meet their earnings expectations, monitor the reaction to the change, and respond promptly to questions. Try to provide the rationale for the change in the context of how changing market conditions or changing sales strategies necessitates the change. It is also important to communicate how the organization will support the required changes and equip the salesforce to be successful under the new plan.

In anticipation of a compensation change, sales management would be wise to seek input from salespeople. It is also a good idea to analyze who would earn what and the total compensation outlay would be under the proposed changes. In some cases, this will require some assumptions, as new compensation plans are based to some extent on future events with unknown probabilities. With reasonable assumptions, however, a decent approximation can be made, and salesforce anxiety can be addressed in a responsible manner.

Communicating the planned change in advance is essential, and in some cases, a phase-in period can facilitate a smooth change. For example, a major bedding manufacturer wanted to change their sales compensation plan from a salary plus individual bonus plan to a salary plus commission plus individual bonus plan. Under both the old and new plan, the individual bonus was based on achieving a preset sales quota. Under the new plan, the salary would be decreased. The company believed that the salesforce had become complacent about pursuing new accounts, and that the salespeople could actually earn more with the addition of the commission element. At the beginning of the year, the new commission rate commenced. In January, salespeople also received 100 percent of their previous year's salary. Each month, the salaries were adjusted toward the new base, so that by year end, the new salary bases were established. These new base salaries were then adjusted according to performance during the year. The plan succeeded, pushing sales effort and results to a higher level and simultaneously encouraging those unwilling to expend effort on securing new accounts to depart.

Sales Contests

Sales contests feature special incentives such as cash, merchandise, and travel to gain increased effort on short-term objectives. Interestingly, sales contests are extremely popular, yet one of the most controversial practices in the sales compensation area. They are popular because they spice things up and provide some excitement over the day-to-day routine. Sales contests, if done properly,

---

BREAK BOX: Reviewing and Relating

The second step in the BREAK process is to review the material and to identify specific ideas that relate to your sales organization. The following questions are designed to assist you in determining relevant ideas and action items for your organization.

1. What are the key roles fulfilled by your salespeople, i.e., what are they paid to do?
2. What evidence do you have that your salespeople are neither underpaid nor overpaid?
3. Are your salespeople paid the right mix of salary and incentives (commissions and bonuses)?
4. How do you evaluate the effectiveness of your sales compensation system?
5. Do you see any need to adjust your compensation system?

---

can build morale and camaraderie in the salesforce. Another reason that sales contests are so popular, unfortunately, is that they are often used to prop up a weak sales strategy or correct for shortcomings in salesforce performance.

Sales contests are controversial because it is often difficult to assess their effectiveness, especially from a return-on-investment perspective. There is also the very real possibility that contests can increase sales during the contest at the expense of future sales. Further, sales contests can lead to undesirable customer pressure to load up during the contest as a favor to the salesperson. If not handled correctly, sales contests can also produce unintended consequences, such as resentment and decreased motivation among salespeople.

To maximize results from sales contests, five key decision areas must be addressed: goals; contest duration and frequency; format and rules; award types; and a contest theme.

Sales Contest Goals

Sales contest goals may focus on improving the sales process, that is, sales knowledge, skills and efforts. More often, sales contest goals focus on sales outcomes, such as sales revenue or customer satisfaction. Goals that focus on improving the sales process require a fair amount of management involvement and monitoring during the contest, while those that focus on outcomes do not. Goals for sales contests should be selected according to strategic priorities, and should consider how not to rob sales from a future time period in order to achieve the contest goals. For example, contests that have goals related to acquiring new customers are less likely to have negative future effects than those that focus simply on selling more, whether it be to new or existing customers.

Duration and Frequency

Sales contests are most useful in the short-term, and thus should not last beyond a normal sales cycle in most cases. For products that are purchased frequently such as high-turnover retail items, the recommended duration is 30–60 days unless there is logical seasonal period during which sales contests are effective. To maximize the incremental motivation effect, do not hold more than two or three contests in a year. An analogy from the retail sector is worth considering when deciding how many sales contests to run. Don't make the mistake that many department stores have made of holding so many consumer promotions and sales that the buying public is no longer stimulated to action by yet another ho-hum holiday sale.

Format and Rules

A clear format and set of rules is essential. In determining the format, one key consideration is whether the contest will be individual or team-based. Contests offer a great opportunity to build teamwork even if team selling is not a formal sales strategy. For example, teams can be based on geography such as sales districts or regions. One unique team approach used by a large communications company was to arrange teams based upon which colleges and universities salespeople had attended. This allowed teaming at two levels, one being at the conference level with teams from the Big East, Big 12, SEC, and so forth, along with a designated independent team. At a second level, alums from individual schools were on a team. The contest began during the final week of college basketball season and concluded with the conclusion of the NCAA Final Four tournament. Tying the contests to a college affiliation built teamwork across regional boundaries and, as expected, increased inter-regional lead referral and new customer acquisition.

To a large extent, a well-run sales contest is a fun, productive game, and rules of the game are important to achieve maximum effort from all participants. A level playing field is important, and individual goals or targets must be set with fairness to all salespeople as a guiding principle. It is crucial that the time period for the contest be carefully specified, as last-minute results are to be expected. If a contest closes at 5:00 p.m. eastern standard time on a given date, there is no doubt that salespeople will be making one more call to their customers that afternoon in pursuit of additional sales. Little things mean a lot when specifying the rules of the game, and it is especially important to detail what counts in the tally and how the tally will be determined. For example, it is not a good idea to count orders taken by a certain time and date, as the term "orders taken" is ambiguous. For example, salespeople can claim that they have a verbal order from a customer and that the written order will be issued in a couple of days. In contrast, it is straightforward and fair to state the rule as "Orders for immediate shipment received in customer service by Friday, September 30 at 12:00 noon will count toward your sales total. Orders may be submitted by e-mail, phone, fax, or regular mail. Additions to orders after the closing time will not be considered in determining the contest totals. Order cancellations after the contest closing time will be deducted from contest totals."

Contest Awards

Determining which awards to use is largely a matter of knowing the preferences of the salesforce. Though awards such as exotic travel and merchandise are often offered, it is hard to beat cash, an award that offers the ultimate opportunity for contest participants to personalize awards. However, constant reliance on cash or any other singular award is not recommended, as the same award time after time does little to add to the excitement of contests. It is also easier to develop an exciting contest theme when something other than cash is part of the award mix.

Contest Themes

Themes add an element of fun and enhance communications before and during the contest. Themes may be tied to contest objectives, the major awards, or both. For example, a regional tire distributor offered the grand prize winner a choice of an all-expenses paid trip to the Master's golf tournament or an equivalent amount of cash. The contest, themed "Drive to Augusta" also included awards such as a gift certificate to an online sporting goods retailer for a wide variety of golf and non-golf items, and one-week's free use of a luxury convertible automobile. In choosing these awards, the management team offered something for everybody and wrapped the incentive package in an award-related theme that succeeded in increasing market share through key retail accounts.

Exhibit 6.4   Tips for Running Effective Sales Contests

1. Strive for performance beyond the norm and plan with a return-on-investment perspective.
2. Set contest goals that are clearly stated and attainable with extra effort.
3. Be fair to all participants, ensuring that winners are top performers, not merely those with easier goals.
4. Recognize that sales contests concentrate efforts into selected activities, and guard against neglect of other important activities.
5. Maximize motivation and morale by allowing multiple winners, but do not set low expectations so that everyone can be a winner.
6. Publicize the contest before it is implemented to build excitement and momentum heading into the contest.
7. Build teamwork by including customer service and sales support staff in the contest.
8. Use variety as a design element, varying themes, duration, and awards.
9. Congratulate the winners in an appropriate manner. A combination of spotlight time at a special event or banquet and a private communication from management such as a personal letter can be especially powerful.
10. Share best practices. Have the winners conduct a training session or share their sales strategies and tactics with the rest of the salesforce.

© Thomson

Once a sales contest is underway, it is crucial to communicate results on a regular basis. This is readily done by e-mail, which offers the sales manager the opportunity to add special congratulations and encourage all participants to work toward their goals. Web-based programs are also good for communicating results. There are companies that furnish web-based sales contests which will facilitate planning, implementation, and follow-up communication of contest results. For tips on running effective sales contests, see Exhibit 6.4.

Team Compensation

As noted earlier in this chapter, defining selling roles is an important step in designing sales compensation systems. It is generally agreed that designing team compensation systems is a more complex process than it is for individual

---

BREAK BOX: Reviewing and Relating

The second step in the BREAK process is to review the material and to identify specific ideas that relate to your sales organization. The following questions are designed to assist you in determining relevant ideas and action items for your organization. Assuming your organization uses sales contests:

1. How do you evaluate the return-on-investment of sales contests?
2. What makes for successful contests in your organization?
3. If your organization does not use sales contests, do you see opportunities to use them in the future?

---

salespeople, partly because there are multiple people who typically play multiple roles. Experimentation is often necessary to find the right pay plan for a team selling. Key questions include:

1. Should individual performance and/or team performance be rewarded?
2. How are permanent team members compensated in contrast to team on-call members who join the team periodically on an as-needed basis?
3. How should those with business development and sales growth objectives be compensated in contrast to those who provide technical support and service?

Team or Individual Rewards?

In most cases, it is beneficial to reward both individual and team results, which again comes back to defining the roles of team members. For example, take a capital goods sales team that sells technical products. A simple team arrangement might have the salesperson as the team leader who is responsible for customer contact before, during, and after the sale. The team leader is also responsible for new business development and takes the lead in making presentations to potential prospects. There is considerable after-sale service, which is handled by a technical support person. This is an important element of customer retention, which is important given the highly-competitive nature of the market and an 18–24 month period before another major sales opportunity arises. A finance expert is also on the team when needed to help determine pricing and customer financing alternatives.

For the salesperson/team leader, the most important performance metrics could be equally-weighted profitability of the sale and percentage increase in sales over the prior year. In this case, a base salary plus a volume-based commission makes sense, with a 75/25 salary/commission mix. For the technical support person, customer satisfaction and customer retention are key performance metrics. This person could be paid 90 percent base salary, with an opportunity for a 5 percent annual bonus based on customer satisfaction and retention and another 5 percent bonus if the team meets its sales volume growth objective. For the finance expert, profitability on the initial sale is an important metric, and to a lesser degree, percentage increase in sales volume over the previous year. The finance team member could be paid 90 percent base salary and 10 percent bonus for meeting the team target for sales volume growth. In this scenario, team member roles vary, and so should compensation.

The assignment of team roles often applies to multiple levels in the organization, especially with national or global account management. For example, a national account team could be responsible for working at the corporate headquarters level for a large retail chain. The key role here could be new product introductions and developing national advertising and sales promotion programs to increase share within the product category. Regional account representatives service the regional buying offices for the chain, working to customize programs according to seasonality differences and other nuances in the regional markets. Local territory representatives provide in-store support in the form of merchandising, supporting special events and product demonstrations, and training retail salespeople. As in the preceding, scenario, selling roles differ, and compensation systems for national, regional, and local representatives should be tied to the various roles, rewarding individual and team results as appropriate.

After selling roles have been defined and corresponding performance metrics set, it is important to establish weighted priorities that establish the importance of each team member's individual and team contributions. Conventional wisdom advises that the number of performance measures per individual be kept low, in the range of 3–5 key performance measures. A conservative number of three key performance metrics reduces the chances of team members disregarding additional metrics. After, all most people can focus intense energy only on a few key initiatives without becoming scattered and ineffective.

Permanent and Part-Time Team Members

The question of how to compensate full-time team members versus part-time team members has no firmly established guidelines. If an individual serves as an on-demand resource for a large number of teams, it would be a good idea to use feedback from those teams as input into that person's performance evaluations. However, it could be cumbersome to tie that person's compensation to the performance of a large number of teams. The summary on part-time team members is that a decision must be made: is this a true team member or simply a team resource? If the individual is deemed a team member, then their compensation should be based in part on team results.

Compensating for Sales Growth

In compensating those with sales growth roles, the incentive portion becomes a more important element than for those who play technical support and service roles. The incentive piece is critical to sustaining maximum motivation over a prolonged period of time. This is especially true when making the initial sale is difficult, for example when selling new-to-the world technologies. This also true when the sales cycle is lengthy, as is often the case with bid business for major construction projects. In such cases, the business development team member may easily work for years before a purchasing decision is made to influence bid specifications, become an approved vendor, and develop a comprehensive proposal.

BREAK BOX: Reviewing and Relating

The second step in the BREAK process is to review the material and to identify specific ideas that relate to your sales organization. The following questions are designed to assist you in determining relevant ideas and action items for your organization. Assuming your organization uses team selling:

1. Are you satisfied that team member roles are sufficiently clear?
2. Are team member roles closely tied to the compensation system?
3. Are you satisfied with the mix of individual and team rewards?

Conclusions and BREAKthrough Directions

In this chapter, we have reviewed the key topics related to the management of sales compensation. Compensation systems should achieve a balance between the needs of the organization, their customers, and their salespeople. More than ever, it is crucial to tie sales compensation to strategic priorities, which can be largely achieved by carefully specifying salespeople's roles and rewarding strategically-relevant sales activities. Sales contests can be used to supplement the core elements of compensation, those being salary, commission and bonus. Team selling is becoming commonplace in most industries with a mix of formal and informal team selling approaches. While most would agree that team compensation is a complicated proposition, the complexity of team compensation can be reduced through hiring the right people who fit with a team culture featuring a customer orientation and cooperation.

Managing the compensation system is part art and part science. Dealing with human beings and their needs is often more art than science, though a basic understanding of the theories of motivation can be useful in understanding the human side of the equation. The science part of compensation management stems mostly from economics, which dictates that sales compensation plans have to be financially sound.

BREAK BOX: Envisioning and Creating

The third step in the BREAK process is to envision how applying key ideas in this chapter in your sales organization might be accomplished and creating the basic steps for this to happen. Identify a key priority for action in each of the following areas and discuss the steps needed to accomplish it within your organization.

1. Improving salesperson motivation through the compensation system.
2. Improving the connections between the sales organization's strategic priorities and the compensation system.
3. Developing additional measures of the financial viability of your organization's sales compensation system.
4. Ensuring that your sales compensation system is consistent with a strong customer orientation.

Progressive sales managers are always alert for ways to improve the performance of their salespeople. Given the crucial role of compensation in motivating the salesforce and, in turn, motivation in determining salesforce performance, sales managers should evaluate their current compensation systems and look for opportunities for improvement.

> Visit The Sales Educators Web site for further BREAK process materials on this chapter's topics. www.TheSalesEducators.com

References and Suggested Readings

Coletti, J.A, and M.S. Fiss (2001). *Compensating New Sales Roles: How to Design Rewards That Work in Today's Selling Environment, 2nd ed.*, New York: American Management Association.

Colt, Stockton B., Jr., (1998). *The Sales Compensation Handbook, 2nd ed.*, New York: American Management Association.

Keenan, William, Jr., ed., (1994). *The Sales and Marketing Management Guide to Sales Compensation Planning: Commissions, Bonuses, and Beyond,* Chicago, IL. Probus Publishing.

Murphy, W.H., P.A. Dacin, and N.M. Ford (2004). "Sales Contest Effectiveness: An Examination of Sales Contest Design Preferences of Field Sales Forces," *Journal of the Academy of Marketing Science,* v. 32 (no. 2): 127–143.

Chapter 7

Getting and Keeping the Best Sales Talent

Introduction

The basic issues in this chapter center on the goal of *getting and keeping the best sales talent*. To build a high performance sales organization, this chapter delineates a comprehensive system focused on the getting and keeping goal, which includes defining the ideal sales candidate profile, developing a set of recruiting sources for creating a flow of candidates matching that profile, and establishing a strategic selection system to ensure that candidates meeting the ideal profile are chosen. The development of a strategic ideal candidate profile takes on even greater importance today as the talent pool shrinks.

With a focus on putting best practices and next practices into action, two approaches for identifying the ideal candidate profile are provided. One approach builds on knowledge of ideal sales candidates from cross-industry research. The second approach is particularly relevant to those leading existing field sales organizations and leverages competitive intelligence for building a new sales organization.

Next, this chapter presents a comparative analysis of many recruiting sources available to today's sales managers and sales organization leaders. The reader is prompted to consider how to best develop and manage the recruiting toolkit using a system for assessing recruiting source yields. With the ideal candidate profile as a foundation, the reader will then be prompted to examine a goal-based selection system and consider how the distinct candidate qualities must serve as the focus for each goal stage. As various selection tools are introduced, the ideal candidate profile serves as a strategic foundation for the process of building the recruiting toolkit.

The last section of this chapter links the work of "getting" and the work of "keeping" the best sales talent. High performance sales managers and sales organization leaders must be focused on improving their "numbers" on both the getting and the keeping parts of the process as they build a high performance sales organization. Since one of the keys to retaining top sales talent lies in getting new sales associates off to a fast start, the chapter includes recent research focusing on the developmental sales hire. Keeping top sales talent in the organization is also a key driver for success, so the chapter closes with a brief discussion of the key levers for retaining top sales talent.

BREAK BOX: Becoming Aware

Step one in the BREAK process involves activating self awareness of personal and collective behavior. The sales manager and sales organization leader is responsible for his/her personal behaviors as well as the shared set of behaviors and beliefs that comprise a sales unit's or an organization's culture. The following questions are designed to help the reader assess both the personal and collective behaviors that are impacting the sales unit and/or the firm.

A) How strategic are you or is your organization in the process of getting and keeping the best sales talent?

   1) Very strategic in this area. We consider the issues of getting and keeping the best sales talent in all strategic planning processes.

   2)

   3)

   4) Doing some things strategically in this area but often operate in a reactive mode.

   5)

   6)

   7) Very reactive or last-minute in considering the issues of getting and keeping the best sales talent in the planning processes.

Comments on the overall strategic approach to getting and keeping the best sales talent:

_____

_____

_____

_____

B) How are you are presently doing (i.e., your results) in getting and keeping the best sales talent?

   1) Very satisfied with the results being achieved in this area.

   2)

   3)

   4) Doing some things well in this area but likely can improve.

   5)

   6)

   7) Very dissatisfied with the results being achieved in this area.

Continued

Comments on your results in getting and keeping the best sales talent:

_____

_____

_____

_____

C) How satisfied are you presently with the effectiveness and/or efficiency of your current recruiting sources?

1) Very satisfied with the results with our current recruiting sources

2)

3)

4) Doing some things well in this area but likely can improve.

5)

6)

7) Very dissatisfied with the results with our current recruiting sources

Comments on the effectiveness and/or efficiency of recruiting sources being used:

_____

_____

_____

_____

D) How standardized is your current selection process? How systematically does the organization capture data at each step in the process?

1) Very standardized and systematic—all prospective sales representatives are treated alike and comprehensive data is captured at each step in the process.

2)

3)

4) Some parts of the process are standardized and some data are captured but this area likely can improve.

5)

6)

7) Very unstructured and few data points are captured on a systematic basis.

Continued

Comments on the current selection system/process being used:

_____

_____

_____

_____

E) How purposeful is your current assimilation process? How systematically do you connect new sales associates into the organization?

1) Very purposeful—new sales representatives are systematically connected into the organization.

2)

3)

4) Some parts of assimilation process are purposeful and systematic but this area likely can improve.

5)

6)

7) Not at all purposeful—new sales associates have to make their way into the organization pretty much on their own.

Comments on the current assimilation process being used:

_____

_____

_____

_____

F) How digestible is your initial training program for new sales associates?

1) Very digestible—new sales representatives receive the right information at the right time with the right level of intensity.

2)

3)

4) The initial training program is pretty good, but this area likely can improve.

5)

6)

7) Our initial training program is like drinking from a fire hose. New sales associates receive too much information too soon.

Continued

Comments on the current initial training program being used:

_____

_____

_____

_____

G) How would you describe the level of psychological and social
(aka psychosocial) support in your organization?

  1) All of our sales associates (long-time associates through new
  sales associates) feel interconnected with one another and
  experience the psychological and social support they need.

  2)

  3)

  4) Some psychosocial support exists for our associates, but this
  area likely can improve.

  5)

  6)

  7) All of our sales associates feel isolated and "on their own."

  Comments on the current psychosocial support in the organization:

_____

_____

_____

_____

H) The management of the culture of our sales organization is . . .

  1) Very purposefully managed and we are building the culture
  (or have built the culture) that we desire.

  2)

  3)

  4) Somewhat purposeful but this area likely can improve.

  5)

  6)

  7) Very much off the radar screen for our managers and leaders.

  Comments on the current culture of the organization:

_____

_____

_____

_____

BREAK BOX: Reviewing and Relating

The second step in the BREAK process is to review the material covered in this chapter and to identify specific ideas that relate to your sales organization. The following questions are designed to help you determine the most relevant ideas in the chapter:

1. In light of the discussion and examples about defining the best sales talent, how can your sales organization do a better job of the three-step process outlined herein?
2. Consider the discussion and examples about recruiting the best sales talent. Does this suggest any new ideas about recruiting in your sales organization?
3. Review the discussion and examples about selecting the best sales talent. Are there opportunities for different approaches to selection in your sales organization?
4. Examine the discussion and examples about developing and keeping the best sales talent. Could there be opportunities for more salesperson development within your sales organization?

Defining "The Best Sales Talent"

Before diving into "getting" the best sales talent, it is important to define "the best sales talent." Creating a high performance sales organization requires that sales managers and sales leaders must identify sales talent that does more than simply meet sales performance goals. The sheer amount of resources required to support a field sales representative demands that sales managers consider each new hire almost like a capital investment. Leaders of the sales organization must require that their investments yield an adequate financial return and create synergies with other capital investments (i.e., other field sales representatives). Turning a field sales organization into a high performance field sales organization operating at the next level requires that sales managers hire new field sales representatives who:

1. Meet the sales performance goals set by the organization AND
2. Get off to a fast start in meeting the organization's sales performance goals

3. Add positively to the field sales organization's culture

4. Remain with the field sales organization longer than industry average

So, the process begins with a focus on sales talent which meets sales goals quickly while positively impacting the sales organization's culture (i.e., builds on the other "capital investments"). The issue of retention (number 4 in the list) serves as a foundational element in this chapter because it is critical that field sales representatives have *continuity* in relationships with external and internal customers and constituents. Relationships by their very nature require time to build and time to nurture. Consequently, the process of developing a high performance sales organization must embrace the issue of continuity or retention. A "next" practice in this area must include getting the best sales talent in terms of what an individual person will contribute to the organization AND how he will synergistically impact the organization.

Identifying the Best Sales Talent: Three Stages

In Chapters 3 and 4 the role the field sales representative must play in today's competitive market was discussed. In the context of devising the firm's go-to-market strategy, organizational leaders identify the role of the field sales representative and in essence craft the framework of the job definition. The work of getting and keeping the best sales talent must be built upon the foundation of those earlier decisions/discussions.

Once the job has been identified and the job description has been developed on the basis on the firm's strategy, the work of identifying the best sales talent begins. To identify the best sales talent, three key decision areas must be managed from a strategic and operational perspective, as shown in Exhibit 7.1.

Establishing the Ideal Sales Candidate Profile

Developing the ideal sales candidate profile (CP) is actually more difficult (and more important) than many books suggest. This is not simply a list of characteristics on paper. The ideal CP guides the present operational work of getting new

Exhibit 7.1   Three Key Decisions in Getting and Keeping the Best Sales Talent

Establish the ideal sales candidate profile ➔ Develop the recruiting toolkit ➔ Establish a standardized selection process

© Thomson

Exhibit 7.2   Elements to Balance in Creating the Ideal
Sales Candidate Profile

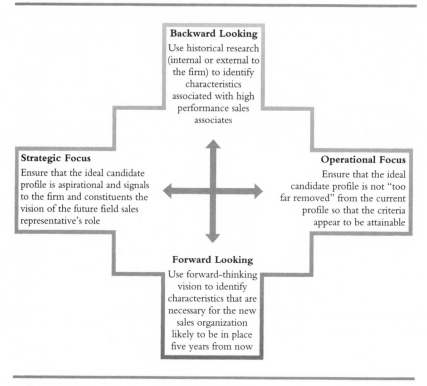

© Thomson

sales talent. At the same time, the ideal CP also must play a strategic role in guiding the sales unit or the firm toward the future. Crafting an ideal CP has both strategic imperative and operational significance. In essence, the work requires that the field sales manager balance four key elements, as shown in Exhibit 7.2.

Strategically, the ideal CP should be a *stretch* from the average profile among the current field sales force. In essence, the descriptors of the ideal sales candidate should be *higher* or *stronger* than the current average and thus serve as a signal to the *level* or *quality* of the field sales organization envisioned for the future. Sharing the description of the ideal CP with sales representatives who are currently on staff should prompt statements or questions, such as "This isn't our sales group." "Who does this describe?" Current sales representatives should perceive the description to be "more" than most representatives in the organization.

However, the strategic or long-term focus—describing the ideal CP in terms of the desired sales organization—must be held in balance with an operational focus. The ideal CP must be perceived as *attainable* by those responsible for recruiting and attracting new sales talent to the organization. This process obviously will create a natural tension.

Likewise, a tension exists and a balanced approach is needed in developing an ideal CP that is both backward-looking (based on historical research either within or outside the firm) and forward-looking. While historical research (from either within or outside the firm) serves as a foundation for this process, it is equally important that the firm's long-term strategy guides the development of the ideal CP. While forward-looking and strategy may appear to be similar, their differences warrant note. The strategic focus prompts the sales organization leadership to *raise the bar* on existing qualities, whereas the forward-looking approach demands that leaders consider the *new characteristics* deemed relevant for the new sales organization being planned two to five years out. Balancing these criteria is necessary to ensure that the ideal CP pushes the firm both toward the future and walks it through the decisions of the day, thereby allowing the ideal CP to leverage the firm's resources in building a high performance sales organization.

Backward-Looking Approach 1

In the rare instance that a firm is building a sales organization from "scratch," the sales organization's leader has limited internal knowledge to draw upon for identifying the ideal sales candidate profile. A job description might exist. Or, more commonly, the job description might be on someone's short-term "to-do list." In this case, examining the roles/responsibilities and the characteristics common to other firms or industries proves to be a useful starting point in this instance.

When internal data is lacking, sales managers or sales organization leaders can turn to published general information. An array of research explores the general roles and responsibilities of sales representatives. Building on academic research starting in the 1980s which profiles the responsibilities associated with various sales roles to more current cross-industry research, ideal sales representatives generally need to possess the following qualities:

- Listening skills
- Follow-up skills
- Adaptable communication/social style
- Organizational skills
- Verbal communication skills
- Written communication skills
- Proficiency in social connections across "levels"
- Able to overcome objections

- Closing skills
- Tenacity and persistency
- Time management and planning skills

Backward-Looking Approach 2

Most field sales managers are likely to be responsible for running an existing field sales organization while devising strategies to improve the organization's performance. While challenging to maintain a day-to-day operational viewpoint *and* to adopt a focus on developing a high performance organization for the future, the manager in this situation has access to an important set of informational assets: current sales representatives.

To identify the historical ideal CP for the entire firm, there are several simple techniques that most will find easy to implement. First, identify the field sales units that are the top performing units for the firm. Top performance may be based on a multiple criteria, where at least three dimensions should be represented when making this assessment: a productivity measure controlling for size of unit (average sales productivity per sales associate), a customer loyalty or retention figure, and a salesforce retention figure at the sales-unit level. Other dimensions that might be considered include: size of the unit (number of sales associates), growth in the size of the sales unit (in terms of number of sales representatives), sales productivity based on a weighted product portfolio, retention of sales associates with fewer than three years experience, growth in new customers, growth in sales from new customers, etc.

After categorizing the organization's field sales units into top-performing units, mid-performing units, and low-performing units, use a relatively simple two-stage survey methodology for identifying the ideal sales candidate profile information. First, ask each sales unit manager to submit his/her description of the ideal sales CP. Have an internal staff member collapse the descriptions across all submissions and develop a list of summary characteristics. At this stage of the process, err in the direction of keeping more descriptors in the list, even though redundancy will exist.

Next, develop a very brief survey and distribute it to these same individuals. Ask the sales unit managers to review the list of characteristics and identify: (1) all the characteristics that are part of their ideal sales candidate profiles, and (2) the top ten characteristics that are part of their ideal CPs. Using very simple analytics (e.g., correlational analysis and analysis of variance to discriminate between the top-, middle-, and low-performing units), a staff member can identify the ideal candidate profile characteristics associated with the firm's top performing sales organizations (see a more thorough description of this process and sample surveys in Dixon, Acito, MacKenzie and Podsakoff, 1995, listed in the chapter references).

To identify the historical ideal CP for an individual sales unit, identify the salespeople that are the top performers for the sales unit. Again, top performance may be based on a multiple criteria, including two dimensions to represent productivity and customer loyalty (e.g., productivity might be captured as sales revenues, sales calls, and/or profits; loyalty might be captured as customer loyalty over the past year, share of wallet in the last quarter, etc.). A third dimension that might be considered is a form of growth, such as growth in sales, sales productivity based on a weighted product portfolio, growth in number of new customers, growth in sales from new customers, and so on.

After categorizing the sales unit's sales representatives into top-performers, mid-performers, and low-performers, develop a summary candidate profile of each of the three groups. This exercise is more qualitative in nature than determining the historical profile at the firm level. However, the insights gained are equally powerful.

Industry Example

In the financial services industry, historical research gathered from over forty companies suggests that more-productive, high-retention field sales organizations have different ideal candidate profiles. Managers of these higher performing sales organizations employ a much richer, more complex description of the types of candidates to seek. The call to action for readers is to determine the ideal CP currently sought by top performing field sales managers in their organizations (or the profile of the top-performing sales representatives in the sales unit), paying special attention to those characteristics statistically more likely to be found in the top profile (than in the profile of the less-successful counterparts).

Forward-Looking Approach

There are as many techniques for identifying a firm's future go-to-market strategy as there are consultants listed on the Internet! Developing the firm's future go-to-market strategy is not the focus of the current chapter. However, the connection between future go-to-market strategies and the development of the ideal CP is often not made. While considering the development or updating of the ideal sales candidate profile, it is imperative that the sales leader touch base with the individuals who are involved in the future go-to-market strategy planning. Seek their insights into how the sales representative's role might be changing. Discuss with the individuals involved in planning the future go-to-market strategy what they perceive to be the implications for the ideal CP under the new strategy (which is typically focused on two to five years out).

Balance the backward-looking approach with the insights gained from discussing the future with colleagues in the organization. Industry trade reports may also provide insight on the future of the sales representative's role in the industry, so do not overlook this important information source.

Operational Approach

The knowledge gained from the backward-looking approach serves as an anchor for understanding the firm's current ideal sales candidate profile. If the low performing unit managers demonstrate a remarkably different profile than their high performing counterparts (or, if the low-performing sales representatives are remarkably different than their high-performing counterparts), the firm or the sales manager may choose to signal an ideal CP that represents a *middle ground* between the two cohorts. It may simply be too much of a stretch to publish and encourage the ideal sales CP from the high performing unit for all sales units.

Strategic Approach

If the discrepancy between the low- and high-performing sales units is not *that great* (i.e., the low-performing sales units are "not that far off"), a firm may choose to encourage the entire organization to increase their expected ideal sales candidate profile. The top sales unit's profile may be used as the new benchmark for all organizations. Specific *levels* of various characteristics may be called out for new performance expectations.

If the discrepancy between the low- and high-performing sales representatives is not *that great* (i.e., the low-performing sales representatives are capable of developing to the high-performing level), a sales manager may publish the high-performing sales profile within the sales unit, encouraging all representatives to assess themselves relative to the profile and to identify areas for professional development.

An Example of an Ideal Sales Candidate Profile

Timothy Murray, CLU, ChFC, President of Executive Benefits, spent several months recrafting his ideal sales candidate profile. In 2000, Murray was leading a sales organization in the financial services industry that generated first-year commissions (new sales revenues) of $1,650,000. In 2001, the organization undertook several strategic initiatives, including the approach described above for building a future focus into the ideal sales candidate profile. One result of that work is the ideal sales candidate profile for Executive Benefits:

- Persons having demonstrated prior success in their lives. The ideal candidate, in fact, demonstrates a history of success in many things that he undertakes. Such success might be in work-related ventures, and/or in leisure pursuits. A pattern of success is evident from the individual's youth through to present day.
- Persons having formal or informal sales experience. Prior sales experience can take the form of a paper route as a youngster, soliciting corporate sponsorships for clubs in college, and so forth. The ideal candidate shows evidence of an ability to interact with the public and be persuasive.
- Persons having demonstrated a need for closure or completion. The ideal candidate's background shows evidence of completing a variety of projects, thus indicating that the individual likes to ensure that his/her commitments are met.
- Persons having demonstrated that they are "givers" and not simply "takers." The ideal candidate's background includes experience, time, and focus on charitable or volunteer-type work, which indicates that he has an "other orientation" and does not solely operate from "what's in it for me perspective."
- Persons demonstrating real drive. The ideal candidate is somewhat aggressive or dominant which is evident in his/her need for closure and for meeting his/her commitments. The behavior is not reflected in an overt fashion (e.g., impatience with others) but rather is reflected in the individual's willingness to "do what it takes" to get things done.
- Persons demonstrating a strong desire to take the ethical high road. The ideal candidate expresses that he makes decisions according to an ethical frame of reference that does not reflect a dominant focus on what's best for "self."

In 2003, Executive Benefits posted first-year commissions (new sales revenues) of $2,875,000, representing a gain of 74% over the 2000 year. Expected first-year commissions for 2004 are $4,000,000. Murray credits

---

BREAK BOX: Envisioning and Creating

What practices in this section appear to be counter to current practice—personally and/or organizationally? Identify here the practices that relate to where the sales unit/organization might go in the future.

_____

_____

_____

_____

---

some of that growth and success to the important work that the organization did in purposefully crafting the ideal sales candidate profile.

Signaling the Ideal Sales Candidate Profile Throughout the Firm

Once the ideal sales candidate profile is determined for the sales unit or for the firm, it is important to purposefully communicate this profile to ensure that it becomes "part of the fabric" of the organization (and is actually adopted into practice). Luckily, if the backward-looking internal research process described above was used, the communication or signaling part of the process is already underway. Those involved in the research understand that important work is being done in this area. Some additional opportunities for signaling the ideal sales candidate profile to the sales leadership team and/or to the sales unit might include introducing the description (creatively) at a leadership meeting, and inserting the ideal sales candidate profile as part of an e-mail signature.

Developing the Recruiting Tool Kit

To develop the most-productive recruiting toolkit, the field sales organization must work with multiple recruiting sources and track the efficacy of each source for the organization. Some recruiting sources (e.g., college recruiting) will work more effectively in partnership with some ideal sales candidate profiles, while other recruiting sources (e.g., headhunters) will be more appropriate for other ideal sales candidate profiles. There is no single recruiting source that is "best" for all organizations or ideal sales candidate profiles.

To assess an existing recruiting toolkit or to build a recruiting toolkit for a new organization, it is important to balance the recruiting sources used.

Recruiting sources can be organized into two types: cold sources and warm sources. Cold sources, such as newspaper and professional journal ads, do not typically pre-screen the candidates. Consequently, cold sources often provide larger numbers of prospective candidates for consideration. Having a "flow" of candidates in the recruiting pipeline allows an organization to work through an actual selection process, meaning more than a small number of candidates are considered in the effort to select and hire one sales representative.

Warm sources, such as referrals from existing employees, typically involve some type of pre-screening of candidates. The employees in the organization understand "the work," the organization, and the customers being served. If the process of getting and keeping the best sales talent is happening according to plan, employees are also aware of the organization's ideal sales candidate profile. Before referring a friend, acquaintance or relative for a sales position, the employee typically weighs the potential referral against such information (i.e., the ideal sales candidate profile, the organization's culture, the expectations, etc.), consciously choosing (or not) to encourage the prospective candidate to proceed. Warm sources involving some type of pre-screening thus serve to ensure that the sales leader is reviewing a pool of candidates who are likely a better fit to the position, the unit, and the organization.

If warm recruiting sources are better, a sales manager might wonder "Why not rely solely on warm sources?" In reality, many organizations are not able to generate a large enough "flow" of candidates through warm sources and find that cold sources provide important increased flow. It is also important to note that warm recruiting sources may not provide a candidate pool that is diverse (relative to the current employee base). So, it is important to include both warm recruiting sources and cold recruiting sources in the recruiting tool kit. The various types of recruiting sources available to the sales manager or organization are summarized in Exhibit 7.3.

Warm Recruiting Sources

Systems can be instituted within the organization and/or sales unit to encourage referrals from current sales associates and/or other employees of the organization/unit. First, the sales manager and/or sales organization leader must ensure that current employees and sales representatives are knowledgeable about the ideal sales candidate profile. Second, these internal partners must know that their referrals are desired and valued. The sales manager must signal that referrals are desired and valued by asking for referrals on a systematic basis. In some organizations, the sales manager accomplishes this task by asking for referrals during quarterly performance review sessions. Some

Exhibit 7.3   Recruiting Sources Available for the Recruiting Toolkit

Warm Recruiting Sources	Cold Recruiting Sources
Sales Associate Referrals	Professional Journal Ads
Other Employee Referrals	College Recruiting
Personal Observation	Job Fairs
Nominators	Newspaper Advertising

Other Recruiting Sources (may include some pre-screening)

Direct Mail

Employment Agencies

Web-based Recruiting

© Thomson

sales managers use face-to-face contact to make the referral ask. Others use e-mail and/or inter-company memos to accomplish the ask for referrals.

Sales managers who are always thinking about adding the best sales talent to the organization will constantly be "on the lookout" for talent. By maintaining an active recruiting mindset, sales managers pay attention to everyone with whom they come in contact. The important part of the personal observation process is that the sales manager has to be ready to transition any conversation and/or encounter with a potential sales candidate into a discussion of the opportunity that is available in the organization.

Similarly, sales managers on the lookout for talent frequently employ others outside the organization in the talent identification process. Nominators are business professionals who come in contact with people likely to match the ideal sales candidate profile. A contact at a customer firm or a trade association representative may both serve as good nominators for a sales organization. To make the nominator process work most effectively, the sales manager needs to ensure that the nominators have a good understanding of the ideal sales candidate profile and the opportunity in the sales organization. Nominators must also feel that their referrals are desired and valued. Those leading high performance sales organizations typically systematize the nominator recruiting process to ensure that all the steps shown in Exhibit 7.4 happen on a consistent basis.

Exhibit 7.4   The Nominator System for Recruiting

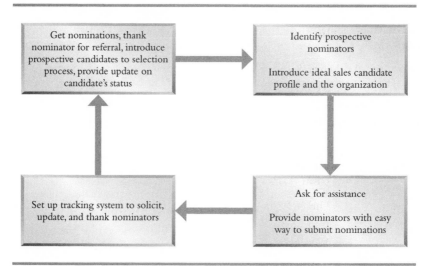

© Thomson

Cold Recruiting Sources

Traditional approaches to generating a pool of applicants include advertising in professional or trade journals and newspapers. Professional or trade journals provide the sales organization with a skills- or experience-targeted audience, while general newspaper advertisements can allow for geographic targeting. In both types of advertising, the copy for the ad should include the title of the position, a brief synopsis of the job, a summary of the ideal sales candidate profile, the name of the company or organization, the geographic location of the position, and contact information for submitting materials. The listing of contact information should direct the prospective candidate to contact the organization in the preferred manner (i.e., sending cover letter and resume via e-mail, fax, snail mail, and/or completing an on-line application). To encourage applications from a diversity of candidates, the advertisement may also note if the organization is an Equal Opportunity Employer (EOE) at the end of the ad and may encourage specific classes of individuals to apply (e.g., "female and minority applicants are encouraged to apply"). Print advertisements may require several insertions in the publication in order to gain necessary visibility and generate response.

Establishing a presence on several college or university campuses can also provide a flow of prospective candidates, particularly if the sales position is an entry-level opportunity. The first step in using this type of recruiting source is to identify the colleges and universities to consider. If the sales organization operates on a regional basis, working through the college and university campuses in that region is probably a logical starting point. In this process, it is important to remember that there isn't one set of "best colleges and universities" for recruiting. The selection of the academic institutions also must relate to the ideal sales candidate profile. If the sales organization operates on a national basis, the profile is even more important as a screening tool for selecting colleges and universities. Consider sending the ideal sales candidate profile to the head of the recruiting process at the college or university. (Recognize that some colleges and/or departments may handle their recruiting process in a decentralized fashion, meaning that a single institution may well have several contacts of interest.) Ask the contacts at the academic institutions being considered whether they believe that students who fit the profile are likely to be available for interviews.

The second step in the process is to engage the recruiting staff on behalf of the sales organization. The recruiting staff at an academic institution is positioned to make the recruiting process more efficient and effective, but they need to be enrolled in the process. They need to understand the ideal sales candidate profile and the position(s) that is available. They can help the sales organization identify an appropriate recruiting schedule and suggest appropriate ways to preannounce the opportunity to students. Pre-announcement opportunities include posters, e-mail (typically sent from the recruiting office—the sales organization simply provides the copy), recruiting fairs, presentations at student organizations, partnering with student organizations, meeting with faculty, and guest lecturing in the classroom.

Developing a presence on a college or university campus does not just happen. This recruiting source requires investment (time and financial) to develop the sales organization as part of the "desired set" for student interviews. Depending on the level of unaided awareness that a company enjoys, it is not uncommon for an organization to build its presence for several years before college recruiting becomes a fruitful source for the investment.

Participating in job fairs provides a sales organization with the opportunity to personally present a position to prospective candidates. This recruiting source also provides a bit of a screening opportunity because a representative of the sales organization can see how the prospective candidate handles himself or herself in making introductions and carrying on a conversation. The quality of the candidates accessible through job fairs depends entirely on the job fair. Some job fairs appear to attract a very highly skilled prospect pool, whereas others attract predominantly an hourly type candidate. Review the materials for the job fair and determine who has participated in the past. Ask for referral contacts and do the requisite homework, asking previous participants how many candidates they identified in the process and their satisfaction level with the candidate pool. Job fairs require a financial investment as well as considerable time investment for staffing a booth. Sales organizations desiring to use this source in their recruiting toolkit must weigh out these investments relative to anticipated pay-offs.

Other Recruiting Sources

Organizations have the ability to purchase lists of prospective candidates meeting a variety of criteria, including experience in sales, experience in a given industry, current household income level, and so forth. Identifying very specific list criteria makes direct mail an attractive recruiting source for many sales organizations; it also makes this recruiting source "less cold." However, the effectiveness and efficiency of this approach also varies depending on the ideal sales candidate profile, the quality of the list (in matching that profile), the quality of the recruiting materials (i.e., cover letter, brochure, etc.) and the frequency of the mailings. Since single direct mailings to a "cold list" (meaning people are not expecting the message) can yield response rates from .5% to 3%, multiple "hits" or mailings may be necessary. The quality of the recruiting materials should be assessed in advance of the mailing. This can be accomplished through a few one-on-one interviews with the target population, asking them to provide honest feedback on the letter (e.g., What do you like about the materials? What don't you like about the materials? If you were to receive this letter in the mail, what images would come to mind upon opening the envelope?, etc.)

Web-based recruiting is gaining in popularity due to penetration of the Internet. By placing the sales organization's announcement on recruiting bulletin boards that are industry-specific, organized geographically, and searchable by candidate qualities, sales organizations can better tailor who views their Internet posting and who is likely to apply. To make this source "less cold," Internet recruiting sites often allow the sales organization to have prospective candidates complete an online application where screening criteria can be programmed into the application file. This means that the sales organization reviews only those applications that truly meet the organization's criteria. Unqualified applicants are captured separately. The sales organization should also include links to job posting information on the firm's home page.

Employment Agencies

To identify experienced sales candidates, many sales organizations turn to professional employment agencies or recruiters. Some employment agencies or recruiters specialize in the sales area, whereas others specialize in specific industries. Identifying potential organizations as partners in this effort can be facilitated by asking current sales representatives for names of employment agencies and/or recruiting firms that might be contacting them about positions outside your organization. Tell the current sales representatives that since they are some of the best in the industry, they would clearly be on target lists for such organizations. Ask them to help identify some of the best, based on their own interactions with the organizations. Then, it is important to share the ideal sales candidate profile with the potential employment agencies and recruiting firms to determine if the agency/firm believes that it might have the potential to identify candidates meeting that profile. The effectiveness and efficiency of employment agencies and recruiters is highly firm-dependent. Sales organizations should avoid long-term contracts with specific organizations until they have proven their ability to effectively screen applicants and provide the sales organization with a qualified candidate pool.

Building a Strong Recruiting Toolkit

Two key principles for recruiting success must be remembered when developing the sales organization's recruiting toolkit:

1) Recruiting activity is a key driver for success. Research documents that higher ratios of "hires" to "screens" yields stronger qualified candidate pools and higher satisfaction among sales organization leaders. A ratio of one hire out of twenty interviewees yields much stronger results and helps the sales leader get better sales talent than typically does a ratio of one hire out of twelve interviewees. The quality of the recruiting toolkit definitely impacts how large these ratios should be. Casting a larger recruiting net and using a larger proportion of "cold recruiting sources" suggests that an even higher ratio (e.g., 1:50) might be needed.

2) The quality of the recruiting toolkit must be regularly evaluated. One of the most meaningful approaches to this process is to track

---

BREAK BOX: Envisioning and Creating

What practices in this section appear to be counter to current practice—personally and/or organizationally? Identify here the practices that relate to where the sales unit/organization might go in the future.

_____

_____

_____

_____

---

every candidate and to identify the recruiting source associated with every candidate. Tally the total number of prospective candidates identified through each recruiting source, the number of hires for each source, the financial expenditures associated with managing each source, and employee time spent in managing each source. To truly build a stronger recruiting toolkit, sales managers must capture the relevant data that allows them to assess, on a cost-benefit basis, the actual data associated with each recruiting source.

Selecting the Best Sales Talent

Establishing a Standardized Selection Process

Instituting a standardized selection process encourages the sales organization to treat all prospective candidates in a similar manner. Ensuring all candidates receive fair and equal treatment through the selection process is necessary to guard against the development of discriminatory hiring practices.

Connecting the Ideal Sales Candidate Profile and the Selection Process

The key purpose of the selection process is to ensure that the sales organization selects the candidate(s) most closely matching the ideal sales candidate profile. To do so means that the sales organization must "connect" each aspect of the ideal CP to specific decisions in the selection process. Research suggests that each profile characteristic should be assessed by more than one selection tool during the selection process to triangulate the assessment on each profile characteristic. Some selection tools to consider building into the selection process include:

- Individual interviews with:
  - Sales organization leader
  - Sales manager
  - Sales representatives
  - Human resources personnel
  - Others in the sales organization (trainer, sales support, etc.)
- Panel interviews (including one or more of the above parties)
- Selection tests delivered via:
  - Interactive voice response systems (telephone-based)
  - Web or Internet
  - Paper
- Assessment center
  - Exercises
  - Simulations
- Application form
- Reference checks
- Credit checks
- Job sampling activities
- Physical examinations
- Drug testing

If the ideal sales candidate profile includes the characteristics that were noted above, the selection process might be linked to those characteristics as shown in Exhibit 7.5.

High performance sales organizations build a "flow" of resumes in cycles so they can manage the selection and hiring process on a cycle. The ultimate goal is to hire the targeted number of new sales representatives to begin their training program with a class of new representatives. Industry research comparing high performance sales organizations to their less successful counterparts suggests that involving multiple parties in the interview process and focusing on the prospective candidate's "fit" improves the outcomes of the selection process.

The Issue of Fit

Focusing on the candidate's fit to the career, to the company, to others in the sales unit and to the culture must all be assessed in addition to reviewing the candidate's ability to do the job and his/her match to the ideal sales candidate profile.

Exhibit 7.5   Linking Ideal Sales Candidate Profile Characteristics to the Selection Process

Ideal Sales Candidate Profile Characteristic	Selection Tools Used to Assess Profile Characteristic
Listening Skills	Individual interviews with: Sales representatives Human resources personnel Others in the sales organization (trainer, sales support, etc.)
Follow-up Skills	Assessment center exercises or simulations Application form (previous sales- or service-related work)
Adaptable Communication/ Social Style	Panel interviews (including several "layers" of personnel) Selection test on social style
Organizational Skills	Application form Reference checks
Verbal Communication Skills	Individual interviews with internal parties Job sampling activities
Written Communication Skills	Assessment center exercises or simulations Application form
Proficiency in Social Connections Across "Levels"	Panel interview in a social setting (e.g., over a meal) Selection tests
Able to Overcome Objections	Individual interviews with trainer (including role play exercise) Assessment center simulation Job sampling activities
Closing Skills	Individual interviews Assessment center exercise
Tenacity and Persistency	Reference checks Job sampling activities
Time Management/Planning	Reference checks Job sampling activities

© Thomson

To ensure that the candidate fits the career, sales managers must provide a realistic job preview during the selection process. Some sales leaders describe this process as introducing "the good, the bad, and the ugly" about the job and the career. Very early in the selection process, the prospective candidate needs to learn how much overnight travel, conferences and trade shows, evening entertainment, and so on, that the sales position involves. The selection process must introduce this information very early on so candidates can choose to opt out early if the position and career isn't a good fit. Otherwise, the selection process becomes costly for the prospective candidate and for the sales organization.

Also during the selection process, the sales organization and the candidate must assess the candidate's fit to the sales organization. To ensure that the candidate is choosing the "right" sales organization, high performance sales managers encourage their prospective candidates to compare multiple sales organizations across an industry. Assuming that the industry selection is on target, the sales manager really must encourage the prospective candidate to invest the time and gather additional data for making the right choice. Sales organizations having a comprehensive selection process signal to the prospective candidate that "this organization is concerned about fit issues." That signal bodes well for the sales organization, even if the organization is operating as a new company.

Fit issues are also important relative to others in the field sales unit and to the sales unit's culture. To determine if prospective candidates will fit with others in the sales unit, the standardized selection process might include interviews with peer sales associates who are purposed with assessing this fit dimension. Sales managers may also find that interviews with others from the sales unit may bear additional fruit down the road. Early connections between current sales representatives and prospective sales representatives can build interconnections leading to informal mentoring relationships which can support new representative on-boarding and training.

If the sales manager takes time in the selection process to discuss the sales unit's and sales organization's history, the prospective sales candidate will have a better understanding of where the organization and the unit have been. Likewise, using interactions with prospective sales representatives to share the sales manager's vision for the unit's or organization's future also provides an opportunity to signal this important information to the prospective sales representative. If the vision does not reflect the kind of organization with which the candidate wants to be associated, it is better for all parties to learn that fact up front, before either party has made a commitment to one another.

Ordering the Selection Tools: Creating a Selection Process Flow

The selection tools used to assess each candidate relative to the ideal candidate profile must be arranged into an ordered fashion. The order of the process should allow the sales organization and the candidate to access the right information at the right time. Early in the process, the organization needs to provide the candidate with enough information so the candidate can begin a self-selection process. At the same time, the sales organization should guard against using time-intensive methods, such as panel interviews, very early in the selection process.

Research contrasting more productive and less productive sales organizations reveals that more productive sales organizations focus on the issue of fit in the selection process. In addition, more productive sales organizations allow themselves the opportunity to stop the selection process with a candidate, even after investing considerable time with that candidate. Less productive sales organizations are less likely to attend to the issue of fit, and they are less likely to allow themselves to stop the selection process with a candidate once the candidate has demonstrated the ability to do the job. Exhibit 7.6 provides an illustration of how the goal-based processes differ across the more and less productive sales units.

Sales managers (or their designates responsible for the selection process) need to develop an assessment form that captures the assessments made at the various steps of the selection process (information gathered from the various selection tools). Such a form, as shown in Exhibit 7.7, should be part of the selection tracking system that is used for all candidates.

Exhibit 7.6   A Goal-Based Selection Process

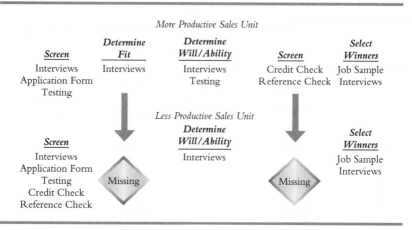

© Thomson

Exhibit 7.7 Example: Selection Rating Sheet

Selection Tool	Profile Characteristic (Behavioral Indicator)	Rating 0–10
Application Form	Organizational skills (Previous position)	_____
	Written Communication skills (Application essay)	_____
	Follow-up skills (Previous sales/service position)	_____
Interviews with Sales Associates	Fit to organizational culture (Personality; citizenship assessment)	_____
	Fit to sales position (Describe details of position and note reactions)	_____
	Listening skills (Assess linking questions to comments)	_____
	Verbal Communication skills (Persuasiveness and clarity)	_____
Testing	Social style/adaptability (Validated test of social styles: test score 0–100)	_____
	Aptitude (Cognitive intelligence test : test score 0–100)	_____
Reference Checks	Organizational skills (Direct question of reference)	_____
	Tenacity and Persistency (Direct question of reference)	_____
Job Sampling Activities	Verbal communication skills (Feedback from ride-along with current sales representative)	_____
	Overcoming objections (Feedback from ride-along with current sales representative)	_____
	Time management/planning (Timely completion of job sampling activities)	_____
Overall Score		_____

© Thomson

BREAK BOX: Envisioning and Creating

What practices in this section appear to be counter to current practice—personally and/or organizationally? Identify here the practices that relate to where the sales unit/organization might go in the future.

_____

_____

_____

_____

Developing and Keeping the Best Sales Talent

To help new sales associates get off to a fast start, the sales manager must work purposefully to assimilate the representatives into the sales organization's culture. The goals associated with this process are to ensure that:

1) New sales associates are connected into the organization so they receive the information and support needed to be successful.
2) New sales associates experience personal support so they feel they individually matter to the organization.
3) New sales associates understand exactly what is expected of them.

Purposeful Assimilation Process

Sales managers must purposefully plan to assimilate new sales associates into the organization. Networks and relationships with experienced sales associates serve new sales associates well in providing just-in-time information when learning is occurring at an accelerated pace. To facilitate the building of these important relationships and networks, sales managers purposefully weave social rituals, such as new sales associates introduction lunches, into the landscape of their sales organizations. In these social settings, seasoned sales associates share with new recruits their stories of what it was like when they started and the fact that they too were overwhelmed when they started in the sales role. Hearing that others experienced this similar struggle, new sales associates gain confidence that their experience is "normal" and that they too can expect to become successful.

Training Presented in Manageable "Chunks"

Rather than try to teach everything at once, initial training programs must focus on the most important "chunks" for new sales associates. What those "chunks" are will depend on the ideal sales candidate profile. If new associates are actually experienced sales representatives, the initial training will likely focus more on sales support systems and product knowledge. For new associates lacking sales experience, initial training is likely to focus on the sales process itself.

In either scenario, to keep the best sales talent, sales managers must battle the natural tendency to make initial training so comprehensive that the new sales associates feel like they just drank from a raging fire hose. More effective sales managers focus initial training on small "chunks" of information, provide an intense or deep dive on those chunks, and incorporate repetition to ensure that the important information chunks are truly learned.

Link Rewards to Behaviors

As new sales associates begin to build their track record with the sales organization, sales managers must find relevant ways to reinforce or encourage desired behaviors. Sales results may not be immediately evident for new sales associates; therefore, specific behaviors likely to lead to desired sales results must be applauded and rewarded. Personal recognition—from handwritten notes to public announcements—can be used to encourage the new sales associates to continue desired behaviors. Sales managers must purposefully define the intervening behaviors that lead to sales results and reward new associates for using and demonstrating such behaviors.

Psychosocial Support

To retain productive new sales talent, the sales manager must ensure that new sales associates receive adequate psychological and social (psychosocial) support to help them through the difficult start-up period associated with a new sales position. The day-to-day interactions that new sales representatives have with their immediate supervisors must establish trust and demonstrate the organization's concern for the new associates. Through a very purposeful relationship-building process, sales supervisors can actively express their faith in the new sales associates. It is powerful for a new sales associate to hear the sales manager express great confidence in the associate's ability to succeed in the role on behalf of the company.

Sales managers in exemplary sales organizations systematize their own behaviors to ensure that this psychosocial support happens purposefully and not by accident. In one organization, new sales associates receive weekly informal contact from their sales manager. Some weeks, this supervisor sends individual e-mails to each associate with a non-business, supportive message. Other times, telephone contact and voice mail are leveraged to build a psychosocial connection. In meetings of the sales management team, high-performance sales supervisors will enlist the support of others on the leadership team to ensure that all new associates receive a personal touch on a regular basis.

The development of a strong, purposeful psychosocial support network in a sales organization can be facilitated through the encouragement of informal mentoring and the designation of formal mentoring and training partnerships. Research on mentoring suggests that informal mentoring relationships yield stronger results; however, waiting for such relationships to occur naturally is not always palatable for results-focused sales managers. Identifying the strong, experienced sales representatives to serve as role models for the more inexperienced sales associates is the first step in developing a mentoring culture, which is often described as a collegial culture. Sales managers who are successful in developing such a culture find ways to promote the right role models to the new associates: using the right role models in training programs, introducing the right role models during sales team meetings, and highlighting the experiences of these right role models through internal communications program (e.g., e-newsletters). Building a culture of sharing and helping one another can also be facilitated by encouraging all new sales associates to work with multiple experienced associates during their first two years in the sales organization. Reporting mechanisms for such teamwork can be included in performance evaluation processes, as intentional behaviors typically occur with regularity when they are measured.

Keeping the Best Sales Talent: The "Moose on the Table"

Sales managers in high performance organizations are willing to talk about that "moose" which less effective managers are unable to voice aloud. Strong sales supervisors tell their associates that feelings of frustration coupled with the sales role are normal. It is also quite normal to experience the desire to quit multiple times throughout one's sales career. A professional sales role can be quite rewarding, but frustration comes with the role. High-performance sales managers recognize that there is a sequence of events that lead up to a sales associate's decision to quit and such supervisors work hard to counter the desire to terminate, before it's too late.

Before the sales associate makes the decision to quit, he goes through several stages in which intervention by the sales manager can make a difference. A visual representation of the termination stage process is shown in Exhibit 7.8. Notice in Exhibit 7.8 that the formal notice to quit comes at stage four, so an observant sales manager has time and cues to help him/her retain the best sales talent.

Exhibit 7.8   The Termination Stage Process

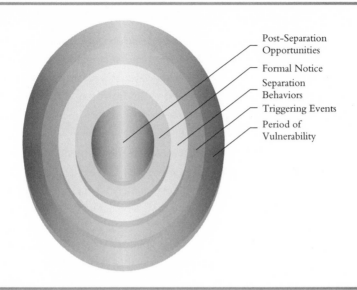

Post-Separation
Opportunities

Formal Notice

Separation
Behaviors

Triggering Events

Period of
Vulnerability

© Thomson

Obviously, a period of vulnerability can occur when a sales associate does not achieve the results that he sets as a goal. However, it is oftentimes less obvious to sales managers that even top-producing sales associates—those achieving all goals and quotas—may be going through a period of vulnerability. Feeling unappreciated by the leadership and the organization can also prompt a period of vulnerability. Receiving less recognition than expected, having lower symbols of status (office size, location, etc.), and even experiencing longer period of status quo (no change) can spark this type of vulnerability. The good news is that sales associates are typically somewhat verbal about these feelings; sales managers must work to distinguish between general complainers and those truly experiencing discontent that can lead to stage two: susceptibility to triggering events.

When the sales associate stops complaining, he has probably experienced a triggering event and moved toward the cognitive thought, "I have to consider leaving." Trigger events can be personal in nature (death, divorce, etc.) or professional (another sales associate leaves the organization or there is a change in the organization's management). Research suggests that effective sales managers use these triggering events to reconnect with associates and to stop the migration toward termination.

If the sales manager fails to address the trigger events and/or the sales associate's potential to quit (this is akin to the euphemism of not talking about something as large as a moose lying across one's table), the sales associate may move toward engaging in separation behaviors. Since most sales positions have some type of variable compensation associated with the role, sales associates planning to quit may prepare their affairs for several months to a year to ensure that they have maximized their financial opportunity. This is probably the most difficult stage to respond to as a sales associate at this point no longer discusses aloud the idea of quitting. Representatives at this stage may be developing personal copies of customer files and creating bridges to other opportunities in similar organizations.

Once the sales associate is prepared to terminate, he formally submits the resignation paperwork, often taking the sales manager by surprise (since the sales associate has been somewhat quiet of late about leaving). A counter-offer may possibly save the relationship but a counter-offer may not be accepted. The mental separation process has been building for a long time and a reactive move is not always viewed positively. However, the sales manager should keep a positive mindset even at this stage of the process. It is not uncommon for a sales associate to see his/her new position less favorably after a period of time. By retaining a positive relationship with the sales associate who chose to terminate, sales managers often have access to experienced talent with proven track records.

The role of sales managers in the process of keeping the best sales talent is multifaceted. Those leading the sales organization or a sales unit must provide important:

- instrumental support—helping associates achieve their professional goals through formal and informal training, relationships, and information sharing
- psychosocial support—creating meaningful connections to the sales representatives' emotional landscape in the work environment
- sales and service support—ensuring that support personnel are trained to be efficient and effective so they are truly supportive of the sales representatives' efforts
- problem-solving support—serving as a primary go-to person who can get things done on behalf of the sales organization
- recognition—building on the understanding that sales representatives (like other professionals) work for more than just the money

Such supports, on the surface, appear to be quite simple. Doing the right simple things every day lays the foundation for the sales manager to keep the

---

BREAK BOX: Envisioning and Creating

What practices in this section appear to be counter to current practice—personally and/or organizationally? Identify here the practices that relate to where the sales unit/organization might go in the future.

_____

_____

_____

_____

---

best sales talent. However, doing what is simple—on a regular basis—isn't always easy. Sales managers need to build systems of reminders to support their own efforts in this area.

Conclusions and BREAKthrough Directions

The critical work that a sales manager must do in getting the best sales talent hinges upon the ideal sales candidate profile. Yet, many sales managers fail to think critically about whom they are hiring now or whom they should be hiring in the future. Getting the best sales talent truly requires defining exactly what that talent looks like. Then, leaders of the sales function must strategically build a recruiting toolkit incorporating several recruiting sources. Establishing a tracking system to gauge the effectiveness of each source is another important step on the road to getting the best sales talent.

The ideal sales candidate profile also serves as the foundation for building a standardized selection process. Each profile characteristic must be linked to at least two selection tools that are organized into a logical system. One of the important goals that must be accomplished through the selection system is to assess the prospective sales candidate's fit to the career, to the company, to others in the sales unit and to the culture. Without ensuring good fit, the sales manager's ability to keep the best sales talent can be thwarted.

Keeping the best sales talent requires purposeful assimilation of new sales associates into the sales organization, and developing an initial training program that breaks down the learning process into meaningful chunks. Again, the ideal sales candidate profile will determine what the focus of the initial training ought to be to ensure that a firm's sales candidates are best prepared for success. Since sales success is not immediate in many sales roles, it is

---

BREAK BOX: Envisioning and Creating

Identify a key priority for action in each of the following areas:

1. Developing or changing the ideal sales candidate profile
2. Building a more effective recruiting toolkit
3. Aligning the selection system to match important qualities from the ideal sales candidate profile
4. Developing and keeping the best sales talent

---

important that sales managers identify and reward the intervening behaviors that lead to sales success. New associates need the positive feedback concerning such behaviors to encourage them to continue to produce the behaviors in the future.

Regardless of where the best sales talent lies (e.g., in the new organization or among existing sales representatives), the sales supervisor must provide adequate psychosocial support to ensure that the organization keeps the best sales talent. High-performance sales people are motivated by more than money and the sales manager is responsible for attending to the emotional landscape and crafting a purposeful culture for the sales organization.

Smart sales managers recognize that keeping the best sales talent may require them to discuss an important issue with their salesforce: the normal desire to consider quitting the role or leaving the company. Creating an open environment in which the supervisor acknowledges a sales representative who may be experiencing a period of vulnerability or trigger event will help diffuse the power of issues when they remain unspoken. BREAK-through thinking may require a sales leader to mention "the moose on the table," in order to get the idea of quitting off a leading salesperson's mind.

Visit The Sales Educators Web site for further BREAK process materials on this chapter's topics. www.TheSalesEducators.com

---

References and Suggested Readings

Dixon, A., C. Walsh, L. Forbes, and J. Gassenheimer (2003). *Systems for Success: Building the Right People.* Washington, D.C.: The GAMA Foundation.

Dixon, A., B. Robertson, S. Schertzer, and C. Walsh (2003). *Systems for Success: Keeping the Right People.* Washington, D.C.: The GAMA Foundation.

Dixon, A., F. Acito, S. MacKenzie and P. Podsakoff (1995), *A Study of Agency Recruiting & Selection Practices,* Washington, D.C.: The GAMA Foundation.

Marshall, G., W. Moncrief, and F. Lassk (1999), "The Current State of Sales Force Activities," *Industrial Marketing Management,* Vol. 28, No. 1 (January), 87–95.

Moncrief, W. (1986), "Selling Activity and Sales Position Taxonomies for Industrial Salesforces," *Journal of Marketing Research,* (August), 261-70.

CHAPTER 8

ENCOURAGING SALES ORGANIZATION TEAMWORK

Introduction

The Los Angeles Lakers had the "best talent" in the NBA. Shaquille O'Neal, Kobe Bryant, Gary Payton, and Karl Malone were current stars and future Hall-of-Famers. The Detroit Pistons had some good players, but not even one player as talented as the Laker stars. Despite their talent advantage, the Lakers lost the 2004 NBA Championship Series to the Pistons 4-1, and the Lakers were lucky to win one game. How could a team with a tremendous talent advantage perform at such a low level?

The basic reason is that the Lakers did not play as a team, and the Pistons exhibited exceptional teamwork throughout the series. Less talented players beat more talented players because success in basketball requires teamwork. The Pistons had it and the Lakers did not. Larry Brown, the Detroit Pistons coach, did a masterful job of creating an environment in which teamwork flourished to produce a dramatic result: an unlikely NBA Championship.

Interestingly, Larry Brown also coached the 2004 USA Olympic basketball team. This team did not have the "best talent," because many of the top NBA players decided not to play in the Olympics. The team did, however, have many good players. Unfortunately, this Olympic team did not play well as a team. This "good talent" and lack of teamwork resulted in a bronze medal and the most losses ever for any USA Olympic basketball team. Although Larry Brown worked hard to create a teamwork environment, the players did not exhibit effective teamwork except in isolated instances. The result was unexpected poor performance at the 2004 Olympics.

It is easy to illustrate the importance of teamwork with examples from team sports. However, even so-called individual sports typically require effective teamwork for success. Take Lance Armstrong as an example. He has won seven consecutive Tour de France races. Although we only see him cycling during a race, he is backed by a team and could not have achieved the success he has without the help of his team.

Just as in sports, teamwork is important to most sales organizations. Typically, salespeople have operated rather independently. It is, however, becoming increasingly difficult for one salesperson to have all of the knowledge and skills needed to meet the complex needs of customers in an effective and efficient manner. Teamwork with other salespeople, sales managers, other business functions or business units, or various selling partners is necessary for success. Just as Lance Armstrong cannot be successful by himself, salespeople need to work effectively with others to be successful. Creating effective teamwork can produce dramatic sales organization results.

Because of the increasing need for teamwork, many sales organizations are establishing formal sales teams of different types. Salespeople and others become "official" members of a specific team with different individuals normally assigned different roles. The purpose of creating formal sales teams is to emphasize the need for teamwork. But, as evidenced by Larry Brown's experiences with the Detroit Pistons and the 2004 USA Olympic basketball team, merely assigning people to a formal sales team or referring to a group as a team does not ensure that effective teamwork will occur.

Producing effective teamwork is not easy. Effective teamwork cannot be mandated, but it is possible to establish an environment that promotes the desired teamwork. It often takes hard work over long time periods to achieve teamwork objectives. For example, Larry Brown was very successful with the Detroit Pistons, but unsuccessful with the 2004 USA Olympic basketball team. One reason for the different levels of success is likely the amount of time he had to work with the teams. He coached the Pistons for two basketball seasons before winning an NBA championship, but only had a few months to work with the Olympic basketball team.

The purpose of this chapter is to examine ways to encourage sales organization teamwork. Chapters 1 and 2 suggested the need for a collaborative sales force as a key element in an entrepreneurial sales organization. Developing and maintaining effective teamwork within a sales organization is a difficult task that requires the proper alignment of all sales management decisions. As discussed in Chapter 3, management activities have an important impact on sales organization teamwork. The types of teamwork required depend upon the customer relationship and the strategic account strategies being pursued by a sales organization. The different strategies have been addressed in Chapters 4 and 5. Compensation plans must also support teamwork as discussed in Chapter 6. The characteristics of salespeople hired can have an important impact on teamwork. This aspect was covered in Chapter 7. Although this chapter will include some material from these other chapters, the main focus is on sales leadership strategies and processes to encourage teamwork within a sales organization.

The chapter begins by discussing the different types of teamwork that might be needed in a sales organization. Then, the concept of social capital is

BREAK BOX: Becoming Aware

The first step in the BREAK process involves becoming aware of the types and current level of teamwork in your sales organization. The following questions are designed to help you assess different aspects of teamwork within your sales organization.

A) How important is teamwork in your sales organization?

1) Extremely important to the success of our sales organization
2)
3)
4) Of moderate importance to the success of our sales organization
5)
6)
7) Of very little importance to the success of our sales organization
Comments on why teamwork is or is not important to the success of your sales organization:

_____

_____

_____

_____

B) How important are formal sales teams to your sales organization?

1) Formal sales teams are extremely important to our sales organization
2)
3)
4) Formal sales teams are of moderate importance to our sales organization
5)
6)
7) We do not use formal sales teams in our sales organization
Comments on the use of formal sales teams in your sales organization:

_____

_____

_____

_____

Continued

C) How important is informal sales teamwork in your sales organization?

  1) Informal sales teamwork is extremely important to our sales organization

  2)

  3)

  4) Informal sales teamwork is of moderate importance to our sales organization

  5)

  6)

  7) Informal sales teamwork is of limited importance to our sales organization

  Comments on the importance of informal sales teamwork to your sales organization:

  _____

  _____

  _____

  _____

D) How satisfied are you with the current level of teamwork in your sales organization?

  1) Extremely satisfied with the level of teamwork in our sales organization

  2)

  3)

  4) Moderately satisfied with the level of teamwork in our sales organization

  5)

  6)

  7) Very dissatisfied with the level of teamwork in our sales organization

  Comments on your satisfaction with the level of teamwork in your sales organization:

  _____

  _____

  _____

  _____

Continued

E) How would you assess the efforts of sales management to build teamwork in your sales organization?

1) Sales management spends a great deal of time and effort in trying to build teamwork in our sales organization

2)

3)

4) Sales management spends some time and effort on building teamwork in our sales organization

5)

6)

7) Sales management spends very little time and effort on building teamwork in our sales organization

Comments on the time and effort sales management spends on building teamwork in your sales organization:

_____

_____

_____

_____

---

suggested as a framework for understanding teamwork. Strategies for building effective social networks in sales organization are identified and examined. The chapter concludes by presenting a process for assessing the impact of various sales management decisions on teamwork and for proactively creating an environment to promote teamwork within a sales organization.

The Importance of Different Types of Teamwork

The importance of teamwork and the need for different types of teamwork depend upon many factors. Of particular importance are the sales strategies being employed and the structure of the sales organization. As discussed in Chapters 4 and 5, different customer relationship and strategic account strategies require different types of teamwork. Effectively implementing these strategies typically requires changes in sales organization structure. The sales organization structure defines the formal teamwork expected, but informal teamwork may also be necessary. The key point is that different sales organization structures impact the types of teamwork needed. For

Exhibit 8.1   Different Types of Sales Teamwork

	Formal	Informal
Within Sales Organization	• Functional sales teams • Salesperson teams	• Field sales manager and sales team • Teamwork across sales function
Outside Sales Organization	• Cross-functional sales teams • Cross-business unit sales teams	• Selling centers • Teamwork across sales channels • Teamwork with selling partners

© Thomson

example, many sales organizations are moving from a product-specialized sales organization structure to one specializing on vertical markets or customers. Salespeople become market and customer experts instead of being product specialists. Although these salespeople develop a deeper understanding of market and customer needs, they typically have to work effectively with others inside and outside the sales organization for the product and technical expertise needed to meet customer needs.

A useful way to view different types of sales organization teamwork is presented in Exhibit 8.1. This figure classifies teamwork according to whether formal teams are created or informal teamwork is required, and whether the focus is on teamwork within or outside the sales organization. Each quadrant in this table represents a different type of teamwork challenge for sales organizations.

Formal Sales Teams

The most obvious need for teamwork is when formal teams are established. Formal teams within the sales organization might be functional sales teams or salesperson teams. Functional sales teams consist of different sales organization members performing different sales functions. This could be teams of telemarketers to perform prospecting activities and field salespeople to call on prospects and close sales. Or, it might be salesperson teams where each salesperson only performs specific sales functions. For example, an IT outsourcing firm creates three-person sales teams to meet the needs of its customers. One salesperson focuses on prospecting, another on meeting with clients to identify needs and develop proposals, and the other salesperson to close the sale. Previously, salespeople worked independently and performed all selling activities. The new approach has produced more sales and shortened the sales cycle significantly.

Salesperson teams can also be used as a way to capitalize on the different personalities and strengths of different salespeople. The salespeople are not assigned specific functions to perform, but work together in a variety of ways to meet the needs of different customers. An insurance company uses this approach when calling on small and medium-sized companies. Salespeople are organized into two-person teams when calling on these accounts. The purpose of these teams is for the salespeople to support each other and to capitalize on different strengths with different customers. The activities performed by each salesperson depend upon the unique situation of each customer and the capabilities of each salesperson. Larger, more structured sales teams are used to serve the firm's large accounts.

Formal teams outside the sales organization can be characterized as cross-functional and cross-business unit sales teams. These teams include members from different business functions and/or business units. National account management (NAM), strategic account management (SAM), and global account management (GAM) teams fall in this category. For example, a large, multi-division industrial manufacturer established a GAM program for one of its large accounts. The complete GAM team consisted of 9 key people at headquarters, 4-10 people from each of the 15 company divisions involved, and 3-6 sales engineers and key account managers in each country. The GAM team had a matrix structure and required extensive teamwork across divisions and countries. Because the GAM team worked together effectively, sales to this large account increased tenfold.

Informal Sales Teamwork

Teamwork within the sales organization is often important even though formal sales teams might not be designated. This could include teamwork by salespeople. For example, the salespeople from a building company sell independently and only come to the office for short meetings three times a week. Nevertheless, teamwork is important in this sales organization. The salespeople support each other by sharing selling ideas and acknowledging the accomplishments of others. The concept of teamwork is reinforced by putting salespeople into "teams" to compete against other "teams" in sales contests. Different "teams" are created for each sales contest as a way to encourage teamwork among all salespeople.

Although field sales managers often refer to their assigned salespeople as a team, this is often an informal sales team. The purpose of this organization is more for sales management span of control reasons and less for the salespeople to work together as a team. However, teamwork among the salespeople and with the field sales manager can be very effective and can be encouraged. For example, the sales manager for a business-to-business telecommunications firm established an environment that fostered teamwork among the eight sales reps and himself. He created a friendly, positive environment and encouraged teamwork at team meetings, training sessions, and conference calls. Salespeople responded by willingly sharing information, challenges, and success stories. This teamwork has helped improve the performance of individual salespeople and the sales unit.

Teamwork outside the sales organization can be critical to meeting the needs of customers. The salesperson is typically the contact point for customers, but cannot normally perform all of the activities required to serve customers well. Thus, the salesperson must be able to "orchestrate" all sales organization resources to meet specific customer needs. This might be in the form of a selling center where individuals outside the sales organization are brought in at different points in the sales process to close a sale. For example, an employee benefits outsourcing company emphasizes teamwork among its salespeople, but also teamwork between sales and operations. The salespeople sell the services and then pass the baton to operations to provide the services. This requires effective coordination and consistent communication among both groups.

Since many firms employ multiple sales channel strategies, teamwork across these sales channels is critical. For example, consider a financial services firm selling a variety of financial products using three different sales channels. The customer selects the desired sales channel, so the firm must have teamwork across the sales channels to meet the complete financial needs of the customer. The sales compensation program must be designed to support teamwork, but other strategies for encouraging teamwork are also needed. Conference calls, meetings, and training programs that include salespeople from all of the sales channels are the types of activities that can encourage teamwork among the different sales channels.

Sometimes, the sales channels include selling partners that are independent entities outside the sales organization and firm. This makes building teamwork more challenging, but also provides opportunities for innovative approaches. For example, a film manufacturer reduced the size of its sales force, but still needed to create teamwork with its independent dealers and resellers. The company developed separate extranets for its dealers and

---

BREAK BOX: Reviewing and Relating

The second step in the BREAK process is to review the material covered in this section and to identify specific ideas that relate to your sales organization. The following questions are designed to help you determine the most relevant ideas in this section:

1. Consider the discussion about the need for teamwork within sales organizations. Does this suggest any new ideas about teamwork in your sales organization?
2. Review the discussion and examples about formal sales teams and informal sales teamwork. Are there opportunities for different types of teamwork in your sales organization?
3. Examine the discussion and examples about teamwork inside and outside a sales organization. Could there be opportunities for more teamwork within or outside your sales organization?

---

resellers. These sites provide order forms, marketing materials, and other useful information. To increase teamwork between the sales rep and dealers/resellers the sites have a customized pop-up from the assigned salesperson. The pop-up includes a picture of the salesperson, contact information, and a personalized message from the salesperson. The reps and dealers/resellers can also communicate electronically about specific issues. This approach has increased teamwork between the sales reps and partners in a cost-effective way.

The need for teamwork is likely to increase in the future. Firms desiring to develop an entrepreneurial sales organization will need to encourage different types of collaboration to be successful. Determining the appropriate types of teamwork within and outside the sales organization to meet the needs of customers in a productive manner is a critical first step for sales managers. Once this is determined, sales managers need to decide on the proper blend of formal teams and informal teamwork for their particular sales organization and to focus concerted effort toward establishing the required teamwork.

Social Capital and Teamwork

Social capital is a concept that has been used by sociologists, economists, and political scientists to understand collaborative behavior in neighborhoods, communities, cities, regions, and nations. It has only recently been applied to organizational contexts. Although there are several different definitions, a useful definition of social capital from a sales organization perspective is:

> Sales organization social capital consists of 1) the number of active connections among people within and outside a sales organization; 2) the trust, mutual understanding, and shared values that bind these individuals and make cooperative action possible.

The first part of this definition is a quantitative dimension. In general, the more active connections established among the appropriate people, the greater the potential for developing social capital. Although some of these active connections might be formal based on a sales organization's structure and organizational chart, many are informal. These formal and informal connections are often referred to as a social network. Thus, the larger the social network, the more active connections, the more potential for the development of social capital, and the more likely collaborative action will take place.

The second part of this definition is qualitative. Even though larger social networks are typically better than smaller social networks, the quality of the connections within social networks is critical. High levels of trust, mutual understanding, and shared values within a social network encourage higher levels of collaboration and teamwork.

Based on this definition, the key to encouraging teamwork within a sales organization is to create large social networks with effective connections within the network. It is important for sales managers to address both quantitative and qualitative aspects of sales organization social capital. This framework is illustrated in Exhibit 8.2.

It is important to note that sales organization social capital is actually created in the day-to-day activities of the workplace. Sales managers cannot mandate the development of social capital, but can establish a supportive environment in which day-to-day activities build sales organization social capital over time. An interesting aspect of social capital is that its value appreciates over time. Sales organization social capital becomes more valuable as more is developed and used. This is in contrast to most physical capital that depreciates with usage.

We will now look at strategies sales managers can use to encourage social networks with effective connections. Although these strategies are presented in terms of building sales teamwork networks and strengthening sales teamwork network relationships, many of the strategies contribute to both areas. The strategies are based on a synthesis of sales research results and best practices from different sales organizations. As discussed in previous chapters, sales organization teamwork can be facilitated by hiring individuals who

Exhibit 8.2   Sales Teamwork Framework

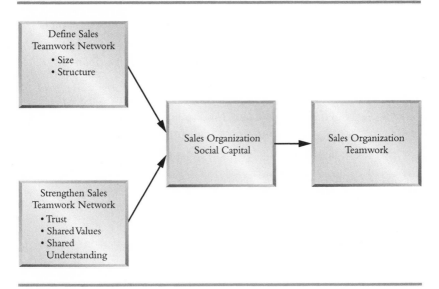

© Thomson

have cooperative personality characteristics and/or have exhibited cooperative behavior in the past (Chapter 7) and by developing compensation plans
that reward teamwork (Chapter 6). Hiring the right sales talent and aligning
compensation plans to reward teamwork are necessary, but not typically sufficient to ensure the desired level of sales organization teamwork.

Building Sales Teamwork Networks

The basic task facing sales managers is to create opportunities for all of the
people who need to work together to get to know each other well. This is
easier for formal teams, because the specific team members are known.
However, there may be individuals outside the formal team that need to be
included in the social network. The task is more difficult for informal teams.
Because there are no formal team members, sales managers need to identify
the key players that should be included within a social network. This can be
accomplished using a formal social network analytical procedure or sales
managers can try to identify the appropriate individuals based on their
knowledge of the sales organization situation. Once the appropriate team
network is identified, sales managers should provide formal and informal
opportunities for these individuals to interact on a regular basis. Several
strategies are presented in Exhibit 8.3.

Exhibit 8.3 Strategies for Building Sales Teamwork Networks

- Clearly delineate the important interdependencies among members of a sales teamwork network.
- Provide opportunities for sales teamwork network members to interact frequently in planned and formal settings.
- Provide opportunities for sales teamwork network members to interact frequently in unplanned and spontaneous informal settings.
- Create an information infrastructure that links all members of a sales teamwork network.

© Thomson

It is important that sales teamwork network members know their specific roles and how these roles fit together to achieve sales organization objectives. This is obviously easier in formal sales teams where specific roles are typically delineated. But, it is equally important in informal teamwork situations. Sales managers need to make sure that everyone knows what they need to do and how what they do is interrelated to what specific others do. In addition, the critical importance of coordination and cooperation to achieve sales organization goals must be emphasized. This might be accomplished by presenting examples of effective teamwork and acknowledging special teamwork efforts. Having sales teamwork network members attend the same training programs and spend time in different members' jobs can be effective in helping everyone understand how interdependent they are on each other to achieve sales organization objectives.

The strategies presented in Exhibit 8.3 include a mixture of formal and informal, and planned and spontaneous approaches for encouraging frequent interactions among those in a sales teamwork network. Person-to-person interactions are the preferred method, but this may be difficult and costly if there is geographic separation among the network. Electronic communication approaches can overcome these geographic barriers. The most effective approaches typically represent a blend of person-to-person interactions and various types of electronic communication. Also, informal, spontaneous interactions can be especially effective. So, sales managers should look for ways to increase the likelihood of informal, spontaneous interactions. This might include locating offices close together, having a convenient room for breaks and lunch, scheduling after-hours social activities with a limited formal program, or anything else that puts members of a sales teamwork network together for informal interactions.

Because of geographical separation and busy schedules, creating an information infrastructure can facilitate the interaction process. This can be very effective if integrated well with other opportunities for person-to-person interactions. Electronic communication tools such as e-mail distribution lists, Intranets, and various conferencing options should be considered. Making a list of sales teamwork network members with detailed contact information, areas of expertise, and preferred contact methods and times is often useful.

There is an opportunity for sales managers to develop creative and entrepreneurial approaches to bring the desired individuals together. For example, the sales manager of a technology company was concerned that many of the technical, sales, and marketing people, who needed to work together, did not know each other very well. She had all of them meet one morning at a public park. Multi-functional teams of 4-5 were created and sent on a scavenger hunt for three hours. The purpose of the scavenger hunt was discussed at lunch concluding the event. Since this event, the technical, sales, and marketing people have been interacting more often with many eating lunch together regularly.

Strengthening Sales Teamwork Network Relationships

Once a complete sales teamwork network has been identified, the critical task is to continuously strengthen the relationships among those in the network. Of particular importance is building trust and shared understanding and values within the network.

Trust is an important lubricant in all relationships. Although trust might be defined in a variety of ways, it is important to have a comprehensive definition that is used by everyone in the sales organization. A useful definition for our purposes defines trust as consisting of five different, but related, dimensions:

1. Consideration
2. Consistency
3. Competence
4. Candor
5. Compatibility

It is important to note that we are applying this definition to each relevant teamwork situation in the sales organization. Thus, members of a sales teamwork network need to develop trust among themselves that each member will work together to achieve sales organization objectives. Building trust within this context is of critical importance.

The consideration dimension represents an orientation toward the interests and well-being of others in the sales teamwork network. Everyone in the network needs to be oriented toward collaboration and not just self-interest. Consistency refers to being dependable. Network members must be able to depend on others to perform desired tasks in an expected way. Competence has to do with the knowledge, expertise, and capabilities of network members to complete assigned tasks effectively and efficiently. Candor involves being honest and open in communications among those in a sales teamwork network. Finally, compatibility is treating everyone in the network with respect and courtesy.

The critical task is to build trust throughout the sales teamwork network by focusing on each of these five dimensions. Sales managers need to support all of these dimensions and be a role model by exhibiting each dimension. They also need to provide opportunities for members of a sales teamwork network to implement these dimensions and should acknowledge and reward individuals for engaging in trust-building activities. The more often each of these dimensions is exhibited, the more trust, and the stronger the relationships within a sales teamwork network.

Creating shared understanding and values is critical for effective teamwork. Everyone within a sales teamwork network must be "on the same page." As discussed previously, the specific role of each member and the impact this role has on sales organization success needs to be understood by everyone. It is also important that the company and sales organization mission, vision, and objectives are communicated regularly and understood by everyone. Specific goals need to be established for each sales teamwork network and progress toward these goals communicated, celebrated, and rewarded.

Several strategies for strengthening sales teamwork network relationships are presented in Exhibit 8.4. These strategies focus on ways to build trust and shared understanding and values among those in a sales teamwork network.

The creation of a sales organization culture and climate that communicates teamwork and ethical and other values as norms is extremely important. The emphasis on a teamwork culture and climate needs to be evident during the first contact with potential employees and continually reinforced throughout the socialization of new employees. Initial orientation sessions should focus on

Exhibit 8.4   Strategies for Strengthening Sales Teamwork
Network Relationships

- Create a sales organization culture that consistently communicates the importance of teamwork in the sales organization.
- Continuously communicate the ethical and other key values of the sales organization.
- Incorporate members of a sales teamwork network into the decision-making process and empower them to make as many decisions as possible.
- Employ a transformational leadership style to increase job satisfaction and encourage commitment to the sales organization.
- Establish attractive careers paths for employees and promote from within the sales organization.
- Emphasize a teamwork orientation throughout the sales organization socialization process.
- Perform employee satisfaction evaluations on a regular basis and communicate the results and any changes made due to the evaluations.
- Engage in innovative team-building exercises.

© Thomson

the company and sales organization values with the emphasis on teamwork highlighted. Stories about effective sales organization teamwork throughout the history of the company can be especially effective.

A transformational leadership style is also important. Sales managers need to incorporate sales teamwork network members into the decision-making process and empower them as much as possible. A focus on professional development, attractive career paths, and promotion from within can help strengthen sales teamwork network relationships. It is also important to conduct regular employee satisfaction evaluations within the sales organization and to communicate the results and to make changes based on these results. This leadership approach is likely to increase job satisfaction and commitment to the sales organization. Those committed to the sales organization will be more willing to help others and will more often put the needs of the sales organization above their own personal benefit. This type of sales organization culture and climate produces an environment in which teamwork is encouraged.

The use of specific team-building exercises can be very effective. However, if these exercises are isolated events, and not backed by many other strategies for encouraging teamwork, they can be viewed as hypocritical and generate more cynicism than teamwork. On the other hand, if sales managers create a supportive teamwork environment, well-designed team-building exercises can have a positive effect. The most effective exercises tend to be those that engage individuals in a variety of different tasks together to produce important results. And, the more fun in doing this the better.

An innovative example is a cooking program offered by one firm. Salespeople are randomly assigned to one of four groups and prepare one course of a gourmet meal with the help of a personal chef. During the hours of this activity, salespeople work as teams in taking risks, dealing with limited resources, building trust, solving problems, setting priorities, and meeting deadlines. Everyone works together for the purpose of producing a wonderful meal that everyone can enjoy with each other. There is a debriefing at the end of the activity to identify how they can apply what they learned in their sales organization.

BREAK BOX: Reviewing and Relating

The second step in the BREAK process is to review the material covered in this section and to identify specific ideas that relate to your sales organization. The following questions are designed to help you determine the most relevant ideas in this section:

1. Reread the definition of sales organization social capital. Does this definition generate any ideas for your sales organization?
2. Consider the concept of sales teamwork networks. Have you ever thought about teamwork in terms of social networks? How could viewing teamwork in terms of sales teamwork networks help you identify all of the individuals who need to work together for your sales organization to produce BREAKthrough results?
3. Review the five dimensions of trust. Can you identify ways to encourage each of these dimensions to build trust within your sales teamwork networks?
4. Think about shared values. What opportunities can you identify to instill shared values throughout your sales teamwork networks?

Sales Organization Teamwork Processes

The creation of an appropriate sales teamwork network is a difficult task. The type of network needed depends upon the situation of a specific sales organization. This can be viewed from two different perspectives. First, it is important that sales managers consider the impact of various decisions on the level of teamwork that exists within a sales organization. Sometimes, sales managers can inadvertently reduce existing teamwork without realizing it. Second, there are often times when sales managers want to proactively build teamwork within a sales organization. This situation calls for a specific approach for encouraging more teamwork. Processes for addressing both of these situations are presented and discussed.

Sales Management Decisions and Teamwork Process

This situation might be considered the "do no harm" approach. Seemingly effective sales management decisions might negatively affect sales organization teamwork, if the impact of these decisions on teamwork is not directly considered in the decision-making process. For example, downsizing and reengineering the sales organization can promise significant cost reductions in the short run, but both can have a negative impact on sales organization teamwork by removing links in a sales teamwork network and weakening relationships within the remaining network. Sales managers should consider the expected benefits from any major decision and the potential impact on sales organization teamwork. A process for explicitly incorporating teamwork considerations into all sales management decisions is presented in Exhibit 8.5.

The first step in the process is to assess the current level of teamwork within the sales organization. Is teamwork currently about where it should be, better than normal, or lower than needed? This is a general evaluation to provide a baseline for the rest of the process. Then, the different sales management decision alternatives should be identified and assessed using the normal criteria and the best alternative selected.

The final step is to evaluate the impact of this decision on the existing level of teamwork within the sales organization. Two key questions should be answered:

1. What impact will this decision have on the size and structure of the sales teamwork network?
2. What impact will this decision have on the strength of the relationships within the sales teamwork network?

Exhibit 8.5 Sales Management Decisions and Teamwork Process

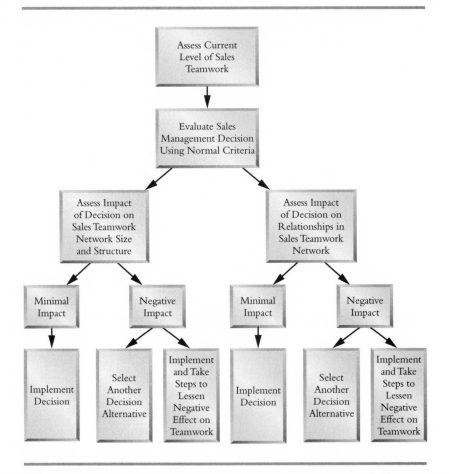

© Thomson

If the answers to these two questions indicate that the decision will not have an adverse effect on the sales teamwork network, then this is likely the best decision. However, if this analysis indicates an unacceptably negative effect on existing teamwork, two options should be considered. First, it might be best to select another decision alternative that offers the best balance in achieving the objectives of the decision and maintaining the desired level of sales organization teamwork. Alternatively, the best decision alternative might be implemented, but specific steps taken to lessen the negative impact on teamwork. This could be accomplished by implementing proactive measures to build sales organization teamwork simultaneously with implementing the sales management decision.

An example illustrates the value of this process. Many sales organizations have significantly reduced or eliminated office space for salespeople as a way to reduce expenditures and to encourage salespeople to spend more time in the field. When this decision is viewed entirely from a cost standpoint, it is normally easy to identify large cost savings from using much less office space. However, if the effect of this decision on teamwork is considered, the cost savings are likely to be offset to some extent by the potential negative impact on teamwork. If sales managers incorporate the effect on teamwork into the decision process as depicted in Exhibit 8.5, the final decision may be somewhat different than the original one. One possibility is that the negative impact on teamwork is viewed to be more detrimental than the cost savings and the office space is maintained. Another possibility is that less office space is eliminated to balance the cost savings and teamwork issues. A final possibility is that office space reduction decision is implemented, but in conjunction with proactive approaches for encouraging teamwork in the new situation of limited office space. The net effect of this process should be a decision that is best for the sales organization.

Many sales managers do not explicitly incorporate the potential impact of various decisions on sales organization teamwork. This can lead to unintended, negative effects on sales organization teamwork. Sometimes, these negative teamwork effects could be worse for the overall sales organization than the expected benefits from the new decision. Employing the process in Exhibit 8.5 will help ensure that this does not occur by directly integrating sales organization teamwork issues into the decision-making process.

Building Sales Organization Teamwork Process

Proactively building sales organization teamwork can be best accomplished by following a process similar to that presented in Exhibit 8.6. This process requires a sales manager to consider the critical areas in developing an effective sales teamwork network and builds on previous discussion in this chapter.

The first step is to identify the type of teamwork that is needed. The basic alternatives within the context of formal teamwork and informal teamwork, inside and outside the sales organization, are illustrated in Exhibit 8.1 and discussed earlier in this chapter. One approach for determining the appropriate teamwork type of teamwork is to use the Sales Teamwork Network Matrix presented in Exhibit 8.7. This matrix makes it possible to identify the types of

Exhibit 8.6   Building Sales Organization Teamwork Process

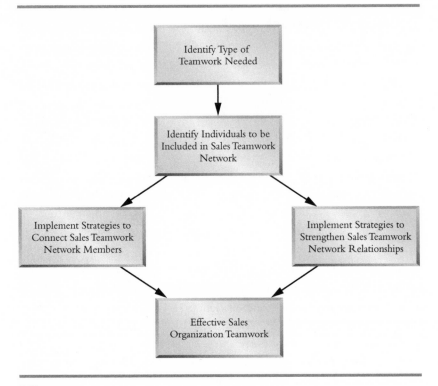

© Thomson

Exhibit 8.7   Sales Teamwork Network Matrix

Sales Process Stage	Type of Teamwork Needed
Prospecting	Teamwork among sales, marketing, and telemarketing personnel
Sales Presentation Planning	Teamwork between salespeople and field sales manager
Sales Presentation Delivery	None
Earning a Commitment	Teamwork between sales and technical personnel
Servicing the Account	Teamwork between sales and service personnel

© Thomson

teamwork needed based on the stages in the sales process. The example in Exhibit 8.7 employs a traditional sales process. This matrix can be adapted to meet the needs of any sales organization by changing the steps in the sales process and by conducting the analysis separately for different customers segments.

The key task is to determine the types of teamwork needed to implement the sales process in the most effective and efficient manner. As indicated in the example in Exhibit 8.7, informal teamwork is going to be employed throughout this sales process. However, teamwork among different functions is required at different stages of the sales process. The salesperson works with marketing and telemarketing personnel to identify the best prospects for sales attention. Then, the salesperson and field sales manager strategize and plan the sales presentation. Although the salesperson delivers the sales presentation, the incorporation of technical people to close the sale is expected. Finally, the salesperson and service personnel must coordinate efforts to ensure customer satisfaction with the receipt and use of the product. The value of the Sales Teamwork Network Matrix is that it forces sales management to think about the type of teamwork required to implement each stage of the sales process effectively and efficiently.

The second step is to determine all of the individuals that need to be included in the sales teamwork network. This is necessary to ensure that the network is complete. In the example presented in Exhibit 8.7, the complete sales teamwork network consists of individuals in sales, marketing, telemarketing, technical, and customer service. The challenge is to ensure that individuals in all of these areas are included in efforts to build an effective sales teamwork network.

The final step is to identify the best strategies for building a strong sales teamwork network. Several strategies are presented in Exhibit 8.3 and Exhibit 8.4. However, this task provides the perfect opportunity for sales managers to be entrepreneurial and creative as discussed in Chapters 1 and 2. Achieving BREAKthrough results typically requires innovative decisions. Doing what has always been done or what everyone else does is likely to produce typical results. Entrepreneurial and creative strategies are often needed to generate radical results.

Conclusions and BREAKthrough Directions

This chapter has addressed the need for sales organization teamwork and a collaborative sales force. The use of formal sales teams and informal teamwork within and outside a sales organization is becoming increasingly important.

BREAK BOX: Reviewing and Relating

The second step in the BREAK process is to review the material covered in this section and to identify specific ideas that relate to your sales organization. The following questions are designed to help you determine the most relevant ideas in this section:

1. Consider several recent sales management decisions you have made. Did you address the potential impact these decisions might have on the level of teamwork in your sales organization? Would you have made a different decision or done something else differently had you assessed the impact of the decision on sales teamwork?

2. Examine the Sales Management Decisions and Teamwork Process in Exhibit 8.5. How might using this process help you make effective sales management decisions and maintain teamwork within your sales organization?

3. Review the Building Sales Organization Teamwork Process in Exhibit 8.6. How could you use this process to identify the appropriate sales teamwork network? What ideas for strengthening relationships within a sales teamwork network might work well in your sales organization?

4. Study the example in the Sales Teamwork Network Matrix presented in Exhibit 8.7. How does your sales process differ from that in the example? How could applying the matrix to your sales process help you identify different types of teamwork for your sales organization?

5. Think about the types of teamwork appropriate to your sales organization. How could you be creative and entrepreneurial in determining the best ways to build teamwork in your sales organization?

Creating an environment that encourages the desired teamwork is a difficult, but critical task for sales managers. This is hard work that requires constant attention and the alignment of a variety of sales management decisions. A process for developing and maintaining effective sales teamwork networks has been presented and discussed. The key challenge for sales managers is to identify the most important priorities for their sales organization and develop an action plan to implement necessary actions.

BREAK BOX: Envisioning and Creating

The third step in the BREAK process is to envision how applying key ideas in this chapter in your sales organization might be accomplished and creating the basic steps needed for this to happen. Identify a key priority for action in each of the following areas and discuss the general steps that would be needed to make it happen in your sales organization:

1. Using formal sales teams in different ways.
2. Using informal teamwork in different ways.
3. Building more effective teamwork throughout your sales organization.

Visit The Sales Educators Web site for further BREAK process materials on this chapter's topics. www.TheSalesEducators.com

---

References and Suggested Readings

Cohen, Don and Laurence Prusak (2001), *In Good Company: How Social Capital Makes Organizations Work,* Boston: Harvard Business School Press.

Doyle, Stephen X. and George Thomas Roth (1992), "Selling and Sales Management in Action: The Use of Insight Coaching to Improve Relationship Selling," *Journal of Personal Selling and Sales Management,* (Winter), 59–64.

Ingram, Thomas N., Raymond W. LaForge, Ramon A. Avila, Charles H. Schwepker, Jr., and Michael R. Williams (2006), *Sales Management: Analysis and Decision Making,* 6th ed., Cincinnati: Thomson/South-Western.

Johnston, Mark W. and Greg W. Marshall (2006), *Churchill/Ford/Walker's Sales Force Management, 8th ed.,* Boston: McGraw-Hill/Irwin.

Prusak, Laurence and Don Cohen (2001), "How to Invest in Social Capital," *Harvard Business Review,* (June), 86–93.

CHAPTER 9

CONCLUSION

As we told you in Chapter 1, this book is about the sales function, and the role it can and should play in 21st-century companies. As you have seen from the myriad examples, BREAK process exercises, and discussions throughout the chapters, not only are salespeople more critical today than ever to the success of your firm, but also strategic leadership of the sales force often provides the competitive edge necessary to thrive in today's super-competitive business environment.

We, as The Sales Educators, are committed to excellence in all aspects of sales management. That is, our primary job is to make *you*—the thoughtful, creative, and innovative sales leader—even more successful. Our assumption is that if you weren't committed to BREAKthrough Thinking for BREAK-through Results, you would not have taken the time from your busy schedule to utilize this book. Congratulations on your commitment to excellence!

Before we invite you formally to continue your journey with us, it is useful to briefly recap several of the stops on the journey so far. We began by identifying core principles reflective of today's radically different mindset about the role of the selling function within the firm, how the sales force is managed, and what salespeople are expected to produce:

- The sales function must become a source of competitive advantage in companies.
- Great sales organizations are run strategically and with strategic intent.
- Sales managers and salespeople must see themselves as entrepreneurs, and the sales department should be the most entrepreneurial area within companies.
- Sales must be an opportunity-driven, rather than a resource-constrained, activity.
- Innovation is a major responsibility of those in sales.
- The ability to create, develop, and manage relationships with customers is the single biggest way in which salespeople create value in the marketplace.
- The sales function is not separate from the marketing function.
- Peak performance in sales is most likely when organizations have dynamic management systems to support the sales force.

As you have seen, these principles are the foundation on which this book was written, and as such they form the core values for BREAKthrough thinking in strategic sales leadership. Getting to BREAKthrough results requires a strong sense of the many changes and external influences impacting you, your firm, and your customers. Today's dynamic business environment truly does challenge much of our existing knowledge and experience about what it takes to achieve excellence in sales. Exhibit 9.1 provides a summary of the critical influences we agreed are impacting our thinking about the field, with the changed sources grouped into four key

Exhibit 9.1   Environmental Conditions and the Sales Force

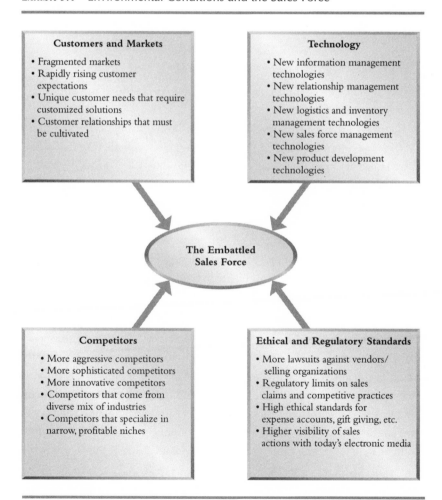

Customers and Markets

- Fragmented markets
- Rapidly rising customer expectations
- Unique customer needs that require customized solutions
- Customer relationships that must be cultivated

Technology

- New information management technologies
- New relationship management technologies
- New logistics and inventory management technologies
- New sales force management technologies
- New product development technologies

The Embattled Sales Force

Competitors

- More aggressive competitors
- More sophisticated competitors
- More innovative competitors
- Competitors that come from diverse mix of industries
- Competitors that specialize in narrow, profitable niches

Ethical and Regulatory Standards

- More lawsuits against vendors/ selling organizations
- Regulatory limits on sales claims and competitive practices
- High ethical standards for expense accounts, gift giving, etc.
- Higher visibility of sales actions with today's electronic media

© Thomson

Exhibit 9.2   A New Model of the Sales Force

The Empowered Sales Force

The Strategic Sales Force

The Creative Sales Force

The Entrepreneurial Sales Organization

The Technological Sales Force

The Expeditionary Sales Force

The Collaborative Sales Force

© Thomson

categories: customers and markets, technology, competitors, and ethical and regulatory standards.

Because of these quantum changes, some business prognosticators in the 1990s made a lot of money on the consulting circuit predicting that selling as a part of the business model would tumble into a free-form decline. It's gratifying to look back now and be able to say that, far from declining, the role of selling has actually been enhanced over the past decade in firms that are cognizant of the sales force's potential to provide a significant source of sustainable competitive advantage. But remember that in order to take advantage of this opportunity, your new sales model should be built around six key elements that, when combined, form the basis for our concept of the entrepreneurial sales organization. These elements are depicted in Exhibit 9.2 and are briefly recapped below.

The Creative Sales Force—Creativity must pervade your organization. Sales leaders must be willing to challenge old assumptions, reject accepted precepts, and eliminate established methods. Salespeople must be provided an environment for creative thinking and sharing of new ideas. Creativity truly must be the soul of the new sales organization. It must be ingrained in the culture and lived every day. BREAKthrough thinking is fueled by creativity—without it, sales organizations are doomed to wither and become irrelevant.

The Expeditionary Sales Force—Creativity breeds *innovation,* the hallmark of the expeditionary sales organization. "Expeditionary" implies leadership, instead of followership, of customers, of competitors, and of one's own firm.

The new sales organization must be a leader in all respects, acting strategically for the benefit of its constituents.

The Empowered Sales Force—A central theme of this book is that sales managers and salespeople must be viewed as *entrepreneurs*. They should be opportunity identifiers, creative problem-solvers, and organizational value creators. Empowerment involves risk and requires trust. It must be built into the design of sales jobs, with salespeople having broad discretion to try new approaches and create novel solutions. This implies, of course, that the salesperson is an "insider" on the organization's goals and strategies—if not, his or her actions may be counter to the direction of the firm.

The Strategic Sales Force—Most traditional sales management books talk primarily about tactical level roles and processes. As you have seen, this book seeks to focus you—the sales leader—on strategic matters. The words "Strategic Sales Leadership" in the title of this book weren't chosen lightly! The entire BREAK process is designed to facilitate alignment—of your internal systems, of various internal business functions, of your firm's overall goals and strategies with those of your sales force, and most importantly of your goals with those of your customers. Today's sales organizations must be strategic and must create and communicate value inside and outside the firm.

The Technological Sales Force—CRM, and database-driven marketing in general, cannot function without the sales force's embrace. For today's salesperson, technology holds both a strategic and tactical role within the job. At the strategic level, the degree to which the sales force is completely integrated into the process of capturing, recording, assembling, and analyzing customer information is a strong predictor of a firm's overall success in the customer marketplace. Salespeople today perform a much broader array of marketing activities for their customers than ever before, most of which are facilitated by their integration into the overall CRM system. At the tactical level, the myriad technology-driven sales tools available provide strong opportunity for "selling smarter"—making the sales job more professionally rewarding, and enhancing customer relationships.

The Collaborative Sales Force—Years ago, we sought out salespeople who were highly individualistic, worked well on their own, and were super competitive one against the other. How sales job requirements have changed! The nature of today's sales organization and customers requires a redefinition of the sales role to one that is largely engaged in obtaining and conveying resources of various kinds among and between constituents—both inside and outside the sales organization. A large portion of the knowledge, skills, and abilities that made for the successful salesperson ten years ago are likely way off from those that comprise the star sales performer today. The move to a collaborative model—team-based selling and all that it entails—captures much of the essence of the changes in the selling model of the 21st century.

Back to the BREAK Process

This brings us back to where we started out. Building the type of sales organization that we all aspire to lead requires change. Change breeds resistance unless a well-reasoned, well-executed approach to the needed change is put to use. Sales leaders need a strong model or framework for making change happen. As you have seen as you worked through the building blocks of sales leadership represented in Chapters 2 through 8, the BREAK process developed by The Sales Educators is a great way to increase the likelihood that your desired sales organization changes will *actually happen*. Upper management requires evidence through analysis that investment in change has a high likelihood of payoff—the BREAK process, through its systematic attention to each step, affords you a convenient mechanism to build your case for change. The steps or stages of the BREAK process are summarized once again in Exhibit 9.3.

Exhibit 9.3   The TSE BREAK Process

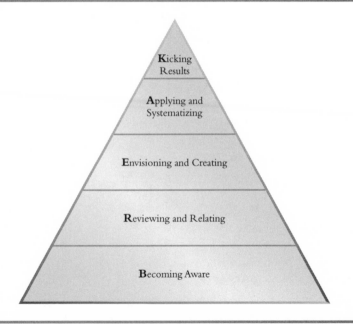

Kicking
Results

Applying and
Systematizing

Envisioning and Creating

Reviewing and Relating

Becoming Aware

© Thomson

So far, you have applied elements of the BREAK process to these key topical areas in strategic sales leadership represented by the content in Chapters 2 through 8:

- Developing an entrepreneurial sales organization
- Achieving peak sales organization performance
- Developing customer relationship strategies
- Leveraging strategic account strategies
- Designing strategic sales compensation systems
- Getting and keeping the best sales talent
- Encouraging sales organization teamwork

For each of these critical strategic aspects of the new sales organization, you had the opportunity to utilize the first three elements of the BREAK process via BREAK boxes throughout the prior chapters in the book: Becoming Aware, Reviewing and Relating, and Envisioning and Creating. In addition, on TheSalesEducators.com Web site you were able to employ the Applying and Systematizing stage, along with additional resources in support of the other three BREAK process steps. Ultimately, our goal is Kicking Results to the Next Level! Let's briefly review each of these stages of the BREAK process.

Becoming Aware—First, the sales leader must truly look inward at their organization and outward at the external environment to create an honest and accurate portrayal of their situation. This is the "seeing oneself as one truly is" phase, and the process was facilitated for each of the content areas above by a series of reflective questions early in the chapter.

Reviewing and Relating—Once you are aware (of shortcomings, opportunities, emerging challenges, new patterns, etc.), the next step is to develop a richer understanding of these developments as they relate to the current mission, structure, capabilities, resources, and policies of your own sales organization. At this stage you began looking for connections—how different facts and insights are connected to one another, why they matter to you and your firm, and the ways in which they are likely to impact the performance of your sales force. The content provided in each chapter, through examples and discussion, provided potent ammunition for you to relate what you have learned to your own situation—the Reviewing and Relating step.

Envisioning and Creating—The awareness and insights resulting from the first two stages in the BREAK process provided the raw material you can use to innovate. At the Envisioning and Creating stage, your goal was to begin to seek out creative solutions to problems and innovative approaches to opportunities that you have identified. Focus was on elements that are most likely to enhance your sales force's performance toward achieving truly high-level—"BREAKthrough"—results.

The Sales Educators are confident that these three steps, when accomplished thoughtfully and creatively by sales leaders across the key topics in this book, provide an excellent road map for the future of your sales organization.

Applying and Systematizing—The great plans you developed through the first three stages of the BREAK process undoubtedly necessitate that new behaviors, revised business practices, changed investments, and overall different ways of thinking be applied to the sales organization in a disciplined and systematic fashion. The changes must also be implemented in a manner that reflects the political and resource realities within your company. Otherwise, new behaviors are briefly (or never) adopted and then quickly fade away. All this requires a great set of action plans for implementation.

The Applying and Systematizing step is *the* action step in the BREAK process. In order to provide the maximum utility and value in this process to sales executives such as yourself. Earlier, The Sales Educators invited you (as a purchaser of our book) to join the community of our Web site to apply and systematize the plans you developed so far from your use of the BREAK process within our book. Our URL is: www.TheSalesEducators.com. Using the Web site for this next step provides you maximum flexibility in developing your action steps, and also allows you to communicate directly with us about what your plans and strategies are. And, most importantly, our Web site allows us to keep the most current information possible at your fingertips so you can continually work toward Kicking Results to the Next Level!

Kicking Results to the Next Level—As we told you in the very beginning, The Sales Educators are not much for quick fix books offering one-size-fits-all solutions. Only through thoughtful, individualized analysis can you achieve the step-change in results you are looking for. We are confident that the reader, working openly and earnestly through the BREAK process, will actually experience a step-change increase in their sales organization's results. Sales professionals reading this text will think about their businesses differently. Becoming aware of one's practices, reviewing and relating best and next practices to one's organization, envisioning and creating the linkages between old and new practices, and applying and creating systematizing connections between the new practices and your sales management systems are key steps to effecting real change. In sum, these are steps toward a healthier, more prosperous, and more strategically relevant sales organization.

On our Web site you will find continually updated ideas, exercises, and approaches for Kicking Results to the Next Level. We want this book, and the BREAK process you have experienced, to become an ongoing, dynamic part of your organization and its leadership and management. Through access and use of the materials on our Web site you can ensure that you are always able to put best practices into play in your sales organization—truly facilitating Strategic Sales Leadership: BREAKthrough Thinking for BREAKthrough Results!

ABOUT THE AUTHORS

The Sales Educators Are . . .

 **Gerald J. Bauer, MBA**   Gerald Bauer is President of Bauer & Associates, a sales training and consulting firm, and a partner in Atlantic Marketing Workshops, a marketing training and consulting firm. In 1999, he retired from the DuPont Company as Sales Competency Leader after 31 years of service. In DuPont, he held a variety of positions including sales, sales management, product management, industry management, customer service management, and purchasing management. Jerry also led a number of intra-company networks that focused on sales management, distributor management, and sales training and development. He was frequently involved in benchmarking with companies regarding sales and marketing topics. He has served as a conference and seminar speaker in the United States, Canada, Mexico, Latin America, Europe, and Asia. His experience also includes involvement in developing many sales and marketing courses and a process for developing sales competency and sales strategy.

 **Andrea L. Dixon, PhD**   Andrea Dixon is Associate Professor of Marketing at the University of Cincinnati where she conducts research in selling and sales management and teaches graduate sales and marketing courses. Prior to joining U.C., Andrea was the Senior Director of Product Development and Marketing at GAMA International. In that role, she developed the Institute for Field Training and the Best Practices Seminar series, programs that provide field sales leaders in the financial services industry with the latest research on leading the sales function. An award-winning teacher, Andrea is also a Research Fellow (2005-2008) at U.C. She serves on the Editorial Review Boards of the *Journal of Personal Selling & Sales Management* and the *Journal of the Academy of Marketing Science,* and is an ad hoc reviewer for the *Journal of Marketing.*

Thomas N. Ingram, PhD   Tom Ingram is Professor of Marketing and First Bank Professor of Business Administration at Colorado State University. Before his academic career, Tom worked in sales, product management, and sales management with ExxonMobil. He has received teaching and research awards, including the Marketing Educator of the Year by Sales and Marketing Executives International (SMEI). He was the first recipient of the Mu Kappa Tau National Marketing Honor Society Recognition Award for outstanding scholarly contributions to the sales discipline. Tom has served as the editor of *Journal of Personal Selling & Sales Management*, Chairman of the SMEI Accreditation Institute, and as editor of *Journal of Marketing Theory and Practice*. One of his coauthored articles in the *Journal of Marketing* was recognized by the American Marketing Association Selling and Sales Management Special Interest Group as one of the "Top Ten Articles in the 20th Century" in the sales discipline.

Eli Jones, PhD   Eli Jones is Associate Professor of Marketing and Executive Director of the Sales Excellence Institute at the University of Houston. He has won numerous teaching awards, including the Outstanding Marketing Teachers' Award (Academy of Marketing Science) and the University of Houston's Enron Award for Excellence in Teaching. Eli has won service excellence awards from the Bauer College of Business and is a Bauer Faculty Fellow (2002–2005) and he serves on the University of Akron's Fisher Sales Institute's advisory board. Before becoming a professor, he worked in sales and sales management for Quaker Oats, Nabisco, and Frito-Lay. Eli serves on the editorial review boards of the *Journal of Personal Selling & Sales Management* and *Industrial Marketing Management* and is an ad hoc reviewer for the *Journal of the Academy of Marketing Science* and the *Journal of Business Research*.

Raymond W. LaForge, PhD   Buddy LaForge is the Brown-Forman Professor of Marketing at the University of Louisville. He is the founding Executive Editor of the *Marketing Education Review*, founding Executive Editor of the Sales Educator Network, has served as Executive Editor, Sales Education and Training section of the *Journal of Personal Selling & Sales Management*. Among the roles Buddy has performed in the business and academic community are the following: Vice President/Marketing for the Academy of Business Education; Vice President of Marketing, Teaching, and Conferences for the

American Marketing Association Academic Council; Chair of the American Marketing Association Selling and Sales Management Special Interest Group; Direct Selling Education Foundation Board of Directors and Academic Program Committee; DuPont Corporate Marketing Faculty Advisory Team for the Sales Enhancement Process; Family Business Center Advisory Board; and Strategic Planning Committee for the National Conference on Sales Management. He currently serves on the Louisville Sales Club Board of Directors and administers the AMA Sales SIG/DSEF Sales Dissertation Grants.

Thomas W. Leigh, PhD   Tom Leigh is Professor of Marketing and Emily H. and Charles M. Tanner, Jr. Chair of Sales Management in the Terry College of Business at the University of Georgia. He teaches in all four of the Terry College's MBA Programs on CRM, B2B Sales Strategy, eCommerce, and Sales Management. Prior to joining UGA, Tom served as faculty director for the Penn State University Executive Management Program (where he received an MBA teaching award) and visiting professor at Ogilvy and Mather Advertising (NY). Tom is Past President of the American Marketing Association Academic Council and is a charter member of the AMA Foundation Leadership Circle. He was the founding director of the AMA's CRM Leadership Program. Tom recently served as Guest Co-editor for a Special Issue of the *Journal of Personal Selling & Sales Management* on CRM: Strategy, Process and Technology. Tom serves on the editorial boards of the *Journal of Marketing* and the *Journal of the Academy of Marketing Science,* and is a member of the Senior Advisory Board for the *Journal of Personal Selling & Sales Management.*

Greg W. Marshall, PhD   Greg Marshall is Professor of marketing in the Crummer Graduate School of Business at Rollins College in Winter Park, Florida. He previously served on the faculties of the University of South Florida, Texas Christian University, and Oklahoma State University. Greg has experience in sales/sales management, product management, and retailing with Warner-Lambert, Mennen, and Target Corporation. He is immediate past editor of the *Journal of Personal Selling & Sales Management* and is on the Direct Selling Education Foundation Board of Directors. Greg serves on the editorial review boards of the *Journal of the Academy of Marketing Science, Journal of Business Research,* and *Industrial Marketing Management.* He received the 2002 Outstanding Marketing Teachers' Award (Academy of Marketing Science), 2003 Chandler Freitz Teaching Award (OSU) and 2005 Cornell Distinguished Faculty Award (Crummer School at Rollins College).

Greg past president of both the American Marketing Association Academic Division and the Society for Marketing Advances.

Michael H. Morris, PhD   Mike Morris holds the Witting Endowed Chair in Entrepreneurship, and is Chairman of the Department of Entrepreneurship and Emerging Enterprises, at Syracuse University. He previously served as Noborikawa Distinguished Professor of Entrepreneurship (University of Hawaii), Cintas Chair in Entrepreneurship (Miami University), and the Gordon Professor of Entrepreneurship (University of Cape Town, South Africa, where he created the Supporting Emerging Enterprises Program). Mike, a former Fulbright Scholar (South Africa), has served as chair of the American Marketing Association's Task Force on the Interface of Marketing and Entrepreneurship and is editor of the *Journal of Developmental Entrepreneurship*. He was twice honored by Pi Sigma Epsilon as national Faculty Advisor of the Year, was inducted as a "21st Century Entrepreneurship Research Fellow," and has received the Edwin and Gloria Appel Prize for the field of entrepreneurship. In 2004, Mike received the Syracuse MBA Outstanding Professor award and the Oberwager Prize, for impacting students beyond the classroom.

INDEX

263

About TEXERE

Texere, a progressive and authoritative voice in business publishing, brings to the global business community the expertise and insights of leading thinkers. Our books educate, enlighten, and entertain, and provide an intersection where our authors and our readers share cutting edge ideas, practices, and innovative solutions. Texere seeks to cultivate, enhance, and disseminate information that illuminates the global business landscape.

www.thomson.com/learning/texere

About the Typeface

This book was set in 10.5 point Bembo. Bembo was cut by Francesco Griffo for the Venitian printer Aldus Manutius to publish in 1495 *De Aetna* by Cardinal Pietro Bembo. Stanley Morison supervised the design of Bembo for the Monotype Corporation in 1929. The Bembo is a readable and classical typeface because of its well-proportioned letterforms, functional serifs, and lack of peculiarities.

Library of Congress Cataloging-in-Publication Data

The Sales Educators
   Strategic sales leadership : breakthrough thinking for breakthrough
     results / The Sales Educators.
       p. cm.
   Includes bibliographical references and index.
   ISBN 1-58799-203-5 (alk. paper)
    1. Sales management. 2. Selling.   I. Title.
   HF5438.4.M374 2005
   658.8'1—dc22

                               2005020350